Handbook of Textile Marketing

Compiled and Edited
by Jean L. Woodruff,
Editor, "Textile Marketing Letter" and
J. Michael McDonald,
Associate Professor, Clemson University

Fairchild Publications
New York

Standard Book Number: 87005-404-X

Library of Congress Catalog Card Number:
81-71630

Printed in the United States of America

Dedication

The *Handbook of Textile Marketing* is dedicated to the faculty, students, and alumni of the colleges and universities comprising the National Council for Textile Education.*

It is our hope that this compendium of marketing knowledge will serve as an inspiration to those who follow in the footsteps of the thousands of men and women who have led the way in the establishment and development of the textile industry in this country since Samuel Slater established the nation's first cotton mill in Pawtucket, Rhode Island in 1793.

Wallace D. Trevillian
Dean
College of Industrial Management
and Textile Science
Clemson University, 1963 - 1980

Member Schools of the National Council for Textile Education:
Auburn University
Clemson University
Georgia Institute of Technology
Institute of Textile Technology
University of Lowell
North Carolina State University
Philadelphia College of Textiles and Science
Southeastern Massachusetts University
Texas Tech University
Textile Research Institute

Table of Contents

Chapter Two—Textile Marketing—Defined and Discussed

Chapter Three—Textile Fibers

Chapter Four—Textile Chemicals, Dyestuffs, and Special Finishes

Chapter Five—The Textile Machinery Industry

Chapter Fifteen—Building The Industry's Future: The Management of Resources and Change

Preface

You might say that this "how-to-do-it" book on textile marketing has been some 56 years in the making, and you would be right. It had its beginning on September 23, 1925 when the writer showed up for his new position as a "textile advertising copywriter" at Fairchild Publications at 8 East 13th Street, New York City. What he didn't know about this mysterious and wonderful world of textile marketing, which touches our lives at so many points, was just about everything. Today, in 1981, the learning process continues as the research and development programs of this multi-billion dollar industry develops new products, new technologies, new methods of distribution.

This book is not the work of one man, one woman or one organization; rather, it reflects the combined achievements of literally hundreds of talented men and women at every level of the industry: mill men and fiber producers, converters and garment manufacturers; retailers, wholesalers, chain stores, and mail order companies; importers and exporters; producers of textile-related products for military, industrial and governmental uses. Today, as always, the real inside knowledge of textile marketing resides largely in the minds of those men and women who are doing the job on a day-to-day basis.

Textile marketing is a difficult and complicated business. There is nothing quite so difficult, quite so multi-faceted in any other major industry. There are an almost infinite number of influences which, at any given time, can influence the sale of a textile or apparel product. The force of fashion, the influence of the retail merchant, the influence of the trade and consumer press, and the continually changing lifestyles of the consumer all play their part. Such matters as timing, seasonal influences, local and national weather conditions must always be kept in mind.

The history of the industry reveals the names of very few men or women who have entered the industry in a marketing capacity in middle life who have made a success in it. (Regardless of the success that they may already have achieved in other fields). It almost seems that you have to be born into the industry and spend a full lifetime at it to be successful. As a matter of fact, many men and women do just that. They start their careers in one narrow segment of the industry and spend their entire careers wrestling with the marketing problems and opportunities in that segment. They become greige goods people, cloth brokers, or perhaps yarn merchants. They spend their business lifetimes marketing natural, synthetic or "man-made" fibers, dyestuffs, chemicals or machinery. Or they may devote their entire careers to the technical world of industrial or military fabrics. There is a vast difference between the marketing techniques employed at various price levels of the industry; between staple and fancy goods; between fine imported woolens and worsteds and their domestic counterparts; between the apparel industries and the home furnishings industries. There are even vast differences between the men's, women's, boys', girls' and children's trade. You can be a genius in one area and a positive stumblebum in another. We've seen it happen.

In collecting and publishing the material contained in this handbook, we have used the word "marketing" in a broad sense to include all of those activities that might contribute to the successful creation and sale of a textile product at a profit: market research and marketing research; the influence of producing organizations at every level of the industry from mill and fiber producer to retailer; the impact of the trade and consumer press and trade associations; the use of fashion publicity, fashion shows and organized fashion groups; the use of trade and consumer advertising; direct mail, trade and consumer publicity. Each of these marketing tools has its place in textile marketing and each must be used in the right way, at the right time, with the right product, alone or in combination with other desirable marketing tools.

We have wished on many occasions that these great industries, these great "Job-Builders" of ours, were not so rigidly segmented. It would be a great thing, we think, if all mill executives could get some exposure to their customers' thinking by working for a reasonable period of time in one of the mill's selling offices. We also think it would be great if every marketing executive could spend some time at the mill so that he could have direct knowledge of what the mill's machinery can do. We call this "mill merchandising." It is the essential bridge between making the right product and moving it through the correct marketing channels at a profit.

Furthermore, this would bring home to the marketing executive in no uncertain terms what the mill man means when he complains about changing constructions or blends too often. Over the years we have known mill men who have had an abundance of marketing experience, and marketing men who have also served their time at the mill. The results have always been beneficial. Likewise, we have observed many situations where the "Big Boss" at the mill and the "Big Boss" in the New York office seemed to think and act as one man, always with excellent results.

We hope this *Handbook of Textile Marketing* will help many beginners as well as many proven veterans along the road to continued and greater success. We also hope that graduate and undergraduate students of marketing will find this book helpful in defining the areas in which textile-apparel-home furnishings marketing differs so dramatically from the simple, straightforward procedures involved in marketing such things as foods, automobiles, and insurance. We also hope that men and women who are primarily concerned with the production or research areas of textiles will find this book helpful in guiding their efforts along the most promising and profitable channels.

It has often been said that the best background for a career in the textile and related industries is to have the advantage of starting in the training programs of such retail organizations as R.H. Macy & Co., Inc., J.C. Penney Company, Inc., Sears, Roebuck and Co., Dayton Hudson Corporation, the K mart Corporation chain, Carter Hawley Hale Stores, Inc. or the Federated Department Stores, Inc. With this we wholeheartedly agree. We have also followed with great interest the successful careers of men and women who got their starts in the highly professional atmosphere of a good trade paper or consumer periodical. We would like to think that perhaps the *Handbook of Textile Marketing* itself will someday also be considered a good and helpful way to introduce talented men and women to these great industries of ours.

John A. Cairns
Clemson, South Carolina
1981

Note: Much of the material in this book has been taken from the columns of the *Textile Marketing Letter* which has been published ten times a year since 1970 by the College of Industrial Management and Textile Science at Clemson University. The *Letter* was started in January 1966 as a service to the industry by the former advertising agency of Chirurg and Cairns, Inc. It was given to Clemson University in 1970.

Chapter One

America's Textile Industry

OVERVIEW

By J. Michael McDonald

Beginning in 1789 with Samuel Slater's tiny spinning mill on the Blackstone River in Pawtucket, Rhode Island, America's textile industry has grown dramatically.

The early days of textiles found the industry primarily concentrated in and about New England with the mills doing the spinning and individuals and small groups being contracted to do the weaving. However, 1813 marked a major change in the industry, for it was then that Francis Cabot Lowell developed a power loom capable of producing cloth much more quickly and cheaply than by hand looms. Lowell's factory in Massachusetts was the first mill in America to put all phases from cotton bale to finished cloth under one roof. The giant vertically integrated textile mills of today owe much of their heritage to Lowell's efforts.

Along with the contributions of Slater and Lowell, textiles owe a lot to other major breakthroughs. Eli Whitney's invention of the cotton gin in 1793 made possible the rapid removal of seed from cotton. With increasing

1

supplies of cotton fiber came rapid growth of textile production. Slater's wife, Hannah, invented cotton sewing thread to replace linen thread. Steam engines replaced water power which in turn allowed mills to locate away from waterways. The sewing machine, originally developed by Walter Hunt and Elias Howe would be replaced by Issac Singer's model, and with Whitney's mass production techniques came the impetus for large-scale growth of the apparel industry.

As the industry expanded to the South in search of cotton supplies in the late 1800's, significant changes would take place both in population shifts and industrialization. New developments in fuel technology, especially petroleum, would lead to major changes in textiles in many areas, including heating, lighting, power, and processing, as well as in man-made fibers. New developments in iron and steel processing would mean better machinery. And new developments in fibers would bring about tremendous changes in the industry.

With the 1930's and the invention of rayon, the industry witnessed radical changes in all areas of textile manufacturing and marketing. Man-made fibers, like polyesters, nylons, and acrylics would mean changes in the way business was conducted, all the way from the making of the basic fiber to finished fabrics.

Perhaps the most interesting factors in the field of textile marketing are the changes the industry has experienced in the United States since World War II. Traditionally the industry was oriented toward turning out tremendous supplies of basic greige cloth which would then be sold to converters for finishing and then on to cutting and finally to garment making and then on down the line to the consumer. This was, as it has been referred to by some, a situation of "selling what the industry produces" (a production-oriented philosophy). However, in an attempt to be more competitive in meeting the needs of consumers, the industry evolved toward "producing what the public wants and will buy" (a market-oriented philosophy). This trend has led to an increasing awareness on the part of textile marketers with regard to consumer needs. Nowadays, for example, the primary textile industry has taken over most of the converting and finishing operations. More and more basic producers are orienting themselves to the ultimate consumer all the way from basic research, to manufacturing, to design, to sales.

The United States' textile industry can be described as large and diversified. It is characterized by being labor intensive, fragmented, and highly competitive as compared to many other industries. There are approximately 6,000 U.S. textile manufacturers operating nearly 7,000 plants. Sixty percent of these plants employ less than 100 workers. Ninety percent of textile companies report sales of less than $10 million annually.

Today, textile mills are located in 47 states with the largest concentration of mills in the Southeast. Nationwide, the textile and apparel industries account for over two million employees. The states most heavily concentrated in textiles are the Carolinas. North Carolina employs an estimated 281,200 textile workers, while South Carolina follows with an estimated 154,200. Textiles have become the South's largest industry, employing 960,000 workers.

Traditionally, most of the marketing, merchandising, sales, design, and fashion ends of textiles have maintained headquarters in New York City. While this continues to be the case to a large extent, many firms have relocated parts of these operations closer to the mills and markets.

Textile sales and productivity have been on the rise nationwide for several years; however, the textile industry is very sensitive to economic cycles. Profits for the industry remain relatively low compared to other American industries. Possibly the best explanation for low profits is fragmentation and competition within this industry.

To try and understand this diverse basic textile industry, it is useful to attempt some segmentation. Kurt Salmon Associates breaks down the industry into the following components: knitting, carpet and rug manufacturers, yarn manufacturers (spun and texturized), textile consumer products (sheets, towels, etc.), woven piece goods manufacturers, diversified textile companies, miscellaneous textile companies, and multiindustry textile companies. Also important are makers of chemicals, dyestuffs, and special finishes; textile machinery; technical groups; fashion groups; advertising and public relations groups; trade papers; consumer magazines and newspapers; radio and TV; and retailers.

The contributions of textiles to overall manufacturing activity in the U.S.A. is sizable. Using the Bureau of Census Standard Industrial Classification (S.I.C. #22), the textile mill industry (as of the late 1970's) ranked ninth in number of employees, eleventh in the amount of payroll, and fourteenth in terms of value-added-by manufacture.

In terms of capital spending, the textile industry averaged over $700 million annually during the 1970's on new plants and equipment. In order to meet competition, improve productivity, and deal with environmental concerns and government safety and health regulations, capital expenditures are expected to increase. For the next decade, capital spending is expected to increase steadily.

Looking ahead, the textile industry faces serious challenges on several fronts. New and expanding technology must be developed, but it must also be dealt with. For those firms slow to respond, the results could be economic decline. Economic and sociological trends will exert tremendous pressures on the industry. Consumer buying habits, largely affected by economic prosperity, will continue to change. Those who can anticipate such changes will likely be the leaders in developing new markets. Ecological and environmental pressures will increase dramatically. The push to conserve energy and develop new, more efficient production processes will accelerate. Energy costs will become a significant item which must ultimately be passed on to the consumer. The government will continue to exert tremendous pressures on the industry in safety and health areas. Product liability will become more and more a force to contend with. And finally, the threat of foreign competition will force the industry to examine new methods of survival.

America's textile industry is indeed a large and diverse gathering of giants and small, specialized operations. What the future has in store for the industry will largely be based on how textile leaders can adapt to and anticipate change.

1. THE WORTH STREET RULES, GOD BLESS THEM

Are Still Very Much Alive and Well and a Day-to-Day Force for Good in the Industry!*

By John A. Cairns, Consultant

It's axiomatic that every basic industry needs an intelligent set of ground rules to guide its day-to-day operations and to remove endless misunderstanding and friction between buyer and seller. This is especially true of an industry like the textile business or the stock market where so much of the business must be handled over the telephone. Here, a person's word must be the binding factor (and no fooling!) or the entire marketing machinery of the industry would quickly grind to a halt.

Thus we were greatly alarmed in the spring of 1975 when word reached us that the American Apparel Manufacturers Association had abandoned their sponsorship of the Worth Street Rules and were in the process of establishing a whole new set of rules to govern their relationships with their fabric resources. We assumed that this would leave it wide open for an unscrupulous buyer to renege on a telephone order given on a falling market and for an unscrupulous seller to renege on a rising market. Again—using the stock market as a somewhat parallel operation—we asked ourselves what indescribable chaos would develop overnight if a buyer of securities were to order 10,000 shares of a given stock on Monday, only to call his broker back on Tuesday and say, "Sorry, I didn't mean it!"

Happily, our fears were unfounded, as these letters from three of the most knowledgeable men in the industry will testify:

From John B. Russell, Jr., executive vice president, Dan River, Inc., and chairman of a committee to consider possible revisions of the Worth Street Rules:

"As to the Worth Street Rules, to drag up an old cliche, the reports of their death are exaggerated. In fact, they are as useful as ever and so far as we can see they will continue to serve the industry effectively for some time to come. *The problem with them* is that they are primarily geared to greige goods sales and have relatively little application to finished goods. For

---

*This article first appeared in the September 1975 issue of the *Textile Marketing Letter*.

example, there is no reference in them to knits at all. It was this deficiency that prompted us to think about a revision. The AAMA's rejection of the Worth Street Rules has caused us to abandon plans for revision in that it is this group that is the major user of finished goods, both woven and knit. We will continue on as in the past using the Rules where they are beneficial to both buyer and seller."

And from Robert E. Eisen, executive vice president of Greenwood Mills, Inc.:

"The Worth Street Rules are still actively used and incorporated in the sales notes of many of the mills in the marketplace, essentially covering greige goods transactions.

"The American Apparel Manufacturers Association recently removed their sponsorship of the Worth Street Rules because, as stated, the Rules cover greige goods primarily rather than finished goods, which is what the garment manufacturer is not interested in."

And, finally, from Arthur M. Spiro, chairman of the board, Textile Distributors Association, and vice president of the Apparel Textile Divisions of United Merchants and Manufacturers:

"The Worth Street Rules are by no means dead. They will continue to be used and referred to as a benchmark between buyers and sellers in dealing with greige goods.

"Certain elements of responsibility in the Worth Street Rules have been used between buyers and sellers of finished goods, and it is anticipated that this will continue in the future.

"All rules are subject to change with the times. There is no revolution going on, just evolution as dictated by practicality and the needs of the marketplace, keeping the best of the past and modifying as necessary."

We are grateful to Messrs. Russell, Eisen and Spiro for their observations and we would be happy to hear from anyone else, at any level of the textile and apparel industries, who might wish to comment further on the present situation as it pertains to the Worth Street Rules. We have always considered that the basic "Worth Street" textile market was one of the most responsible of any major marketplace in the world. And we are most happy that there is no apparent reason for us to alter our thinking in that respect.

2. THE "BACKWARD" INDUSTRY MYTH*

By J.B. Goldberg, Consultant

Those of us who have been associated with the textile industry for a great many years are well aware of the caustic criticism leveled at all of its

---

*This article first appeared in the February 1981 issue of the *Textile Marketing Letter.*

branches by labeling the industry as "backward," lacking initiative in research activities, and utilizing outmoded equipment and processes. Ignoring the fact that textiles and clothing are second only to the food industry in the volume of business generated annually in this country, it has been frequently suggested that we look up to the multi-million dollar automobile industry as one which has always been a leader in research and engineering programs to create new and improved products to benefit the consumer.

If we were to enumerate the commercially successful developments in fibers, fabrics and finishes, as well as machines and processes which have been introduced by the many segments of the textile industry during the past 50 years, this dissertation would easily fill every page of this book. What is even more significant is the fact that the ultimate beneficiary of this multitude of achievements, the consumer, has not been gouged to such an extent that he could not afford to purchase and enjoy the many improved textile and various industrial applications. To cite just a few of the industry's accomplishments, we call attention to such innovations as permanent-press, crease-resistant apparel fabrics, stronger and longer wearing, a complete spectrum of colors with superior light and wash-fastness, stretch fabrics, both fashionable and utilitarian, static-free synthetics, whiter whites, durable water and stain repellency, flame-resistant fibers and fabrics, moderately-priced "fur-like" fabrics, longer-wearing and reasonably-priced soft floor coverings, a wide range of home furnishing materials, to say nothing of a host of military and industrial textiles—from parachute components to more serviceable tire cords, weather-resistant awnings and tarpaulins, and industrial filter cloths.

We have yet to read of *millions* of textile items "recalled" by the manufacturers because of some defect or hazard to the buyer. We are not overlooking the TRIS incident, but the dollar loss was relatively trivial (as compared with the auto industry's experiences) and the question of the real hazard to the individual's wearing of such finished fabrics is still not completely resolved.

In brief, all of us associated with the textile and allied industries can hold our heads high and point with pride to scores of achievements to explode the myth of ours being a "backward" industry.

3. WHAT IT TAKES TO START A NEW TEXTILE BUSINESS*

By John A. Cairns, Consultant

For many years the textile and related industries have employed more people, paid out more money in wages, fringe benefits and taxes, and have

---

*This article first appeared in the April 1978 issue of the *Textile Marketing Letter*.

contributed more to our national well-being than any other major industry. Can this situation continue? It is our understanding that no new textile business of any important size has been established over the past ten years, or longer. There appears to be many reasons why this great basic industry of job-creators and job-builders is now reluctant to move forward with anything like the tempo that it has displayed in the past. A survey of trade associations and individual firms suggests the following:

Picking the Right Spot for a New Business. Anyone exploring the desirability of expanding an established business or establishing a new one must pick out a location with great care. There is not much sense in going to all of the expense of investing in new production and marketing machinery unless there is a reasonable expectation of getting back something a bit better than a new dollar for an old one. The entrepreneur today faces intense competition from both domestic and foreign sources, with very little hope for more tariff protection. He is also extremely conscious of the fact that fashion trends come and go; the double-knit profit opportunity of the 1950's can look something less than attractive in the 1970's. New products and new ideas for new markets are constantly needed.

Does the Return Justify the Gamble? Most Americans seem to think that the average corporation makes a profit of from 25 to 50 percent after taxes, and that dividends are used solely to "line the pockets of the rich." Very few people realize that a corner filling station or mom-and-pop type grocery store might very well show a larger percentage of net profit on sales than a huge textile organization like Burlington Mills, Deering Milliken, Dan River or J.P. Stevens. They find it hard to believe that a net profit of 5½ percent after taxes is considered to be pretty good going, even in a good year. Politicians seem somewhat loathe to tell the true story.

What About the "Price of Admission?" Like everything else, the cost of starting up a new venture in the textile industry has skyrocketed in the past decade. According to figures supplied by the well known management consulting firm of Kurt Salmon Associates, Inc., the mill that cost $14 million to build in 1967 would have cost something like $24 million to build in 1975 with the same technology, and $28 million to build with 1975 technology. Investment required to set up a single job in such a mill has escalated from $40 thousand per job in 1967 to as much as $150 thousand per job in 1975!

Added to those costs are the newer costs imposed by government regulations. According to Mr. O'Jay Niles, Director of Technical Services of ATMI, "Current and proposed regulations in the areas of wastewater treatments, air pollution, solid waste disposal, toxic and hazardous substances, noise, cotton dust and worker safety are probably primary considerations. Not only are capital requirements for plant and equipment a major factor, but annual operation and maintenance costs would be tremendous. In the area of wastewater control, for example, it has been estimated by the National Commission on Water Quality that the textile industry will have capital expenses of $528 to $785 million between 1977 and 1983, plus annual operation and maintenance costs of $50 to $81 million." These, we submit, are sobering figures.

What About Labor? Everyone knows that the textile business is a "labor intensive" business, so the attitudes of labor are of major significance. On the one hand, the prospective investor is aware of the fact that "big labor" appears to have been losing membership steadily over the past ten years. On the other hand, he is almost certain to study with care the Farah Manufacturing story, the J. P. Stevens story, the Darlington story, and others. Can he count upon the support of union and non-union labor, if he starts a new business or provides new jobs? Will the NLRB (National Labor Relations Board) be on his side, or will he be likely to feel that it is a hindrance, rather than a help, to his new business? The answers to these questions can be all-important.

What About Attitudes of Local, State and Federal Governments? Even if all the previous questions have been answered to the satisfaction of our prospective job-creator, this last question can be the one that either makes or breaks the deal. Will the official attitudes be basically friendly or unfriendly? Can he count on the sympathetic support of local business, political, religious and educational leaders? Is the younger generation for or against the type of enterprise which he expects to establish?

In the event of protracted strikes or other disorders, can he count on the protection of his plant and his products by local and state police, and if need be, by Federal military authorities? Our so-called "Free Enterpriser" would like to know.

4. SOME SUBJECTIVE VIEWS ON NONPROFESSIONAL ATTITUDES TOWARD TEXTILES*

By Leon E. Seidel, Consultant

Except for an occasional brief encounter with the single, lead editorial page found in most business publications, those of us who write about textiles or any other industry must keep their work concise, technologically based, and always objective. But many situations arise both in our professional and social lives which arouse the urge and need to express opinions. Since this kind of communication is, or should be, just as fact-based as any article one writes on weaving mill modernization, for example, writing a subjective analysis of something in or around the

*This article first appeared in the January 1980 issue of the *Textile Marketing Letter*.

textile industries that is obviously disadvantageous to our industries is not to be avoided.

The greatest harm dealt our industries usually comes from nonprofessional quarters. The lack of knowledge and experience doesn't deter the amateur, especially if there's a dollar to be made. The following observations were made during the year 1979. They were based on the activities of the nontextile communicator: a consumer magazine, a movie maker, and a union newsletter.

In many cases, and this is one of them, when the professional textile writer communicates with the professional textile businessman, it amounts to one agreeing with one's self: the editor is, or should be, a mirror of the best thinking extant among readers. But our views are presented to readers of the *Textile Marketing Letter* to hopefully provide ammunition with which to fight those who misread us for one reason or another, then proceed to damage our image as seen through the eyes of the public at large.

On Fast-Fact Consumer Journalism. This observer recently asked a newly appointed president of a $70 million privately owned multi-technology mill, "With chronically slim profits, the cost of money, and the need to comply with a maze of plant-product regulations, how can you spend several million dollars on modernization so that it can be priced in cloth as performance-aesthetic plusses? The answer, of course, was "With great difficulty."

These problems—and more—were given skewed attention in an April 9, 1979 *Business Week* story entitled "More Gloom For U.S. Textiles." And for good measure, the writer threw in references to textile labor intensity, anti-union motivated mill "paternalism" and employee job hopping from textiles to a higher paying industry.

The article was but another example of bad news journalism as it concluded that the projected $22.5 billion to be spent in the 1980's will be largely for elimination of labor intensity, 10 percent of it just for compliance with OSHA (Occupational Safety and Health Act) cotton dust standards. The result: loss of one-third of our companies, 7,000 of our plants, and one-third of our work force; some 40 percent of U.S. textiles will be made by the top 15 companies.

Medium and small mill acquisitions by large ones, mergers between medium-sized mills, and the flat-out demise of small mills are the mechanisms by which this projected attrition will occur. And while it does, we will be harassed by snowballing imports by the Chinese dragon and questionable policing of our import agreements by Washington. There wasn't a word amid this glop about our burgeoning exports or anything else positive about textiles for that matter.

This is the sort of copy that sells newspaper stories about the lurid private lives of public figures, movies featuring ignorant, southern policemen and even TV junk food commercials. And commercials are just what

Business Week used as fast-fact sources for the story rather than traditional fact finding and careful research.

In this case, the fast facts were obviously drawn from a few of our Spring '79 textile forums such as the ATMA (American Textile Machinery Association) and AATT (American Association of Textile Technologists) during which big mill industry leaders proclaimed that the mighty are about to inherit the textile world.

In this case, nothing could be further from feasibility and there's plenty of history to prove it. In the mid-1950's, Textron made its classic move to buy American Woolen textile dollar assets for paper stock and the merger evolved in today's nontextile Textron enterprise. During that same time, Burlington was acquiring smaller mills in a big way, many of which it shut down. Neither of these large-scale merger-acquisition actions made a dent on the size, composition, profitability or keen competitiveness of the textile industries. Yes, mills and people in them were displaced but new mills grew up in concert with technological progress in tufting, texturing, knitting, and dry-laid fabric forming (nonwovens).

Fifteen companies controlling 40 percent of textile output? Not a chance as long as 75 percent of it is fashion oriented, ripe for the picking by mills of any size alert and mobile enough to spot and serve the style trends. And as long as a free enterprise system exists in the U. S., no big companies will drive out small ones by sheer force of capital expenditure clout, latter-day government regulations on health and safety notwithstanding.

The *Business Week* recitations of big textile company party line politics and the fast facts on which it was based, like fast foods, are junk.

On the Exploitation of Activity Causes. It can be difficult to know where legitimate latter-day sociological causes such as auto safety, pollution, land/energy/wildlife conservation and ethnic/sexual rights leave off and faddism and self-serving public relations among activists begins.

It may be that it depends on whether one is the "causer" or "causee." For an example, involving management-labor "justice," this observer applied for and got his blue card in what was then CIOTWUA when working as a third-shift worsted mill quilling department floor hand in the summer of 1941. Ten years later, out of school and in service as plant manager of a filament yarn weaving company, union membership yielded to management corps membership and tough negotiations if not "union busting" activities began.

So be it. But when current industrial-sociological activists exploit their chosen cause of the moment, their fad, it's time to pause. When they do so strictly for the money, it's time for the target of exploitation to protest for a change. And no amount of rationalizing that it takes tough consumer talk or action to overcome a tough government, industrial or other consumer-class problem excuses activism for pure profit.

Such is the case of the motives surrounding a movie released in the Spring of 1979 called "Norma Rae." *Time* magazine, March 19, 1979 issue, best describes the content of the film because it's characteristically as accurate as a review can be: "...(It's) the story of a trashy white woman (Sally Field), a textile worker in a small Southern town (Opelika, Ala.) who discovers that she actually has a social conscience (she comes to believe in justice for labor) when a labor organizer (Ron Liebman) arrives at her mill to establish a union."

The review goes on, "...His winning out over her suspicions...and their joint triumph over a union-busting mill management are the bases for a film that is serious and intelligent...."*Time* goes on to analyze actor performance, screenplay writing, its transformation to film, and the characters themselves. And so it should, but it couldn't resist adding a little color and moralizing. "...(The movie shows) company goons on the attack...the death of Norma Rae's father from overwork...We need more movies about the realities of workaday life in America."

Nobody ever said that any kind of workaday life was or is particularly comfortable. Again harking back to some informative years, this editor does recall fainting from heat and humidity while checking loom speeds in a 1040 machine cotton weaveroom in the summer of 1942. But what was said and implied on a TV talk show in an interview obviously intended to promote "Norma Rae" was untrue and unfair.

The interview took place between Mike Douglas and actress Sally Field (Norma Rae) during one of Douglas' regular shows. Obviously under legal department instruction, Miss Field gingerly stated that the movie's depiction of textile mill conditions was not the objective of the makers of the film. Oh no, it was an exhibition of character development. But in the next three breaths, which couldn't have taken more than three minutes, she established before the TV audience of a very well rated show:

- That the noise in the mill was unbearable, so much so that actors had to wear ear microphones to hear the lines being spoken (presumably shouted) to them.

- That employees in the mill were given ear plugs to wear but that they did no good.

- That she (Field) had an attack of asthma in the warping department from flying lint and had to be revived with a vaporizer.

The movie "Norma Rae" will no doubt soon be forgotten. But the kind of cheap exploitation used to put it together and promote it does industry damage and should not be condoned.

On Fallacious Union Public Relations. In the March '79 issue of *Social Justice,* the monthly Amalgamated Clothing and Textile Workers Union (ACTWU) house organ, that union celebrated the 16th birthday of its "campaign for justice" at J. P. Stevens, its one and only ongoing editorial subject.

The things that characterized the union's "struggle" began on March

1, 1963, have been the reckless melodramatics of its public relations campaign and its relentless misuse of the NLRB (National Labor Relations Board) and the courts. Here's a sample of both as quoted from *Social Justice:* "There was no 'New Deal' for textile workers when Franklin D. Roosevelt was president, and the majority of them worked in New England and the Northeast. The National Labor Relations Act (NLRA) guaranteeing the right to organize, became law in 1935, but companies like J. P. Stevens merely marked the occasion by starting to devise ways to voice existing contract protections and run away to wherever cheaper labor and anti-union atmosphere could be exploited (the Southeast)...J. P. Stevens wasted no time in responding to the campaign that began in 1963. The response was harsh and swift: workers who sympathized with the union were fired on the spot. The first of a long line of cases against Stevens...was soon underway.....The NLRB has gone to court again and again, trying to restrain Stevens from its tactics of fear and intimidation....No one outside the company can accurately reckon the total cost...of Stevens' efforts to 'crush the union movement'...but whatever the costs of keeping the workers down, Stevens has chosen to bear them to this day." And the chronicle goes on, laced with such terms as company harassment, election tampering and surface bargaining, concluding with proud descriptions of the current boycott of Stevens products.

Stevens has remained publically silent through the 16 years. As explained to this observer by one of its executives, it has done little good for management to respond to fallacious public relations flak and leading questions. The company never lost its cool, nor has it ever stopped serving the public with value-quality fabrics at a profit.

But in mid-April 1979, Stevens issued the first of a series of news releases concerning its ACTWU inflictions. As might be expected, it and others which followed dealt with confirmed fact. And for a refreshing change, the Stevens viewpoint was given equal time. Quotation from one of the bulletins (4/27/79) illustrates this.

"The ACTWU formally withdrew a request for a (NLRB) order to certify the union as bargaining representative at the United Elastic plants...

"The case had been in trial for 30 days and had approximately five days to go until completion. More than 425 witnesses had already been called to testify...The sworn testimony in the record was replete with incidents in which the union organizers harassed employees into signing union cards and lied to employees about the purpose of such cards. The union withdrawal of the request for a bargaining order was taken to protect only the interests of the union. The evidence produced during the hearing would not have entitled the union to a bargaining order and the union was well aware of the fact. Furthermore, the union was facing a company subpoena for documents dealing with methods used by the union to get cards signed and the strategies employed by the union to deprive Stevens employees of their right to vote in an NLRB election on the issue of union representation. The union has refused to produce the relevant documents and the NLRB was preparing to enforce the subpoena in the Federal courts...."

In mid-May of 1979, an "extra" edition of *Social Justice* was published. It interpreted five recent "ruthless and lawless" incidents involving Stevens employees. It concluded, in part, "The company's new public relations posture of being 'born again' is exposed for the hoax and sham it really is."

More than likely, ACTWU is being startled, confused, and overcome by facts rather than fallacy.

5. WANTED: A NEW KIND OF INDUSTRY LEADERSHIP*

By The Editorial Staff of Textile Industries

"All enterprises, be they political, institutional or profit-oriented, require leadership and direction. As we see it, a key problem in the textile industry today is the fact that for many years the major fiber producers provided strong leadership, market orientation and product innovation." These are the thoughts of Trevor Finnie, Werner Management Consultants, Inc. He continues:

"Historically, the industry was production-oriented and production led. Then, beginning with the 1950's, companies became more market and product-oriented and the leadership shifted toward the fiber producers which provided expertise in product marketing and product innovation as well as distribution. Today, this leadership role is declining and the fear exists that the fiber producers, for sound and justifiable reasons, will have to seriously reduce or abandon this function. Unfortunately, we do not see any other segment of the industry taking over the leadership role and giving direction to this multi-segmented textile system.

"The need for leadership is paramount, not only because of the complex market conditions which exist and the technical and operating challenges ahead, but because the industry is faced with substantial capital requirements in the future. Thus, it becomes incumbent for the textile industry to look inward toward its own financial expertise of outsiders to cope with problems that are fiscal in nature: cash management; capital shortages vs. R. O. I. (Return On Investment); effects of on-going debt services in cyclic slowdowns; planning and monitoring of business opportunities; identification and monitoring of recently acquired cost centers such as energy and pollution control.

---

*This article first appeared in the September 1978 issue of the *Textile Marketing Letter.*

"It is perhaps interesting to note that in certain European countries, banking institutions have assumed rather direct roles in influencing and guiding their domestic textile industries. This is not only true in the developing nations where massive financing by government and private banks are necessary in the building of new plants and expansion of older ones, it is also the case in highly industrialized textile economies such as those of Germany, the U.K., France and Italy....."

Chapter Two

Textile Marketing— Defined and Discussed

OVERVIEW

By Jean L. Woodruff

On the subject of marketing versus manufacturing, the January 17, 1972 issue of *Time* quotes Paul Hoffman as follows: "One illusion is that you can industrialize a country by building fortunes. You don't. You industrialize it by building markets."

To all this, we at the *Textile Marketing Letter* say "Amen." It is the gospel we have been preaching right from the start—that marketing is the force by which industries grow and prosper. For in today's economy the consumer, not the company, is at the center of the business universe. Companies revolve around the consumer, not the other way around.

In 1960, Robert Keith wrote:

> "Growing acceptance of this consumer concept has had,
> and will have, far-reaching implications for business,
> achieving a virtual revolution in economic thinking. As the
> concept gains ever-greater acceptance, marketing is
> emerging as the most important single function in
> business."*

---

*Robert J. Keith, "The Marketing Revolution," *Journal of Marketing*, national quarterly publication of the *American Marketing Association*, January, 1960, p. 35.

Twenty-one years later, I think it is safe to say that Mr. Keith was right.

Exactly what is "marketing?" Over the years, the *Textile Marketing Letter* has gathered, among others, the following responses:

> "Marketing—the performance of business activities that direct the flow of goods and services from producer to consumer or user."
>
> *—American Marketing Association*

> "Marketing—the total of all the phases of business activity directed towards, and resulting in, the flow of goods from the original producer to the final customer. In the broad sense, this includes not only selling, but advertising, packaging, research, and other nonmanufacturing activities."
>
> *—Harvard University Graduate School of Business Administration*

> "Marketing is a comprehensive system of business action that directs the company's activities to meet customer needs and desires profitably.
>
> It is no longer possible for a company to prosper merely by producing goods and services and attempting to sell them. In today's competitive marketplace, organizations must start with the needs of potential customers, then direct the resources of the company toward meeting those needs at a profit."
>
> *—American Management Association, Inc.*
> *Lars Lofas*

There are many other definitions of marketing, each different but all with a common theme. In a following article Cash M. Stanley, Jr. of Dan River Mills has collected additional definitions from knowledgeable people in the field.

One might now ask, "Is textile marketing different from the marketing of other commodities?" To answer this question we include below some definitions of "textile marketing" and following, several articles which address themselves particularly to the question.

> "Textile Marketing is more than selling. It starts with market research to discover present and potential profit opportunities for the company and its customers; plans a strategy of exploiting these opportunities; creates and prices the needed products and services; and distributes by methods which enhance relations with present customers and win new ones."
>
> *—Anderson & Cairns, Inc.*
> *Williard C. Wheeler*

"I believe the basic rules of marketing pertain to all
industries depending on whether or not they are producing
consumer goods or industrial goods. Since the textile
industry is made up of companies which market different
types of products such as woven goods, etc., our job is to
acquaint the student with the basic principles of marketing,
slanted somewhat toward textiles, so that when the student
becomes a trainee in the industry, he has a sound working
knowledge of marketing. As a trainee he will be taught
exactly how his company markets its goods."

> —*Philadelphia College of Textile & Science*
> *H. Lawrence Laupheimer*
> *Associate Professor*
> *Business Administration*

To ensure that textile marketing is properly understood, we have
included articles in this chapter which not only define the concept but
which also discuss its use and importance to the industry.

One article is devoted to profiling "a textile marketing man." Other
articles deal with changing patterns in textile marketing, and check points
which should be used in evaluating the effectiveness of a firm's marketing
program. Taken together, these articles will hopefully provide the reader
with an insight into textile marketing—the concept itself, its application,
and its importance.

6. MORE DEFINITIONS OF MARKETING*

By Cash M. Stanley, Jr.,
Dan River Mills, Inc.

Over a considerable number of years I have collected and filed textile
marketing definitions and concepts from books and publications. From
these I have selected a few that seem to me to apply particularly to the
textile industry. They are the following:

> Marketing is considered a profession in most non-textile
> companies, and is the responsibility of a man who not only
> knows field sales problems and merchandising, but who also
> understands the roles of advertising, market research, and
> sales training as well. He knows how to coordinate all these
> functions and manage them profitably.

> —*John W. Barry, Marketing Consultant*

---

*This article first appeared in the January 1967 issue of the *Textile Marketing
Letter.*

Marketing concept—
1. Explore, discover and analyze markets suitable for development.
2. Organize a marketing system suitable to accomplish the above, and develop products meeting marketing requirements.
3. Develop tools and techniques for market evaluation and product commercialization

>   —*John C. MacIlroy, Chicopee Mills, Inc.*

There seem to be as many definitions for the marketing concept in industry as there are people who are interested in it.

>   —*T. A. Kaiser, Michigan Consolidated Gas Co.*

A company guided by the marketing concept must become customer-oriented rather than product-oriented. Greater emphasis must be placed on profits rather than on mere volume of sales. Essential is the intelligent and enthusiastic participation of all members of the organization.

>   —News Front, *August, 1963*

The ideal marketing man of the '60's must examine change eagerly for the opportunities it creates, and should never resist or view it as something to adjust to later.

>   —*A. C. Stoneman, President, Purex Corp.*

The marketing man must possess an expanded frame of reference and bring a greater perspective to his task. This must be supported by his knowledge and understanding of his business and industry in three principal areas: economic, technological and philosophical.

>   —News Front, *August, 1963*

Devise marketing stratagems which will result in new products, new services, new market segments. The faster this is done, the more lead time there will be for enjoying a competitive advantage, sales gains and gains in percentage of market share.

There are not more than three or four mills in the entire industry that are able to gauge correctly just what their sales mean.

>   —*Paul Bernhardt, Market Research Manager Chicopee Mills*

"The Marketing Concept" is defined as a managerial philosophy concerned with the mobilization, utilization and control of corporate effort for the purpose of helping consumers solve selected problems in ways compatible with planned enhancement of the profit position of the firm.

Ideas which proved most likely to be successful were those which came from customers and salesmen; those least likely— from the company's own top management. Who was going to refuse further consideration of an idea suggested by a vice-president?

—Science in Marketing *by George Schwartz*

The marketing expert is a man who possesses special skills in reaching and moving consumers through the creation, production and distribution of goods and services. He is a specialist in people and products, and in fitting the latter to the needs and desires of the former.

The advertising expert is a man who possesses special, highly developed skills and talents in reaching, touching, interesting and stimulating consumers through the media of mass communications. By contrast, he is a specialist in people and messages, in knowing how to plan, create, and place messages which will move people.

The marketer's role is creating new markets, not simply getting a larger share of existing ones. You charge not what the market will bear but what will help expand the market and still yield a good profit.

—*Thomas B. McCabe, Chairman, Scott Paper Co.*

7. WHAT'S SO DIFFERENT ABOUT TEXTILE MARKETING?*

By John A. Cairns, Consultant

Let me list just a few of the meets and bounds of textile marketing which are now second nature to textile people, but which the average person outside the industry can seldom put together as a workable piece of marketing machinery.

First—The Product Itself—The Epitome of Product Differentiation. Historically the textile business changes its product every spring, summer, fall and resort season—but today change is a daily, not a seasonal affair.

---

*Condensed from an address by John Cairns before the Third Annual Textile Marketing Forum, Clemson University, May 20, 1970. It subsequently appeared in the June 1970 issue of the *Textile Marketing Letter*.

Distribution. Many industries talk about 80 percent or 100 percent distribution and they are not happy until they get it. In this business, 100 percent distribution can be fatal. The biggest garment manufacturer in the business probably has no more than 12,000 retail outlets, nationally.

The High Cost of Fame. In every other business, marketing people think in terms of product identity and consumer demand. Those are nice-sounding words to textile people, too. But, here we think in terms of consumer acceptance rather than consumer demand, and we never lose sight of the fact that the better known you are, the greater chance you run of having your product footballed to death by merchants who will use it as a loss leader.

The Importance of Price. Here's a weird, mixed up subject if ever there was one. Recently we saw the astonishing situation where polyester high modulus rayon blends were selling for less money than the rayon-cotton blends, despite their greater utility and greater cost. Looking back over the years, I can recall many, many cases of textile and apparel products that were rescued from oblivion by wise marketing people who raised their quality, and boosted their prices.

The Force of Fashion. These industries are not known as "the fashion industries" for nothing. Fashion is perhaps the most important single selling force in the business. Starting as the most important fact of life in the apparel field, it has now spread out into linens, domestics, home fashions, automobiles, plumbing fixtures, pleasure boats, airplanes, what have you.

The Influence of Competitors and Suppliers. Marketing people from outside the industry are accustomed to thinking of their customers as the source of all profits, the reason for all of their business successes—and, of course, we in these industries cherish and pamper our customers, too. However, we can never afford to lose sight of the fact that many of our most exciting profit opportunities have come, and will continue to come from our suppliers in the chemical, fiber, machinery, dyestuffs, yarn or fabric fields.

The Importance of Teamwork. In most other businesses, the process of getting distribution is a relatively simple three-step affair: from manufacturer to distributor, to retailer, to consumer. The manufacturer gives the product its final form and in many cases packages it for retail distribution. In our business, firms at every level of the business need help from the right firms at every other level, for maximum success.

The Power of the Press. Here, in our industries we are blessed with something like 30 trade papers whose columns carry the day-to-day news of the industry as well as a continuous flow of profitable ideas for our respective businesses. Out beyond them we have the fashion magazines for men and women, the Sunday supplements and magazine sections, the general magazines like *Life, Ebony,* etc., which carry news from the fashion world, radio and television commentators; plus fashion columns, women's pages and home furnishings columns in literally thousands of weekly and daily newspapers.

The Impact of Technology. Today you have to be familiar with something more than the raw commodities markets to get by. We're living in an age of chemistry, an age of machinery development, an age of electronics, an age of invention and patent development. The permutations and combinations of new fibers available to the fabric designer run into the billions. The marketing man must know something about the new technology and must study it daily. Likewise, the mill must study marketing and customer relations. And together, they must learn to build national brands in which the consumer may have confidence—since technology has made this the most complicated business in the world.

Tenth—Last—And Most Important of All—The Position of Retailer. If there is the slightest doubt in your mind as to who is the Big Boss in the textile, apparel, and home furnishings field, let me let you in on a very important secret. Regardless of their source, all of the goods of this vast industry flow through the hands of the retailer en route to the customer. There are only two significant exceptions—industrial and military goods.

Finally, integrity must not be forgotten as a vital marketing force. It's the foundation on which everything else rests.

8. PROFILE OF A TEXTILE MARKETING MAN*

By George E. Linton, Ph.D., Consultant

In Marketing, three things are essential—the individual, his ability, and his knack of salesmanship.

First, the individual; "character" cannot be defined, as attested by the fact that many luminaries of the underworld were devoid of it but still made the headlines even if in an unsavory manner. "Personality" is not definable, as well; all of us know persons who seem to have no "personality" but still do become prominent in a positive way.

It is individualism that makes or breaks anyone. You have it or you do not. The individual, to succeed, must have ability and be able to sell his product, as well as himself, to the prospective purchaser. And today it may be stated that everyone, generally speaking, has to be a good salesman to

---

*This article first appeared in the April 1967 issue of the *Textile Marketing Letter.*

market his product and succeed in this world of storm, stress, strife and competition.

The greatest thing in the mind of man is a tool to work with; the greatest thing in the hands of man is a tool to work with. A person, especially in Marketing, must use his engineering and imagineering skills to the utmost.

Psychology is defined as a study of the human mind in its relations to all the things about us, whether for good or evil. Philosophy is a study and knowledge of the things which cause, control or affect facts and events. To succeed in Marketing, the individual should use these tools, consciously or automatically, in his daily business dealings.

There are six steps in the lives of all of us that have to be followed in everything we do—

1. Consciousness

2. Sensation

3. Perception

4. Comprehension

5. Apperception, which is recall for past experiences.

6. Voluntary Action, whereby we approve or disapprove, accept or reject, buy or not buy, which applies to the wares we are trying to market. They will be bought or rejected by your customer. Your individualism is paramount in promoting your wares and often does provide you with fruitful results, if you can persuade your prospect into finally giving you the order.

There are "Ten M's in Industry;" Manpower, Material, Machinery, Money, Mill Engineering, Mill Management, Manipulation, Maintenance, Marketing and Merchandising. It may safely be said that every worker will fit into one of the ten categories. If you *know how to do something*, you will have a job or position. If you know *why it is done*, you will be a supervisor or executive.

In the textile fields, the individual should be trained in raw materials, construction, color and the finish given to fabrics. Today, in addition, he must be aware of the marriage, now about twenty years old and still going strong, with the great apparel industry. He should be conversant with the cut-make-trim in this industry. His finished fabric is the raw material for the apparel industry. He ought to know what is done with his finished fabric when it comes to manipulation by the apparel manufacturer.

Six Points for Marketing Success. The good marketing individual, to be successful, should also be aware of the six points that can make or break the marketing of his wares; his fabrics.

He should know the season of the year for which his fabrics are ideal;

the occasions for which the cloth will be suitable; the weight of the fabric; and the effect of color, weave, and finish of his goods in order to aid him in marketing the materials. Season, occasion, and weight are the three vital essentials. Many fabrics attract prospective purchasers because of their color, their weave or their finish, or a combination of two or more of these three selling points.

The smart marketing individual in textiles should also be aware of mass production, uniform sizes, and job assembly lines in apparel. And, in the custom apparel trade, he should be well versed in job specialization.

He should realize that the value and price of fabrics and apparel items are based on the quality of the raw material, the textile fibers used, and the skill and techniques of all operators or workers from the raw material stage to the finished article.

Lastly, in women's wear, he should keep in mind the two great vistas to success in marketing his goods in that field—the "forced obsolescence" which women use as a reason for buying something new, and that "anticipation is greater than realization."

The Five F's of Textile Marketing. The clever individual in the field of Marketing should always keep in mind the "FIVE F's". If he does, he should be aided much in his field in being a top-notch individual in Marketing. He should know as much as possible about the FIBER, FABRIC, FINISH, FASHION, and the FUTURE. His future depends to a great degree upon these factors.

9. THE CHANGING PATTERNS OF MARKETING TEXTILES*

By Irving B. Cohen, J. P. Stevens & Co. Inc.

The title of this talk concerns marketing...mind you, the subject is marketing and not selling. To define the difference between marketing and selling, I cannot do better than quote from Theodore Leavitt's stimulating treatise "Innovations in Marketing," in which he defines it thus:

> "The difference between marketing and selling is more than semantics. Selling focuses on the needs of the seller; marketing on the needs of the buyer. Selling is preoccupied with the seller's needs of converting product into cash; Marketing with the idea of satisfying the needs of the customer by means of the product, and the whole cluster of things associated with creating, delivering and finally consuming. A purely marketing minded firm tries to create value-satisfying goods and services that customers will want

*This article first appeared in the October 1968 issue of the *Textile Marketing Letter.*

to buy. It is vital for all businessmen to understand the view
that an industry is a customer-satisfying process... not a
goods-producing process."

Today, the tools of marketing are forged from the wealth of information available to the marketing-minded company. It may start with a
product, or it may start with the needs of the marketplace. Marketing
research is able to determine in advance, the size of the market; the
composition of the market; the advisable pattern of pricing for effective
marketing; the existing competition within the marketplace; the sales
potentials and the profit possibilities in relation to investment capital
required; the life expectancy of the product; the selective list of direct and
secondary customers that offer us the greatest sales opportunities; and
specific selling strategies for each particular market, and for each major
customer potential.

Even the share of market expectancy for the product can be estimated
in advance, before going into production. Selling techniques, distribution
patterns, advertising plans, sales promotion programs, and effective use of
sophistication and showmanship in product presentation, can be more
gainfully developed after all the apparatus of marketing research and
analysis have determined the product feasibility.

Most of us in the textile industry have realized the importance of
knowing a great deal more about our markets. Most of us are doing more
in the field of marketing research, consumer research and consumer
motivation. As an industry we are approaching the point of marketing
professionalism that will enable us to achieve the most effective exploitation of our products within all areas of the marketplace. This fundamental
premise differs only by degree, whether we are selling greige goods,
finished goods, or consumer goods... whether we are dealing with the
narrowing market of greige goods selling, the expanding markets of design
and fashion, or the extensive realm of retail distribution. The underlying
principles remain constant, in the search for more effective techniques of
enhancing sales by means of the most compelling marketing process.

While the textile industry has progressively moved away from its older
identification as a commodity market, we still operate under the restrain-
ing influences of price competition within·our own industry... thereby
giving our customers, and the ultimate consumer, the best intrinsic values
among all American manufacturing industries.

How very fortunate we all are to be part of the textile business during
this period of dynamic progress and growth.

The previously orthodox view of production concentration within a
narrow marketing area appears now to be somewhat outmoded. The
versatility and pre-eminence of the newer textile fibers and blends have
together made planned diversification imperative to a profitable production and distribution pattern for our industry.

As recently as last year, the dangers of product concentration were fully exposed, as the pricing of polyester cotton blends took a nose dive. Every textile company suffered; but those mills that were saddled with a total commitment to full scale production, inventory buildup, and concentrated distribution within limited markets suffered most.

In contemplating the whole spectrum of sophisticated textile marketing influences, we believe it is necessary to examine the key factors of decision-making that contribute to the formulation of policy and program. As I see it, they include: The Changing Consumer ... The Population Explosion ... The Impact of Young People ... The Revolution of Retailing ... The Potency of the Corporate Complex ... The Revolution in Fiber Consumption ... The Importance of Research and Development ... The Selling Power of Improved Product Performance ... The Technology of Communications ... The Overwhelming Influence of Fashion ... The Authority of Consumer Preference Studies ... The Competence of Share of Market Studies ... The Techniques of Pinpointed Selling Strategies. We might uncomplicate matters by considering all of the foregoing in terms of Consumer Motivation, Market Research and Customer Analysis. Let's try to dissect and analyze some of these significant factors.

The Changing Consumer. The present consumer revolution is distinguished by a unique transformation in the sociological, cultural, psychological and economic aspects, attending a wholly new philosophy of human behavior, standards and values. The consumer today is an independent shopper with a higher taste level and a higher income level and a higher educational level ... which together have combined to make her a smarter and more sophisticated shopper. With family formations rising, housing starts projected for increases, and consumers continuing to enjoy record increases in personal incomes ... consumer goods markets present unique opportunities for expanding sales in textile products. Our record of holding the line on textile prices should help us in obtaining a better share of the consumer dollar, in the face of the inflationary trend.

Consumers are presently in a buying mood. The all-time highs being achieved in retail stores of soft goods bodes well for the textile industry and is already reflected through significant increases in forward bookings, on top of substantially higher sales reported by leaders in our industry.

Despite all these favorable indicators relating to consumer spending for non-durables, the textile industry should be vitally concerned with the apparent inevitability, that for the first time in our history, our country will be spending more for consumer services than for consumer goods. This is likely to occur in the early 1970's. Since 1957, the increase in consumer spending for services has been 92.3 percent. The total growth in personal consumption expenditures, over that 10 year period shows a 74.7 percent increase. Of great concern to us, is the growth pattern of non-durable goods, which have grown but 60.5 percent since 1957.

Aware of the challenging competition for the consumer dollar that surrounds us, the more forward-looking textile producer came to the objective determination that more direct lines of distribution to the consumer were economically feasible and in fact imperative. During the past decade, several of the larger and perhaps more enlightened manufacturers of fabrics and textile products decided to verticalize their structure, so that consumer products could be efficiently fabricated from basic yarns, through packaged consumer goods, on a wholly integrated basis within the corporate framework. This marketing concept, of reaching the consumer more directly through the retailer, opened a whole new world of growth opportunities through diversified and stabilized expansion. Among some of the larger and more diversified textile producers, consumer end products ready for retail distribution accounted for as much as 25 percent of their total net sales during 1967.

The enormous changes in the nation's population have results in far-reaching economic and social transformations over the past two decades. They reflect an extraordinary revision of demographic data relating to the composition, family income, living standards, and the reclassification of age grouping within our national consumer population.

The spectacular progress of technological developments, achievements through the massive research efforts of American industry; the rapid rise of our economic resources; the expanding volume of discretionary spending as personal incomes rise, as younger households increase, and as more families gain a higher total income... suggest that the growth rate of the U.S. economy as a whole holds great promise for continuing acceleration in the marketing of textile products, as we move towards the 1970's.

There are challenges to be sure. Hotly competitive markets may become more intense, as the giants of industry at every level of our industrial and service economy contest for a fuller share of the consumer dollar. The textile community would be well advised to sharpen the tools of marketing and distribution, if our penetration of the bigger and more affluent consumer markets is to keep pace with the favorable economic climate that surrounds us.

Impact of Young People. The big population surge in the '70's will be the 15 to 29 age group. The impact of teenagers on marketing is steadily expanding as they spend more for apparel, entertainment and food. They are venturesome and exert a compelling influence on fashion trends.

The teenager is commonly thought to be between 13 and 17 years of age. As I talk with teenage merchandising specialists and editors, I get the feeling that today's teenager starts at 10, and surely by the age of 12 is a knowledgeable shopper, and highly fashion conscious. More magazines are now being published with their appeal concentrated on the teenager. Their circulation is rapidly growing and the response to their editorials and advertising is sometimes hard to believe.

The young adults in this age group are those who are going to work, getting married, buying all the things a family needs, and are very fashion conscious. With prospects of rising incomes, these young adults have a way of expressing their own individuality and detachment from parental influence, by nonconformist buying habits, for themselves and their homes, that open up wide horizons for marketing textiles and textile products, that are in tune with their tastes in spending.

As we all know, retailers everywhere have Young World Departments with trained specialists who are constantly in touch with the pulse of foreseeable buying trends among young people.

The point of all this lies in the fact that 54 percent of our 1970 population...forecast at 207 million people...will be under 30 years of age.

A direct appeal to the youth of America demands a more complete involvement with their thinking, their tastes and their living habits for everyone in our business who hopes to get more from this Horn of Plenty.

Revolution in Retailing. From the viewpoint of textile marketing opportunities, it is obvious that the multiple forces of modern retailing establish more direct lines for reaching the explosive consumer markets, through all the multiple channels of retail distribution. To recapitulate, they include Traditional Department Stores...Junior Department Stores...Giant Catalog Chains...Low Margin, Mass Merchandisers (the discounters)... Specialty Stores of all types...Chain Variety Stores...Direct Mail Companies...The Premium business ($ billion worth)...and the combination of food and non-food supermarkets. There are others, but, let these suffice.

One of the most essential ingredients, other than research and product development, is the comprehensive knowledge of long-in-advance timing, as practiced by the central buying specialists among the leading retail organizations. It is no longer enough to develop a new fabric, a new finish or a new consumer product. All the other elements of effective selling strategies must be present too...including styling, quality, performance and value to which must be added the additional factors of packaging, designing, point of sale presentation, sales personnel education, fact sheets, laboratory testing reports, advertising and sales promotion recommendations, audio visual techniques where necessary, plus a planned program of delivery, scheduled to meet anticipated requirements of the retailer. From the viewpoint of textile marketing, we are right back to the ever present factor of Total Involvement. "There are No Free Rides."

Importance of Research & Development. The American Textile Industry keeps renewing itself through reinvestment of its earned assets into new plants and equipment at an average of about $1 billion annually over the past three years; plus a 70 percent increase in Research and Development Expenditures, between 1962 and 1967.

There is one component of great importance concerned with R. & D. growth that is being closely examined by corporate textile management. This is the matter of products produced at the laboratory level and on a sample basis only. Unless that product can be translated into commercial feasibility on a volume production line, research and development discoveries will at times result in unnecessary problems. This is a danger that research and development directors are surely alert to. It is the marketing person who has to be certain of commercial feasibility before prematurely moving into the marketplace.

Is it not possible that the present re-evaluation of soil releases on lighter weight polyester/cotton blends with a durable press finish, might have been avoided many months ago, if the finishing process could have been thoroughly proved out on a commercial basis, before the marketing team rushed in? The frustrations and problems must have left a lot of scars in customer relations between the textile producer, the manufacturer and the retailer. To paraphrase an old cliche, the marketing men should have "made haste more slowly." Every good merchant knows that there is not virtue in being first, if the product hasn't been perfected.

Technology of Communications. As the science of electronic communications continues its dynamic advance forward, today's systems of marketing and retail distribution may become archaic, in little more than ten years from now. The long range planners among enlightened retailers recognize the overwhelming importance of shopping conveniences to the consumer by bringing their goods through multiple branches right to the consumer's backyard. They are also adjusting shopping hours to suit the needs of the consumer's family, as a complete entity. Plans are already being blueprinted, which enable the consumer to shop even more conveniently, without ever leaving home, through the wonders of electronics via the TV set, the audio visual telephone, and Lord only knows what other wonders will develop through the use of satellites and whatever succeeds them.

Influence of Fashion. The impact of fashion is moving our textile industry forward as never before, and, at an ever-quickening pace. Fashion continues to be a major factor in the sale of all consumer products. Believe it or not, contemporary fashion, styling and good taste take precedence over performance in the selection of consumer goods in textile products for apparel and for the home.

Consumer Preference Studies. By now, we are all aware of the significance to our textile industry of consumer research. It appears obvious, that with 83 percent or more of our textile products ending up ultimately as consumer or household items, we should incessantly follow the pattern of consumer textile and apparel preferences, in as much depth as possible. Through the use of computers, many of us are enabled to obtain pertinent and accurate consumer buying information, which measures current trends of purchasing by the public.

As many of you know, these detailed studies are obtainable from outside professional service organizations which employ a national consumer panel diary approach. The consumer preference information which is provided, can involve only textile products if desired. It includes the following data:

> Consumer Product Purchased...Retail Outlet Where Bought...Price Paid...Number of Units Purchased ...Fibers and Fabrics or Materials...Brand Names... Color Information...Special Finish for Better Performance...Age of User.

Target Accounts—Customer Analysis. As the concentration of business falls into fewer and bigger companies, it becomes incumbent upon everyone interested in textile marketing, to analyze the quantitative composition of their active customer lists to determine the factual distribution of corporate sales, in this period of bigger business establishments. Among primary producers of textiles, would you believe it possible that one percent of your active customers might contribute as much as 50 percent of your total sales? Those of you who keep such records will agree that these proportions are not far fetched.

Today, we are in a business of fast moving change: new fabrication developments, new yarns, new processes for dyeing, finishing and texturing the appearance of our goods. It is no longer a dry goods business. It is the new Textile Industry, with greater sophistication and greater importance in the world of fashion, in the world of industry, in the world of home living. To all of which I would add one further essential of marketing; and that is "customers must be thought of as an extension of our own business—which they certainly are; because without customers we wouldn't have any business."

Chapter Three

Textile Fibers

OVERVIEW

By Leon E. Seidel

When Reavis Cox of the Wharton School, University of Pennsylvania, wrote his authoritative *The Marketing of Textiles* in 1938, textile fiber marketing was simple. Indeed, so was all textile marketing. In those days marketing meant movement of product from point of origin to the mill, storing it at various locations in between, sorting and grading it, and pricing. Of course, Dr. Cox was describing our key natural fibers: cotton, wool and silk. The thing that differentiated marketing of rayon, our most important man-made fiber at that time, was that less storage was involved, transport was less complicated, natural fiber growing seasonality did not exist and pricing was simplified because rayon was not subject to erratic weather, plant/animal disease and so on. But rayon was indeed marketed quite like natural fibers and promotion of the filament form as artificial silk and staple as artificial wool or cotton, created one of the classic stigmas in textile history. How things have changed since World War II!

Interestingly, the current concept of marketing—total profitable business planning and administration—was also adopted early on by the

Wharton School. But what has evolved in the marketing of textile fibers is the sole creative product of American fiber producers, man-made *and* natural. For cotton has its marketing arm, Cotton, Inc. and wool has its Wool Bureau. These groups, the 13 major U.S. man-made fiber producers, and their trade association, Man-made Fiber Producers Association, Inc. are providing an in-depth multiplicity of marketing services to themselves, to their mill customers, to customers' customers and so on through the physical market to and including the ultimate consumer.

These external services are rendered for reasons far from altruistic. In U.S. man-made fiber production, highly capital intensive fiber forming units are necessary to compete in domestic and world markets and so is a broad, sophisticated product mix. Unlike other parts of the world, in the U.S., fiber production cannot survive as made from a 20 million pound a year plant turning out garden variety polyester, for example, in a simple range of deniers, lusters and deniers per filament.

Even with their considerable financial clout, our fiber producers— including the marketing arms of cotton and wool growers—must move fiber in enormous volume, relatively consistently to achieve the kind of return on investment demanded of American industry. The situation is even more difficult for the man-made fiber producer because few, if any, of the manufacturing facilities and the products they output are usable outside of the textile industries. These compelling forces have grown even stronger as government regulation and law and oil price increases have forced fiber producers to spend increasingly more on the research and development and processing involved. The net result, uniquely and notably American, have made textile fibers one of the biggest bargains in any economy and the range of products and marketing services that are available are unprecedented in international commerce.

Product Development

The palette of man-made fiber variants as they existed in 1977 was published in *Textile Industries* for May 1977, later as the monograph *Textile Fibers And Their Properties* by American Association for Textile Technology. Involved are descriptions of 20 generic man-made fiber categories and seven natural fibers. The variant listing for nylon alone numbers 183 types. The total fiber mix active in the U.S. at any one time represents successful efforts at the fiber producer research & development level to generate products, each of which is at once suitable to specific yarn and fabric forming mill processing and the coloring and finishing that follows, suitable to the end product made by our mills *and* their customers, and suitable to the competitive economics of fibers, yarns, fabrics and made-up consumer or industrial end products.

These scientific achievements of U.S. fiber producers have mandated a new need among line sales representatives of the fiber producers and among many classes of textile mill personnel. The need is for product knowledge: knowledge of the behavior in the mill of members of the current fiber product mix and the textile engineering knowledge required to put this behavior, fiber properties, to best use in the mill and in the market. Today, product knowledge is the keystone of textile fiber marketing. The road from "test tube" to market-ready fiber is expensive, long and arduous. There is no budget at the fiber producer level to pursue "laboratory curiosities." The product must serve specific end product functional and aesthetic needs as defined by the market research arms of fiber producers. At the same time they must process on conventional textile machinery, much of which was designed to run natural fibers.

The middle ground between lab and full-scale man-made fiber production is the prototype production line and its output is tested and evaluated variously depending on the fiber producer involved. Some producers have full-scale textile manufacturing labs as does DuPont at its Chestnut Run facility and sufficient captive personnel to conduct statistically significant use (wear) trials. But it's almost certain that most fiber makers get newly developed fibrous products into the mills and into the markets as soon as possible. There have been numerous fiber producer in-house triumphs that were greeted by big yawns when finally released to the textile industries. While certain of these developments were perhaps introduced before the mills and markets were ready for them, the point is that they failed.

Tracking

To minimize costly failure of new product introduction, not only are new fiber variant developments based solidly on processing or end product reasons, but the producers live with them until they become obsolete. More than any other fiber marketing technique practiced by producers, the business of tracking product spells the difference between a major and a minor fiber maker. By this process, technical service can be applied at the mill or in the establishment of one of its customers to prevent rejection because the fiber doesn't get through the process. By tracking, the fiber producer can tell when the new product needs a promotional push or a merchandising pull; when developmental fabrics, garments or other made-up end products must be made available to demonstrate new product use.

In home and apparel fashion, new fiber developments are often seeded in major markets in Europe and in the U.S. That's the way Qiana was launched: in a Paris couture, no less. And when the June or January home furnishings markets are taking place around this country, especially in Chicago, one can be sure that several of our fiber producers attend, not just for entertainment of customers, but to track some new carpet fiber variant in a customer's line, frequently to help them introduce it.

Another practice used in the tracking process is getting the opinion and buying the attention of name designers in the home furnishings and apparel fashion world. Thus the endorsement of half a dozen American fashion leaders, secured by ITT Rayonier when it launched a major 1978 program to reacquaint America with the new *and* old rayon fibers of its customers for wood pulp, was instrumental in helping the whole program succeed. And in the early stages of any products introduction, the products are so fragile, so vulnerable to fall-out that producers literally live with them.

This observer was not above patrolling the counter of a New York retail store displaying a body suit containing a new man-made fiber for which he was responsible, getting consumer reaction and particularly sales person advice.

All of this activity is just as important to new fiber development as is the complex physical chemistry that goes into its synthesis or regeneration. Of extraordinary current interest in the man-made fiber development activity being engaged in most developed nations is reemphasis on the cellulosics, and development of variants on the big three of synthetics— polyester, nylon and acrylic—that will make fabrics more cotton-like, silk-like and wool-like. If it would seem that we have come full circle back to the fibers of Reavis Cox's day, there is no question that the way these products are being marketed is uniquely different and extraordinarily sophisticated.

Protecting The Mark

Many times the main difference between one trademark and another, both representing about the same fiber, is the way the mark is presented and protected. Again, American fiber producers have spent a lot of time, money and talent on this critical facet of marketing fibers.

Part of the reason for this is purely legal: preventing unauthorized marketers past the fiber producer level from mislabeling and misrepresenting a trademark when indeed the fiber it represents is not in the fabric. A more important part of the reason is maintaining a quality image in market products bearing the mark built so carefully and at such high cost by fiber producers through manufacturing care and marketing science, particularly promotion.

The law generally states that if product is available, the producer cannot refuse to sell it. But it can refuse to allow use of the trademark if fabric *or* made-up end product does not measure up to producer standards. These standards have been carefully quantified by most fiber producers. Those of Celanese are outstanding because they are comprehensive, reasonable and specific end use oriented.

All fiber producers have lab testing programs to measure market products against end use performance standards and approve or reject them vis-à-vis trademark use. The most meaningful whip used is promotion: no lab approval, no promotional support from fiber producers. While wool and cotton have similar trademark programs, the natural fibers are not nearly so sensitive to misuse as are the man-mades. If some mill makes a poor cotton denim cloth, the jeans cut from it, also poor, are just another bad buy at retail. But if a trademarked polyester gets into a poorly styled and formed double knit and a poorly cut pair of slacks, the whole market shakes, consumer groups rally around an example of "plastic cheapness" and TV comics make jokes about it.

Researching Markets

It's been demonstrated time and again that the laws of supply and demand won't be repealed. It's thus urgent that fiber producers measure demand in specific textile end use sectors and develop programs to supply as much of it as possible. This measurement, market research, is another expensive business. Certain information is in the public domain, placed there by trade associations for specific textile sectors by the government, and by publications such as *Textile Organon*. This aspect of the subject was discussed in some detail in *Textile Industries* for February 1980 in the article "Textile Mill Sellers' Guide" and won't be repeated here.

Much market data is quite difficult to come by and fiber producers, as usual, make the investment required to get it. They have their own research specialists and they regularly engage the services of a host of low profile consultants, each usually with a specialty machine class market such as carpeting, texturing, nonwovens, etc. Few mills can afford this marketing service and as with so many functions, fiber producers share market research data with responsible mill customers.

If the research under discussion pinpoints end use and machine class markets for today and tomorrow in terms of fiber pounds, the international per capita pound fiber usage is currently under more serious consideration by fiber producers than ever before. Our generally improved export picture for soft goods and particularly the sharply improved man-made and cotton fiber export picture is based largely on the devalued dollar plus the efficiency of U.S. fiber makers (and growers) and marketers. Longer range, fiber producer targets are the developing nations and the rich potential to be realized as they boost their per capita fiber consumption from five pounds. Our benchmark in U.S. consumption is 65 pounds per capita.

Promotion

We define promotion as the imperfect science of attracting customers to one's products essentially via advertising and public relations. It's imperfect because it's quite difficult, often impossible, to measure results in fibers and textiles and products made from them in bottom-line dollar sales terms. The closer the product gets to the consumer, the easier it is to measure the results of promotion on it. Ready-to-install carpeting is easier to promote and measure than is nylon staple for use in carpet yarns, for example.

In this effort, again fiber producers have the financial clout to launch comprehensive promotional programs. Consumer advertising seems to be the favored medium and both institutional and product/customer-specific methods are employed. Since so many fiber makers are also chemical company giants, they can and do engage in multi-product TV advertising. Owens-Corning's glass used in draperies was introduced *and sold* initially on national network TV by master huckster Arthur Godfrey.

But the preferred promotional method used by the fiber producer is the newspaper ad in conjunction and cooperation with apparel and home furnishings retailers.

In recent years, fiber producers have recognized the value of trade magazine advertising to promote a corporate image and to convey that rapidly changing technology cited earlier in this overview: product knowledge.

Perhaps one of the classics in all of American business was development of the cotton logo by Cotton, Inc. and the "natural look" promotion engaged by it on behalf of its cotton grower constituency. At the program's outset in 1972, this observer was called into the ad agency handling the account for consultation. The agency executive was wearing a denim business suit. Shocking! And so were his views on cotton use, and most of them were disputed by this observer with all sorts of irrelevant facts. What Cotton Inc. knew that the rest of us didn't was that there was a whole, huge, young demographic sector of the U.S. *and* international population that was ripe to fight the establishment with natural foods, natural habitats and *natural fibers*. As known to most, the cotton program was and is a big success and it happened because the promotion was superbly and broadly executed, based on solid market research and backed by technology generated in the company's Raleigh, N. C., headquarters. It was and is an example not just of promotion but of total marketing with a bit of good timing luck thrown in.

Merchandising

Technically, merchandising in fibers and textiles and soft goods made from them is secondary selling, helping one's customer sell. It's the most often confused aspect of marketing: some think it's direct selling, some think it's promotion. And in the organization charts of some fiber producers, merchandising is used interchangeably with marketing per se.

The merchandising of fiber is a workmanlike, nitty-gritty job and it often spells the difference between success and failure of a fiber maker's program. Merchandising is a vivid example of tracking: retail-wise specialists start with the fiber producer customer list and follow the fiber through to the consumer, persuading and aiding sales all the way. Many tools are used besides the personal call: ad reprint mailing, in-store training and fashion shows, and resource listing, to name a few.

Direct Sales

In the book, *Applied Textile Marketing* (Seidel), fiber and textile sales was termed the highest calling in all soft goods business. There are still those fiber producers and mills who feel that given some other strength such as product development or raw materials procurement, the salesman is merely an order taker. Not so! If anything, the accelerated rate of product generation in the 10 short years since *Applied Textile Marketing* was published have made the salesman's lot even more important. For he is a line representative, particularly in fibers, of the whole complex of techno-marketing company know-how and he must represent it correctly from the standpoint of bottom sales and from the legal standpoint.

Considerable time and effort has been spent by fiber producers in organizing and reorganizing sales departments first by end use, then by fiber, and then back to end use. Perhaps it doesn't matter if the quality of the salesman is high enough to properly represent his company, its programs and its products to mill customers.

Controls

Of the various industrial controls we use—quality, inventory, production and credit—none currently assumes greater importance than does inventory control. The reason: the soft goods inventory disaster of the 1974-75 recession. Textile mills learned well from it and so did fiber producers. Should there be any doubt that excess, devalued, static inventory is a drain on profitability—thus the total marketing effort—the reader is urged to review financial statements of textile and fiber companies during the days to come.

For the fiber producer, living in a continuum of escalating petro-chemical feedstock (raw material) costs, inventory contol has become even more sensitive an issue than most other marketing functions. Difficult as it is to start and stop fiber production lines, start and stop them fiber producers do when inventory build up is excessive.

International Business

Fiber producers are as astute as any industrialists when it comes to producing and selling off-shore. According to a 1979 *Organon* report, some 14 U.S. fiber makers had a total of 42 investments in manufacturing facilities in countries other than the U.S. On exports we quote from the same source, "...The (positive) export balance for man-made fiber manufacturers (fiber, yarn, fabric, apparel, home furnishings) during the first quarter of 1980 totalled 60.3 million pounds, up 23 percent from the export balance of 49.1 million pounds recorded during the fourth quarter of 1979 and almost three and a half times the export balance of the corresponding 1979 period... The export balance of man-made fibers (cellulosics, non-cellulosics in tow, staple, monofilament and (multifilament) yarn form at 283.7 million pounds...was 11 percent above the export balance obtained during the first quarter of 1979."

These numbers say more than can hundreds of words. What fiber producers have programmed to do and what they and their customers (man-made fiber manufacturers) have done is a product of good marketing and good manufacturing, not—as EEC nations claim—the product of "subsidized" petrochemical feedstock prices.

The Future

The marketing progress made by American fiber producers in the last 35 years as overviewed herein encourages and guides the student and professional alike. But a host of new problems face the U.S. man-made fiber producer. Key among them are:

The ongoing petrochemical cost-mill price squeeze dictates construction of even less labor intensive, more energy-efficient fiber plants. At least one producer, American Enka, is close to bringing one such plant on stream.

Legislation regarding chemical toxicity (TOSCA) is a sleeping giant soon to fully awaken. All fiber producers have for years been *policing themselves* to eliminate the use of hazardous chemicals and Monsanto has launched a broad, consumer promotional program to help the uninitiated understand how seriously these potential problems are taken.

Developing nations are building modern fiber producing units as quickly as they can. No longer will these off-shore fiber mixes consist of crude cellulosic and non-cellulosic staple and filament yarn. This is perhaps the most difficult problem of all and it will be solved by a combination of increased manufacturing efficiency and variant development to make man-made fibers more "natural fiber-like," filament yarns more spun-like, and to achieve more attractive and practical styling (color) effects in the dyebath. True to form, fiber producers will continue to attempt and succeed in helping mill customers develop apparel, home furnishings and particularly industrial end use oriented fabrics for which there are viable markets in terms of pounds, yarns and *dollars of profit.*

10. A REBIRTH OF COTTON*

By Ursula Holahan, Associate Professor of Home Economics, Clemson University

The rebirth of cotton may be a spin-off from the popularity of cotton denims and jeans and interest in things natural. But as one looks in

---

*This article first appeared in the June 1976 issue of the *Textile Marketing Letter.*

apparel shops or fabric shops, one sees very little, if any, 100 percent cotton, or blends of at least 60 percent cotton with other fibers. It appears the rebirth of cotton is only in the embryo stage. Why? There are presently new developments available for cotton fabrics on which industry is not capitalizing to their full potential. Also, much more could be done in producing more cotton fabrics if industry and cotton growers would put more money into future developments for cotton.

What's Happened to Cotton? Some consumers are asking, Why is cotton so expensive? Why can't I get an all cotton tennis outfit? Why can't I buy an all cotton dress shirt for my husband? They also ask, Why can't I buy an all cotton sheet? Why can't I buy lightweight all cotton flame retardant nightwear for my children? These are questions that cannot be easily answered, but they show the consumer interest and desire for cotton. Questions regarding the lack of lightweight all cotton flame retardant nightwear also raises a frightening issue in view of the fact the consumer has no choice in summer weight children's nightwear. She must buy polyester which melts and sticks to the skin if it gets near any source of ignition such as charcoal or the heating element on a kitchen stove. And now questions are being raised about toxicity of the flame retardant chemicals used in polyester nightwear for children. Some individuals would rather put their children in all cotton nightwear but they cannot buy it for summer wear unless they make the garment, and then they have little choice in all cotton yard goods.

There is an imbalance in the apparel field between natural fiber fabrics and synthetic fabrics. Consumers are waking up to the fact that they now have little choice of cotton garments if they want them and they are asking why.

Manufacturers and cotton growers say there is not enough profit in cotton. What have they done to create the market for it in the volume trade? If one can buy a man's quality dress shirt of all cotton for $30, or a ladies cotton blouse for $25 or more, why are there not more in the volume lines? If manufacturers can make all cotton jeans and shirts to sell at retail for $15 to $18, why not more all cotton pants suits, men's slacks, dress shirts, ladies dresses, and lightweight flame retardant nightwear? If more all cotton, or 60 percent cotton, permanent press fabrics were made available at volume prices, they would sell.

Manufacturers tell consumers the retailers don't want cotton because the garments won't sell at the high price and retailers tell consumers the manufacturers do not make cotton garments because cotton is too expensive. Is cotton that much more expensive than synthetic fibers? The fuel shortage is now closing the price gap between the synthetics and cotton. Fabric mills need to be more creative in their use of fibers, including the natural fibers.

What Are the Volume Sales? Let's look to what age level our volume sales are today. Are they below 30 years of age, or above 30 years? Those below 30 years are having a romance with the natural fibers, particularly cotton. They were 53 percent of our national population in 1970, and they are a large bulk of the volume business today. But what of the population over 30 years of age? Most of these individuals were born when cotton needed to be dampened and ironed, or remember the wash and wear cotton durable pants that abraded and easily wore out. Have these consumers been educated to the new cotton—the permanent press cotton that can be washed, dryer dried and worn without ironing? Do they realize the blends of 60 percent cotton can be more comfortable than the 35 percent cotton blends, and wear well? Do they realize the all cotton flame retardant garments won't melt and stick to the skin in a fire or when exposed to high temperatures? Do they realize that some of the synthetic fibers will melt and cause deep skin burns, often requiring skin grafting?

Those in marketing should get on the bandwagon, use more cotton, and educate the public to the advantages of cotton. Let consumers know about the new improved cotton and they will buy it. Cotton can be made easy care and attractive.

Can the price be reduced if more cotton is available and production streamlined to keep costs at an efficient price? Let's stop blaming each other for the high prices and get together to communicate and cooperate on what can be done to get more cotton products to the consumer who works in high temperature conditions, or with fuel, or where machinery gives off sparks; the consumer who is allergic to synthetic fibers; the consumer who wants the comfort of cotton in sportswear and for general use. The consumer has a right to choose between cotton, a blend of cotton, or all synthetics. The synthetic fiber industry has done an excellent job in selling the advantages of their fibers. Now the cotton industry, mills, garment manufacturers, and retailers need to let the consumer know the true facts and advantages of cotton—then cotton can sell itself.

A survey of mothers with children aged 2 to 13 taken in January through March, 1973 indicated the majority preferred dungarees, slacks, shorts, sport shirts and other tops that were made of a blend of cotton and polyester because if requires little or no ironing, is long lasting, and is neat looking. All cotton was preferred for nightwear because it is cool, absorbent, soft, long lasting and easy to wash. In 1976, new developments enable better permanent press on all cotton, or the blends with 60 percent cotton. It is almost impossible in 1976 to find summer weight all cotton nightwear for children. Researchers and mill men need to get together to engineer more satisfactory lightweight all cotton flame retardant fabrics for nightwear. When it is available, marketing and advertising people need to get together to inform the retailers and consumers about these new reborn cotton fabrics.

Information At All Levels. Few consumers know what lies behind the textile product they view in a store. Take a dress, for example. Someone designed it; another person—a buyer—selected it for her department; the store itself buys it, advertisers it, and sells .it. Many of the individuals that are involved in marketing and selling do not truly know the potential of cotton. Before they can develop and market successful cotton fabrics they need to know more about cotton and the processing of it.

Open communication and cooperation between cotton growers, marketing men, mills, designers, and all those involved in bringing the garments to consumers is essential for a successful product and market. Total marketing involves service and feedback of information at every stage in the creation, manufacturing, merchandising and sale of a product.

Marketing surveys have shown that price, color, and style are important to consummate a sale. But when the consumer starts to wear and care for a garment, then they look for comfort, easy care and durability. These latter qualities keep consumers going back for your product.

All cotton or blends of high percentages of cotton can provide comfort, easy care, durability and attractive colors provided they are properly engineered. This means working closely with all those involved with the production of fibers, to the fabric, to the garment manufacturer, to produce a product that is appealing pricewise, aesthetically, and for quality.

Over-the-Counter Trade. Some attractive cotton fabrics have been appearing in stores lately but much more can be done to provide more cotton to the home sewer. There needs to be more variety of fabrics for various activities. For example, the tennis player cannot find much in attractive cotton fabrics for tennis clothes. There is little to select in cotton flame retardant fabrics for home sewers to make clothes for their children. Little is being done by the mills and retailers to tell the home sewer about the easy care and durability of cotton. Cotton Incorporated has been working hard to let the consumer know more about the advantages of cotton. However, the mills and retailers have not made cotton readily available to the consumer. Home sewers are often frustrated and are not satisfied with what is available to them. They need reliable information on how a fabric will wear, how to care for it, whether it is shrink resistant, how it will drape on the figure (is it crisp or soft), and how it will sew. The home sewer needs and wants care labels that are informative which she can sew into garments.

Total Marketing. Total marketing involves service and feedback of information at every stage in the creation, manufacturing, merchandising and sale of a product. There are new cotton developments available today from which engineers, designers, and manufacturers could make more cotton fabrics that would appeal to a large number of consumers. Consumers have a right to easy care cotton as well as to the synthetic fibers. They also have a right to wear cotton for comfort when air-conditioning is reduced to save fuel or to cut energy costs. There is a whole new aspect for cotton that can make it a profitable fiber for wearing apparel. But don't try to fool the public by putting small percentages of cotton in fabrics and playing up the comfort factor of cotton. Consumers soon learn when some products are not what they are advertised and will not return to the marketplace for that product. Durability features, like abrasion resistance and pill resistance, can be engineered into some fabrics. It takes communication and cooperation to build better cotton fabrics for the marketplace.

11. "WOOLENS AND WORSTEDS ARE GETTING A SIGNIFICANT NEW DIRECTION"*

Says William H. Myette, Boston Wool Merchant in an Interview with Julia Morse

One questions today what has happened to the phrase "All wool and a yard wide," a phrase that summed up a concept of quality that prevailed in America and in England for generations.

With the present consumption of wool in America standing at one and a half pounds per capita, unless consumption turns sharply upward, the phrase might well be diminished to "Part wool and an inch wide."

Today's outlook for wool is defined for the *Textile Marketing Letter* by William H. Myette, a Boston wool merchant, whose experience in this field covers 38 years. He sums up the situation as follows:

Wool is alive and well in the carriage trade market. Its contribution to elegance and good living are realized as essential to the good life— specifically its warmth, resilience and richness of texture and color.

In America, the most substantial market for wool is women's apparel, a more innovative field for wool than men's apparel. A small percentage of the total supply of wool is used in rugs and draperies where wool's fire-resistance and resilience are valued highly.

Wool merchants are bullish about the possibility of an upturn in the consumption of wool, noting an increase in sampling of woolen goods by New York cutters. With the future of wool hovering around the dollar mark per pound, and assuming stability in wool price, the demand for wool should show steady growth, responding to the increasing appreciation of quality by the consumer, spurred by the recession economy.

To understand this optimistic turn of mind held today by the wool merchant, a review is necessary of the factors which brought about the downtrend in wool for the past two decades. These appear to be:

1. **The American Lifestyle.** The swing to convenience products, with "wash and wear" the keynote of sales and promotion.

---

*This article first appeared in the June 1975 issue of the *Textile Marketing Letter.*

2. **The "Pricing Out" of Wool.** Wide fluctuations in
   the price of raw wool. During the Korean War,
   wool never returned to a practical price
   foundation. Speculative binges increased price
   instability. Wool never fully recovered its market.

3. **Competition from Eastern Countries.** Japan is the
   second largest consumer of wool. Wool is an
   important export product of Japan which excels
   also in fine quality wool fabrics, notably worsteds.

4. **Strong Promotion of Synthetics.** Fiber industry
   promotion budgets accelerated—in fact created—the
   rapid growth and development of the synthetics
   markets by means of sophisticated marketing
   techniques.

5. **Shrinkage in Wool Manufacturing.** Many of the
   family-owned mills in New England which were
   the foundation of the American woolen textile
   trade are gone.

These are some of the factors leading to the market downtrend, not only of wool but of all the natural fibers. All natural fibers are equated today with high price. In the retail store we find a cotton blouse is priced as a luxury fashion.

Wool appears in such exclusive designed lines as those of Anne Klein, Oscar de la Renta and Bill Blass, contributing to the value which warrants high price. Because of design uniformity, the only distinction between a woman's gray flannel slacks priced at $110 and one selling for $49.50 is the quality of the workmanship and the fabric of 100 percent wool.

The wool merchant's optimism over the growth of the wool market involves a realistic attitude concerning the factors which created the mammoth synthetic market. It is based also on observation of changing factors important in American life. To be considered are:

1. The oil shortage has alerted attention to the
   natural warmth of wool. During the first winter
   shortage in 1974, retail stores were unprepared for
   the consumer call for wool garments. Another
   aspect in the limitation of the oil supply is, of
   course, the effect it will have on both synthetic
   fiber supply and pricing.

2. Flammability is an issue of increasing importance
   in legislation. Flammability laws should result in
   the use of more wool in drapery fabrics and in
   children's apparel. Wool has innate inflammability.
   In Canada this realization has resulted in greater
   use of wool. Awareness of this is limited in

America because there has been no cohesive effort
to inform the consumer as to the inherent
advantages of wool.

3. The retailer is alerted to the boredom experienced
by the consumer in being confronted with rack
after rack of polyester dresses. He is concerned that
clothing expenditures for the family may soon
drop below the consistently held level of eight
percent of the total spendable family income.
Retail merchants are aware, too, that the consumer
is becoming more selective and quality conscious
in her buying habits.

On balance, the optimism of the wool merchant is based on the realization that a new quality era of consumer purchasing will bring into sharp focus the values of wool: its beauty, warmth, resilience and fire-resistance.

To accomplish this, a coordinated effort is required on the part of the weavers and knitters of wool fabrics, apparel manufacturers and retail merchants.

The consumer has indicated her readiness to pay a fair price for the qualities represented in wool.

The question that we in the industry have to answer is: Will we let her know its values and where it can be purchased?

And, finally, is the wool industry prepared to make this effort now that time is opportune?

12. SILK'S ANCIENT ROAD IS OPEN AGAIN*

By Julia Morse, Consultant

Silk runs an erratic course in textile marketing. Since Japan has disappeared from the scene as an exporter of silk, the Orient is still proving a productive source for silk fabrics, both solid colors and prints, originating in Mainland China.

The International Silk Association, with headquarters in New York City, was disbanded in 1977. Its principal function since the end of World War II has been to foster the use of silk in America. Japan was the major source of promotion funds as the largest exporter of silk to the United States in the post-war period. But now the home market absorbs all the silk produced in Japan and, surprisingly, Japan too is an importer of silk from China.

---

*This article first appeared in the May 1978 issue of the Textile Marketing Letter.

As the role of New York in fostering a silk market has diminished, another East Coast city has picked up the challenge and is developing it with enthusiasm and high expectations. Boston, known for its beans, codfish, and blizzards, now has an association with that symbol of elegance—silk.

China views Wellman, Inc. of Boston as one of the largest importers of silk in this country. First undertaken as a venture, Wellman, Inc. found silk to be an important commodity in the apparel market and in the over-the-counter trade. In commenting on silk, George J. Ertlmeier, manager of the International Trading Division, said that its high price has not been a marketing obstacle. He found that silk has a fresh appeal for the flourishing home sewing market where it offers a new luxuriousness. And as for the American couture trade, it never really abandoned silk, relying on France and Italy for imported fashion fabrics.

Wellman, Inc. is an old and honored textile name in Boston, its founder having built the family fortune in the last century as a woolen merchant. More recently, Wellman, Inc. opened textile mills in North Carolina, specializing in synthetic fibers, with fill-fiber the largest operation.

Distribution of its silk lines is handled by Wellman, Inc. through sales representatives to both high- and medium-priced apparel manufacturers, with about 80 percent of its current volume going to over-the-counter trade.

Silk's traditional drawbacks—high price and impracticality in contrast to easy-care synthetics—have not daunted the new home sewer whose high standards are an upgrading force. "Luxurious silks from the Orient," according to Mr. Ertlmeier, "provide the allure that is sought now that over-the-counter is a quality market."

"Our people select the goods in China," he explains, "from a splendid variety of solid and printed silks. To get the Chinese to use American designed patterns is difficult, though not impossible. At this stage, this is not essential as their print styling is good and offers the American market fresh ideas."

Future marketing of original designs is planned by Wellman, Inc., offering the advantages of Oriental craftsmanship combined with American creativity. "In the days ahead, the market will be looking for a broad-based appeal," explains Mr. Ertlmeier, "and we intend to be ready."

As these plans go into action, Boston will become a central source of silk fabric and the freshness of American design. Wellman, Inc. sees an accelerating business. Currently the Wellman exclusives are broadening the range of silk fabrics available to the fashion world. These include decorative fabrics, scarves and accessories, as well as fabrics for apparel. An example of this broad range of ideas is the new line of silk umbrellas with patterns designed by Francie of Wellman's Design Division, who has a special flair with silk without reference to traditional Oriental styling.

The ancient road to the Orient is now reopened. The silk trade is very much alive. Always the most luxurious of the fibers, its course in textile history has not run smoothly. Yet, as it loses ground in one market, it accelerates in another. Over the years, the elegance of silk has been essential to fashion, and fashion is the mainspring of textile marketing.

13. UNIQUE ARE SOME OF THE USES OF MAN-MADE FIBERS*

Medical: Artificial Organs. The idea of using artificial organs to sustain and improve human life is not new. In 1542, a Flemish anatomist studied the use of reeds from tall grass to replace sections of arteries in animals. Over the centuries, some progress was made. However, during the past 20 years amazing breakthroughs have taken place.

It is estimated that about 100,000 Americans are living with artificial organs. Some surgeons believe that eventually it will be possible to replace more than half of the human body with artificial devices. Many materials are now being used for artificial organs, and some of them involve man-made fibers.

Polyester, for example, can be woven or knit into a fabric or made into the thinnest mesh or web for surgical uses, such as artificial blood vessels, patches for arteries, innerlinings for some artificial hearts, or covering material for the metal rings and struts of artificial heart valves. Many artificial hearts utilize a polyester mesh fabric as a reinforcing agent for silicone rubber or other polymers.

Flurocarbon fiber is used to build up receding chins, to improve the shape of deformed noses, and to repair the bony socket of the eye. This fiber, closely woven fabric, also has been used to patch arteries and holes in the heart. Nylon mesh is used for hernia repairs.

Textile Membranes Improve Roadways. Surface cracking is a prime problem and expense for road and highway maintenance officials. Cracking occurs when moisture seeps into the foundation of a road and then freezes, expands, and cracks the asphalt pavement. When ice forms within the broken surface, it also can quickly tear pavement apart. Potholes develop and the road must be repaired and resurfaced. Some roads

---

*Most man-made fibers are designed for use in general apparel, home furnishings, and industrial products. Some, however, find their way into quite unusual and different applications. While these do not represent the industry's major markets, they do illustrate the amazing versatility of man-made fibers and the limitless possibilities for improving products through their use now and in the future. Reprinted from "Focus on Man-Made Fibers," Man-Made Fiber Producers Association, Inc., 1150 Seventeenth Street, N.W., Washington, D.C. 20036.

This article appeared in the January 1977 issue of the *Textile Marketing Letter.*

receive so many surface layers that curbs are virtually buried, yet the cracks can be expected to reappear within a few years.

Highway maintenance departments can now solve this problem by using a nonwoven fabric layer as a stress-relieving membrane between the roadbed and the surface pavement. The fabric is made of nonwoven olefin, polyester, or nylon fibers. It is waterproof, decay and tear resistant, and indifferent to freezing temperatures or the heat of melted asphalt.

After holes and cracks in the existing pavement are repaired, then the fabric membrane is laid, saturated with asphalt and bonded down. This provides a flexible moisture barrier. A black-top overlay is then applied and the road is ready for use.

Follow-up surveys after five years show that roads with textile membranes remain about 94 percent crack-free. Officials report that road repairs can be made more quickly and economically with this new method because road crews can place the fabric layer rapidly and use a thinner topping of asphalt than would normally be required. This technique also is used to protect bridge decks from freeze-thaw damage and from corrosive salts.

Spunbonded man-made fibers also are used as support membranes for aggregate surfaced access or haul roads during construction, logging or mining projects. The support membranes increase the load-bearing ratio of silty or clay soils, thereby reducing the amount of aggregate and maintenance required. Spunbonded nylon mats are used to protect against water and wind erosion. They are used to cover steep slopes, line roadside ditches, and reinforce stream and lake shorelines.

Fabric membranes also are used on railroad track beds, parking lots, tennis courts, and driveways.

Body Armor for Crime Fighters. King Arthur's knights, and more recently airmen of World War II, donned heavy body armor as protective clothing. Today, a man-made fiber called aramid, which is lighter and tougher than steel, is used to make a fabric that provides protection against bullets from certain types of firearms.

Specially designed undervests, made from layers of finely woven fabric of aramid yarns, are used mainly by police departments. It is estimated that nearly 40,000 policemen are using this new body armor.

One style, a seven-layer undervest, weighs only two and a half pounds and scarcely impedes movement. It can deflect a knife slash and stop a .38 caliber bullet traveling at a velocity of 850 feet per second (typical velocity at a distance of 10 feet). The ".38" is one of the most commonly used handguns in the United States. A .38 caliber bullet will dent, but not penetrate, the vest.

Another model, a 23-layer vest, is two-thirds of an inch thick and will stop a .44 magnum slug. Neither vest, however, can stop a high power rifle bullet at relatively close range.

Fibers That Reinforce Plastics. Specially prepared rayon or acrylic yarns or tow can be slowly heated and stretched in a way that drives off most elements except carbon, leaving fibers that are more than 95 percent pure carbon.

These fibers, often called graphite fibers, are embedded in plastic resin to form a thin, flexible, gumlike material. This material can be formed into sheets, rods, tubes, or other usable structural forms, then heat set into a variety of shapes ranging from guitars to golf club shafts.

Carbon-fiber-reinforced plastics are used as substitutes for metals because they offer high strength and rigidity at a fraction of the weight of metal. For example, for equal volumes, they are one-fifth the weight of steel while exhibiting equal tensile strength.

Graphite laminates have been used widely in spacecraft and missiles because of their lightweight strength and stiffness. They also provide industry with a new material for high-speed machinery parts, automotive components, construction and piping equipment and precision instruments.

Aramid fibers are also used in reinforced plastics as a substitute for structural fiber glass. These high-strength, stiff fibers behave much like carbon fibers in reinforced plastics.

The consumer finds this new family of strong, lightweight materials in sporting goods, such as tennis rackets, fishing rods, ski poles, and the hulls of sailboats and canoes.

Artists Discover a "Hidden" Fiber. Sometimes a product finds its way into a market totally different from the one originally intended for it. Such is the case of a spunbonded polyester sheet structure originally intended for "hidden" uses, such as apparel innerlining, underlays for carpeting, and backing for vinyl wall coverings. When artists began using the polyester material as a "canvas" for watercolors, oils, acrylics, and inks, they discovered some unusual effects. Traditional watercolor techniques were altered, because spunbonded polyester is nonabsorbent and water evaporates leaving only particles of the paint's pigment on the surface of the fiber. Colors dry lighter in shade giving a different effect from a conventional watercolor. Artists found that when using this material, oil paints resemble pastels and India ink takes on a charcoal look.

Fibers in the Sporting Field. More than 50 million fishermen will spend in excess of $200 million on rods, reels, lines, and lures this year. Many of the rods will contain carbon fibers and most lines will be made of nylon. There is new nylon monofilament fishing line that has built-in fluorescent glow that makes it easier to see and control. It also is modified for extra knot strength, since knotting can greatly weaken a line. In addition, it combines such properties as abrasion resistance, proper limpness, controlled strength, and good shock resistance. Carbon fibers are used in golf clubs to create lightweight, strong shafts. Many golf bags are also made of nylon.

Man-made fibers are utilized in many ways by boating and sailing enthusiasts. Sails are generally made of polyester because it offers lightweight strength plus quick-drying and mildew-resistant qualities, as well as durability against sunlight and salt spray. Floatable olefin ropes make retrieval easier; nylon nets and boat covers are quick drying and strong.

Footballs, baseballs, and basketballs are sewn with nylon thread. Uniforms of most professional football players are made from blends of spandex with nylon or rayon while the majority of baseball uniforms used in the major leagues are polyester warp knits. Artificial turf, on which most major sporting events are played, is made from nylon. Spunbonded nylon mats are sometimes planted several inches under an artificial or natural turf surface on athletic fields, playgrounds, or recreation areas. They are an excellent condition in that they resist soil compaction, maintain soil porosity, and promote uniform moisture distribution. Even the cheerleaders' pennants are made of man-made fibers.

Silver Threads Among the Nylon. Some nylon carpet fibers are coated with silver to prevent the buildup of static electricity. Other specially designed, electrically conductive fibers have been developed that also reduce static discharge. The use of only a small amount of these special fibers in a carpet will control static problems. Carpets represent the largest single non-apparel market for man-made fibers, as 98 percent of all surface fibers used in carpets are man-made fibers.

Fibers in Construction Projects. Huge, lightweight "skins" of man-made fiber fabric can be shaped into dramatic forms that provide coverings for stadiums, theaters, car parks, outdoor restaurants, and other public gathering places. Many of these futuristic structures and domes are air supported and can be erected more quickly and less expensively than regular buildings. Inflatable air structures may serve as permanent or temporary housing. Graceful canopies made of man-made fibers can be stretched over an open area giving an impression of lightness and airiness. Others may appear as bubble-shaped domes. Still others may be foam coated into rigid, permanent structures. Knitted or woven fabrics of man-made fibers also can be coated and used as a major building material. They are stronger and lighter than metal and, in most cases, less expensive.

In Hawaii, high-strength, rubber-coated nylon fabric has been used to line that state's largest reservoir. More than five million square feet of the specially engineered nylon was sunk, without tearing, under 50 feet of water to the unstable volcanic soils of the reservoir floor.

Another unusual application of man-made fibers is in connection with the placement of piers and pilings in harbors. Polyester or nylon zipper bags are placed around wooden pilings by divers, then filled with cement. This hardens in place, thus eliminating the necessity of building cofferdams.

Slotted plastic drain pipes are often used along highways, adjacent to shopping centers or in other areas subject to heavy water runoff. If the surrounding soil contains fine particles, it can frequently clog the pipes causing water overflows. The use of man-made fiber fabrics in subsurface draining systems has been proven to be more effective, less expensive, faster to install, and easier to maintain than pipe drainage systems. Trenches lined with nonwoven fabrics of man-made fibers and filled with aggregate carry off excess water. A drainage pipe is not required since the fabric serves as a soil filter. The fabric also is decay proof, unaffected by temperature extremes, and inert to, most soil chemicals.

Nylon safety nets have been used on some of the biggest construction projects of the last decade including the World Trade Center in New York, the Sears Tower in Chicago, NASA's Space Assembly Building, and the second span of the Delaware Memorial Bridge. The net catches the workers in the event of a fall. A new cable lock stitch was developed that can withstand the force of a 350-pound sandbag dropped 70 feet (24,500 foot-pound impact). The construction of the diamond-shaped net contributes to slower deceleration of a falling object, thus resulting in a softer landing and safer working conditions.

Past, Present, Future Fibers. Thirty years ago, man-made fibers accounted for less than 15 percent of the raw materials used by American textile mills. Each year since 1945, the use of these fibers has increased. During 1975, man-made fibers provided 70 percent of the total fiber requirements of U.S. mills.

Man-made fibers have been the motivating force behind new ideas for textile products. They have brought the American public the widest selection of the most beautiful textiles in history with added features of easy care and greater durability. They have given industry the strongest fabrics for better products, enabling them to use textiles in applications never before thought of.

In the future, new man-made fibers and variations of existing ones will be developed to meet new needs. There may be clothing that is color changing and temperature adjusting, sports shirts that allow one to suntan, draperies that heat a room, or textile membranes that melt snow and ice from roads. There may be a greater use of textiles in constructing homes and buildings, and, in years ahead, complete temperature-controlled domed cities covered by a single sheet of fabric. Many new and unusual products will certainly surface and the man-made fiber industry will play a leading role in their development.

14. THE MARKET INTRODUCTION OF QIANA NYLON FIBER*

By James S. Rumsey, Qiana Marketing Manager,
E.I. du Pont de Nemours and Co., Inc.

One thing E. I. du Pont de Nemours Company did not forecast accurately when it devised its marketing plan for Qiana nylon was the plot

---

*This article first appeared in the September 1969 issue of the *Textile Marketing Letter.*

of Danny Bendit-Cohn, the communist-anarchist, who caused a major strike affecting the entire French economy for three weeks, but our forecasters for new product ventures have promised to do better next time.

Red Danny nearly brought the entire introduction program to a halt when fabrics woven in the deepest of secrecy in the South of France could not be dyed and finished in the French plants which were shut down as a result of the general nationwide strike in May 1968.

The story of this fiber goes back more than 30 years ago when a couple of du Pont chemists found an entirely new long chain fiber-forming chemical polymer which they felt had an impressive balance of physical and chemical properties.

I know you no longer visualize that in a situation like this a chemist rushes into the office of his supervisor with a test tube in his hand and yells, "Eureka, I've got it," because, as you know, the problem is not finding new chemical formulations but determining which of the thousands of formulations provide the best balance of properties and economics and warrant the expenditure of enormous amounts of time and money to reduce them to practice. This decision was made on Fiber Y, as QIANA was first known, and a supersecret group was assigned to its development.

Next, Textile Fibers Management concluded that the fiber had demonstrated its potential in internal testing all the way through to the finished fabrics and garment wear tests, and the Executive Committee approved the proposal to invest in equipment to manufacture it.

The Marketing Plan which constituted an important element of the proposal to top management took nearly a year to develop.

A key element in the plan involved risking laboratory size samples of yarn, perhaps prematurely, in commercial fabric development effort. This we decided to do in Europe where we could avail ourselves of the cottage industry type manufacturing which means, as the word implies, a number of small weavers who are really farmers, who make cloth on leased looms during off-farming hours, giving nearly complete attention to the fabric.

The Fabric Development Stage. The fabrics produced by these people, located in France, Italy, and Switzerland, are nearly perfect and it was a natural as it turned out for QIANA because they could work with very small quantities of the new variable yarn from our laboratory and produce the very nearly perfect fabrics of QIANA which the world saw for the first time in July 1968 in Paris.

We wanted to conduct this operation in strict secrecy, so that if a deficiency was discerned, we could have the opportunity to correct it in our laboratory before proceeding. We also wanted to complete the filing of some of the key end use patents which were to become an essential part of our marketing strategy. And lastly, we found that it is hard to preserve any lead time over our vigorous competitors unless we keep them as much in the dark as possible.

The maintenance of secrecy about this operation was very difficult. We started the program by assembling a conference of the officials of five of the best silk mills in the world who had never, before then, been in the same room together. We asked them to sign a Secrecy Agreement before inviting them to the meeting, which turned out to be quite a difficult thing to accomplish. Nevertheless, they all signed the agreement and they all came. We had decided that the best way to get a sharp assessment of the fiber and at the same time get the attention of these experts was to run a small contest. We showed the group nine fabrics, six of QIANA, three of silk and told them we would award a magnum of champagne to anyone who could distinguish the silk fabrics from QIANA without melting the fibers or using a pocket microscope.

The tension in that meeting for the next thirty minutes was just about as high as it could get. The silk men were striving for champagne and the Du Ponters were fearful that the ability to distinguish between silk and QIANA would be too easy—but this did not prove to be the case. Less than half the members of the conference made the distinction correctly and, in any event, by the time the little contest was over, we had their undivided interest in the new fiber.

For seven months we had a technical service force of sixteen men working in the tiny hamlets in France, Italy, and Switzerland, where the cottage industry weavers were located. And believe me, it isn't easy to keep the presence of so many Americans in Europe working on a new fiber a secret from some pretty smart competitors and from very smart newspaper people.

Introduction to Couture Houses. Now came the problem posed by Red Danny, because in May 1968 many of the fabrics were woven and required dyeing and finishing and none of the textile plants were working in France because of the general strike. It is interesting, though, that the farmers could continue weaving fabrics during a strike because power to the farm houses where the farmers had the loom was continued, while power to the dye plants was cut off. This gave us the problem of getting a finished cloth out of France into Switzerland and Italy for dyeing and finishing, and then back to France for fabrication into garments with only a few days to spare. By the time the streets were cleared in Paris and the designers' seamstresses went back to work there were only fifteen working days for the couture houses to complete anywhere from one-half to two-thirds of their collections.

The Simultaneous Announcement. Now to leave the designers for a moment, I would like to deal with the mechanics of the introduction. The trademark name was an enormous problem—a little harder, we think, than inventing the new chemical. We started with a list of 6,500 artificial words punched out by a computer which was instructed to take the twenty-six letters in the English language and print out a combination in a series such as consonant vowel consonant vowel, consonant consonant vowel, consonant vowel, etc. We practically memorized this list, searching it for those words which would have a glamorous, exotic look, a pleasing sound and which would neither be in conflict with other registered trademarks nor mean something unpleasant in some language such as Japanese, Phillippino, or Swahili. Hundreds of these marks were searched and dropped by the wayside because of conflict. Several remained and the Du Pont Company Management had to elect one of these for the new fiber.

We chose a bit of international drama for the trademark introduction. The fiber was introduced to newspapers, magazines, radio, TV, and wire service people in eight cities of the world in five languages at the same instant, so that at 7:00 AM in Los Angeles and 10:00 AM in Buenos Aires, New York, and Montreal and at 3:00 PM in London, Paris, Dusseldorf, and Milano over 1,000 editors saw the experimental fabrics which had been woven and finished at our Chestnut Run Laboratories and heard the trademark name.

We were very fortunate with the publicity we got from this effort. It generated nearly 15,000 inquiries from different elements of the textile industry and from a number of colleges and universities—all curious about the properties and potential of the new product.

There are really only a few more things to say about the introduction. We had the problem during the secrecy period of introducing the material to the French couture designers without disclosing what it was, and yet we wanted, of course, to be honest with them. The system we used was for the fabric houses to show fabrics for initial placement identified only by number, which is standard practice for the fabric house lines at this stage. Later, when the first sample cuts had to be delivered, the couture was advised that if they ordered fabric number so and so, on the premise that it was silk, that they could withdraw the order because it was not silk; it was a new fiber. There were no withdrawals that we know of.

I must say also that we wanted the introduction in the July 1968 Paris couture to come as a surprise so we did not say during the trademark introduction in June 1968 where the fiber would appear in the first commercial garments. You may be sure this led to a number of aggressive questions by our alert friends in the news media. As a matter of fact, we couldn't quite keep this secret either because Fairchild Publications found out about this one, and printed a story a few weeks before the fact that several of the key French couturiers were working with QIANA.

Now just to give you a little bit of summary of the introduction: more than 116 garments were shown by the top Paris couturiers made of QIANA, and response by retailers was excellent. This was followed by the introduction in the U.S. designers' spring clothes in November 1968 when QIANA appeared in nearly 100 garments made by top designers in the United States. Next was the third round—the Spring/Summer clothes in Paris and Rome collections shown in January 1969 in which QIANA appeared in 80 costumes.

What's Ahead for Qiana? As you may already know, we license the use of the QIANA trademark to identify the new yarn *only* in those finished fabrics which meet Du Pont's quality standards.

We plan to sustain a heavy program on quality throughout the years so that the mills, manufacturers, and retailers will be able to depend upon consumer demand stemming from favorable experience with quality merchandise. We want the industry to have the opportunity to deal with a "pre-sold" item to the extent that we can make it happen. This means working hard on all those things which go with development and maintenance of an image of high quality for the new fiber.

15. FIFTEEN STEPS IN THE MARKETING OF NEW SYNTHETIC FIBER*

By R. Richard Carens, Director of Merchandising,
Beaunit Fibers Division, Beaunit Corporation

It has now become essential to the fiber producer to make a thorough analysis of the market, to zero in on a particular end use, to isolate the components of demand, to determine the exact nature of the need and THEN to develop a *compatible* product which comes as close as can be practically achieved to fill that need. A product *compatible* with the technical requirements of the mills and finishers, *compatible* in blends with other fibers and *compatible* with the day-to-day necessities of the consumer. But whichever way you look at it, it amounts to a specific development for a *specific end use*.

To highlight the marketing span in today's fiber business, let us follow step by step a typical sequence of operations that would move a fiber from test tube to fabric and from fabric to consumer:

1. Research laboratory produces new fiber.

2. Fiber potential is evaluated by fiber producer for performance and spinnability.

3. Fabric samples of the new fiber are tested to investigate possible end uses.

4. Fabric development suggests modifications of the fiber for various end uses.

5. Experimental lots of fiber are sent to mills for test runs; problems of spinning, dyeing, and finishing are cooperatively solved between mills and fiber producer.

*This article first appeared in the May 1967 issue of the *Textile Marketing Letter*.

6. Fiber producer's consumer testing and fabric development groups determine minimum standard requirements for fabrics.

7. Marketing Research recommends primary end use markets for new fabrics.

8. Fiber producer establishes a merchandising strategy and a campaign theme and broadcasts the plan to mills, converters, manufacturers, and retailers.

9. Consumer advertising and public relations tie-in with merchandising group.

10. Fiber producer's licensing department sees that product specifications are maintained.

11. International and domestic "couture" houses are sometimes asked to create new fashions of the new fiber.

12. Fiber producer's retail representatives set up displays in major stores and provide training and point of sale material for sales personnel.

13. Consumer Education program is instituted to promote further familiarity with the new fiber.

14. Market Research feeds back information to marketing department on consumer reactions and attitudes toward new product.

15. Research and Development diversifies fiber end uses and develops further improvements.

...And during all this time, the merchandising staff keeps knocking on doors. So goes the cycle....

16. FIBER ADVERTISING ISN'T AS EASY AS IT LOOKS*

By Bernard Rosner, Copy Chief,
Chirurg & Cairns, New York

Suppose you're a fiber producer and you're planning to come out with a new fiber on a licensed brand name marketing basis. Let's see what you're up against in terms of the consumer.

---

*This article first appeared in the March 1967 issue of the *Textile Marketing Letter*.

The Competition. Your competition is anyone who is currently trying to penetrate the public consciousness with a fiber name of any kind. Not only has the number of generic names swelled during the last two decades, but there has been a brand name explosion as well.

To get an accurate picture of what the consumer is being faced with today, glance through a copy of *The New York Times Magazine.* Any given issue is likely to turn up the following names: Avril rayon; Avisco acetate; Dacron polyester; Acrilan acrylic; Herculon olefin; Arnel triacetate; Creslan acrylic; Estron acetate; Kodel polyester; Orlon acrylic; Verel modacrylic; Celanese nylon; Caprolan nylon; Enkalure nylon by Enka; Crepeset nylon by Enka; and others. Unless the reader is a textile engineer, he or she is lost. (So are many textile engineers.)

Choosing a Name. With that in mind, your first job is to find a name for your fiber. Most of the people who have gone this route before have chosen completely meaningless names, and tried to endow them with meaning through advertising. If the name "Arnel" suggests crease retention, it's not because of the name itself, but what the name was made to stand for. (A notable exception is "Tough Stuff," Beaunit's new name for their vycron polyester.)

How to Advertise Your Fiber. Okay, you've now got a fiber and a name. You've developed a marketing strategy that includes a profile of the audience you want to reach and what you want to stand for to that audience. Now you've got to find a way to get there. A way that will make your voice stand out from the crowd. Maybe you need a slogan.

Slogans seem to result in higher brand name registration than non-slogan fiber advertising. In a recent survey, an advertising agency with a fiber account took one of the fashion supplements of *The New York Times* and masked out all trade and company names. The issue was then routed among the agency's staff and among their client's staff. The highest degree of brand or company name recognition came from Avril, Klopman, and Riegel. All examples of slogan-type advertising.

One popular route is that of the "franchised concept." An example is "Actionwear," a concept originally built around the fiber Blue "C" Nylon. Any time the consumer bought an Actionwear garment, she was buying Blue "C" Nylon.

It's interesting to note that even with a concept as seemingly clean-cut and simple as "Actionwear" the ads are still sprinkled with specific names: Actionwear; Blue "C" Nylon; Chemstrand; Monsanto, the name of the mill or converter who made the fabric; the name of the garment manufacturer.

A Different Route. Recognizing the difficulty of trying to embed a new name in the public's mind, two manufacturers chose to take a different route entirely. Joyce fabrics launched a campaign under the theme: "Poor Joyce. Nobody remembers her name." And Courtauld promoted Fibre and

Coloray as: "The fibers nobody remembers;" and "Fibers you can forget about."

The Power of Advertising. In the face of this highly competitive and confused picture, would you be better off selling your fiber as an un-branded commodity? Not if you want to hit the jackpot. For despite the clutter of brands in the fiber arena, nearly all of the great fiber successes have been achieved through promotion.

The trick is to out-promote the next guy. And that doesn't mean you have to out-weigh him. It means you have to out-class him. For good advertising is the most effective way of separating one fiber from another.

A good advertising program should contain enough "institutional" advertising to educate your audience to the merits of your fiber. Far too frequently a fiber advertiser spends his entire budget promoting other people's fabrics or garments.

Despite the proliferation of new fibers, one thing is certain—more fibers will come. Even so, there's plenty of room for your fiber provided you're willing to give it the benefit of good advertising. And if you want to know what good advertising is all about, sit down and talk with a good advertising agency.

Chapter Four

Textile Chemicals, Dyestuffs, and Special Finishes

OVERVIEW

By Michael James Drews

It is possible that no other segment of the textile industry faces the spectre of change that confronts the one loosely grouped under the headings of textile chemicals, dyestuffs, and special finishes. With the exception of finishes such as Scotchguard® or Zepel® and the sanforization process, these products are generally not consumer oriented materials. In terms of a market, they have little identity of their own, are often supplied by small companies and generally do not have a significant level of research and development behind them. They have been marketed by personal contact, advertising in technical journals, and at technical conventions. Whether or not this marketing strategy will continue to be successful in the 80's may depend on a variety of factors which in the past have not been very important in this segment of the textile industry.

As will be shown later, there are some indications that future changes in this market may be less likely to come from the marketplace itself, as from other factors such as changes in processing technology and increasing government regulation. Before these are discussed, a brief look at where chemicals are used in the textile industry and what they do may help to define the diversity of this market. This discussion is not meant to be comprehensive at all, but only an indication of the range of chemical applications used in this segment of our industry.

Excluding the chemicals used in the production of some of the natural fibers, the first extensive use of chemical additives occurs in the spinning of synthetic fibers. The chemicals used in this process are called spin finishes and they are applied immediately upon stabilization of the fiber structure during manufacture. They serve as lubricants during subsequent yarn processing and as agents to reduce the buildup of static charge on the processing equipment. Spin finishes often contain other additives and are usually complex and proprietary mixtures. They are difficult to chemically analyze and tend to be designed for specific end use applications and processing steps.

The next major use of chemical additives is in the sizing of the warp yarns in preparation for weaving. The principle purpose of applying warp sizes to yarns is the protection of the yarn during the weaving process. Size formulations, while tailored to specific applications, can be more easily identified as to their chemical content than spin finishes. The principle ingredients in a size formulation may be starch, polyvinyl alcohol, or a starch/polyvinyl alcohol combination, along with lubricants and film forming assist additives. A newer class of size that is beginning to be used more extensively in the industry are the water soluble polyester warp sizes. Because sizing tends to be an energy intensive process, there has been considerable interest in new technology for the application of sizes; the two most promising techniques are foam application and hot melt sizing.

The next three chemical steps are generally applied to the woven fabrics and, depending on the fabric and its intended end use, may vary in sequence, but are generally in the order of desizing to remove the warp size, scouring as preparation for further finishing and bleaching. These processes are often referred to as the fabric preparation steps. The major chemicals employed in these steps are enzymes, mineral acids, and peroxides in desizing; caustic, soda ash, and surfactants in scouring; and chlorine containing, peroxide or perborate bleaches in bleaching.

The next step in this generalized processing scheme for the production of the textile fabric would be dyeing. The application of dyestuffs to textile goods is perhaps the most complicated, and accordingly the most sophisticated, of all the textile wet finishing operations. The variety and number of dyestuffs available to the dyer can be almost described as limitless. This is indicated by simply considering the classes of dyestuffs available for general use on the major natural and synthetic fibers used in textile applications.

The final step the fabric is generally exposed to is the series of operations generally referred to as finishing. In these operations a variety of textile chemicals are used to impart specific properties to the fabric, for example, the application of permanent press resins to cotton/polyester

TABLE I
DYE CLASSES USED WITH MAJOR TEXTILE
FIBERS

Fiber	Dye Class
Acetate	Disperse
Cotton/Rayon	Direct, Reactive, Vat, Sulfur, Azoics
Nylons	Disperse, Acid, Premetallized
Regular Polyester	Disperse
Deep Dye Polyester	Disperse, Basic

blend fabrics to gain wrinkle resistance and the wash-wear characteristics demanded by the American marketplace. While permanent press is probably the most familiar of the textile finishes, a variety of other specific chemical applications may be added to the fabric, such as soil release finishes, antistatic finishes, flame retardants, hand modifiers and water repellents.

Up to this time we have considered the use of chemicals in the preparation of a textile good in respect to specific finishing steps. In addition to the primary ingredients, such as the dyestuff, the permanent press resin, or the bleaching agent, in all of these processes there are usually added a number of chemicals often referred to as auxiliaries. This class of textile chemicals is the broadest of the categories, and many of them may be used only in specific processes, such as carriers in dyeing. Others are employed generally in wet processing, such as defoaming agents which may be used in finishing, dyeing and certain preparation steps, etc. These materials tend to be produced by the smaller suppliers and often little technical information is available about these products. Some of the more important textile chemical auxiliaries are the accellerants/carriers, retardants, and gums and thickeners (or viscosity modifiers) used in the dyeing of textile materials. In addition, with the increased activity in foam processing, there are agents specifically designed to enhance foam formation while other chemicals are added to prevent foam formation. Of course, one of the most generally applied of all classes of textile chemical auxiliaries are the surfactants. These fall into three general classes: the nonionics, cationics and anionic surfactants, and may be employed in any textile finishing operation where an interaction occurs between a chemical and a fiber surface. There are a host of other additives such as lubricants, antistats, waxes, etc. that are employed in various specific applications.

An important class of chemicals finding increased applications in the textile industry are the latex emulsions. These are used for carpet backings, binders in pigment printing processes, and increasingly as binders for nonwoven fabric structures. Again, these materials are often more or less tailored to a specific end use application; however, their chemical structure falls into one of four general categories. These are the polyvinyl chloride or PVC latices, the SBR or styrenebutadiene rubber latices and the acrylate and acrylic latices.

By this time it should be apparent that this particular segment of the textile industry is exceedingly important and extraordinarily diverse. This diversity makes the development of a specific marketing strategy extremely difficult. In addition, the nature of the products and the lack of inherent technical information has led to a personal contact-price structure marketing approach. However, there are three factors which are becoming increasingly important in this segment of the industry, as in the American chemical industry in general, and these factors may have a significant affect on the way the products are used in the textile chemicals, dyestuffs and special finishes segment of the textile industry. These three factors listed in no specific order are government regulation, the shift in basic research and development emphasis, and new machinery process development.

The government regulations having particular impact on this segment of the industry can be identified as four: the Occupational Safety and Health Act, which controls worker exposure to chemical additives in the textile plant; the Toxic Substances and Control Act, which regulates the disposal of the waste products generated during wet textile chemical processing; the Environmental Protection Wastewater Recovery and Clean Air Acts and finally the Consumer Products Safety Commission's regulation of consumer exposure to potential carcinogens. An example of how these have already affected the marketing of dyestuff materials can be seen as a result of the scramble which has occurred to not only replace benzidine based dyestuffs in various applications, but also to certify the absence of benzidine containing intermediates in the production of various dyestuffs. As a result of these regulations, performance and disclosure of chemical composition are becoming more important than price/personal contact and advertising in the use of certain additives in the plant.

In the past, the textile industry has depended heavily on its suppliers in the chemical, fiber production and dyestuff manufacturing areas for much of its basic research and development, and consequently often lacked the technical capability to evaluate many of the products used in their plants. As these basic industries shift their research activities from new product research to more customer service/product development research, the textile industry is having to develop a higher level of in plant technical expertise. With this new expertise will come the ability to make more performance related evaluations of potential new products in their mills.

New machinery developments will also have an effect on the marketing of textile chemicals in general. The machinery manufacturers are being prodded by four specific incentives both in the development of new dyeing and finishing machinery and also in process modifications.

These can be identified as: (1) the increased importance of energy conservation, (2) the trend towards increasing processing speed by replacing batch processes with continuous ranges, (3) the need to reduce the chemicals needed for a specific step, and also the more efficient application of expensive chemicals, and (4) the reduction of labor costs resulting from increased automation. New machinery creates the need for new chemicals and, perhaps more importantly, eliminates the need for other chemicals that have been used successfully in the past.

In conclusion, it appears that as we look into the 80's in this particular segment of the textile industry, we might expect the marketing to become more technically oriented in the future. We might also predict a lessening of customer demand as a force for creating the impetus for new product development. Two current examples of the effects of the above factors on changing the marketing of textile chemicals can be seen in the development of low and no formaldehyde permanent press resins in response to possible formaldehyde legislation and in the tremendous increase in interest in foam dyeing and finishing as energy costs continue to soar.

17. DAN RIVER DOES IT AGAIN!

All-Cotton "Sanforset" Shirtings A Big Hit
With Trade and Consumer*

By John A. Cairns, Consultant

Back in 1947, Dan River introduced its registered trade name, "Wrinkl-Shed." Although Tootal, Broadhurst and Lee's "T.B.L." finish had prior market success in linens and spun rayons, Dan River's "Wrinkl-Shed" was generally considered to be the first durable finish to achieve market success on 100 percent cotton constructions. But it took a full year to get "Wrinkl-Shed" properly placed in the market and successfully launched.

"Wrinkl-Shed" was first introduced in shirting fabrics at a price premium of something like 5¢ to 8¢ a yard, but the shirt trade just couldn't see it. At that time, the Arrow Trump Shirt, at a retail price of $1.95, was about the biggest selling branded shirt in the market and a number of other shirts were being offered at that same price. Shirt manufacturers argued that "Wrinkl-Shed" at a price premium of from 5¢ to 8¢ a yard would not fit into their established wholesale price ranges and could therefore not be offered at retail at the big selling price of $1.95. So another approach had to be made and Dan River's Dress Goods Department came to the rescue.

Under the able leadership of Bill Fullerton and his #1 assistant, Jim Gardner, "Wrinkl-Shed" was soon successfully launched in a full line of ginghams for the women's wear trade. (It was necessary to stick pretty much to "square" constructions since the new finish tended to weaken

---

*This article first appeared in the June 1979 issue of the *Textile Marketing Letter*.

unbalanced fabrics.) Suffice it to say, "Wrinkl-Shed" took off in the women's and children's trades and soon made a lasting name for itself. If memory serves properly, first year's sales amounted to some 6 million yards. This was a period of fabric and market testing. Second year's sales jumped to 19 million yards as garment manufacturers and retailers alike became impressed with the virtues of these new Dan River offerings. And third year's sales hit some 33 million yards. Sales for the fourth year were 51 million yards, the full capacity of the mill at that time for that kind of finishing.

There were some interesting sidelights to this market success. Manufacturers soon found that "Wrinkl-Shed" saved them a lot of money in their showrooms and on the road. After a busy day in the showrooms with a new line, manufacturers had always had to iron and sometimes launder the line before showing it again the following day. The same problem beset the salesmen who were showing the line on the road. It wasn't long before these manufacturers discovered that dresses made of "Wrinkl-Shed" fabrics stayed fresh on the racks much longer and saved many dollars in refinishing. The same thing, of course, applied to the sale of "Wrinkl-Shed" dresses at retail. So manufacturers and retailers took those new fabrics to their hearts and they remained big sellers until the polyester blends came along and gradually began to replace the all-cotton constructions. It might be said in passing that housewives loved both types of fabrics because of their lasting good looks, their comfortable hand, and their easy-care qualities. So much for past history.

In 1978, Dan River did it all over again. In collaboration with Cluett, Peabody and Company, owners of the "Sanforset" patents and trademarks, Dan River introduced a whole new line of combed all-cotton shirting materials under the "Sanforset" label. According to Linwood Wright, Dan River's Director of Research and Development: "The fabric is first treated with liquid ammonia...the chemical finishing which is added to this cloth is the culmination of all the thermosetting resin research which has taken place over the past 30 years. The problem of cross-linking cotton is the same as it has always been—strength loss versus improved wrinkle resistance...We are enjoying good market success and acceptance at retail...The consumer does appear to want minimum care properties in a comfortable, luxurious hand, 100 percent combed cotton shirting fabric." To all of this, we say, "Amen!"

During the past several years there has been a notable revival in consumer interest in fabrics made of natural fibers, cotton, wool, and linen, as well as silk. If the prices of these natural fibers can be more carefully controlled so that the mills can buy with confidence and the growers can raise them with confidence, we believe that they will enjoy steadily increasing market success. Meantime, our hats are off to Dan River, Inc. and to all those other textile firms who are doing so much on a daily basis to make this a better country in which to live and work. Research and development programs can be expensive, and sometimes disheartening, but they are most certainly good for everyone when they pay off as they have in this instance with Dan River's "Sanforset" fabrics.

18. PERMANENT PRESS—THE BEGINNING OF A MULTI-INDUSTRY REVOLUTION*

By Dr. W. E. Coughlin, Manager, Consumer Education, Celanese Fibers Marketing Co.

It is possible that no development in the textile industry has ever had such an impact on other industries as has the introduction of permanent press fabrics. It has been generally noted that the development of special pressing and oven-curing equipment for the production of garments with permanent creases or pleats, as well as shape retaining qualities, has put many garment manufacturers in the "finishing" business because they now carry out an essential operation formerly performed by the finisher: namely, curing of the fabric. This, however, was only the beginning of a chain reaction of developments that have affected many industries and products related to the care and maintenance of textile items. Among some of the industries and products affected are the following:

Home Laundry Equipment. For years the editors of home service magazines have been urging their readers to fully realize the dividends on their investment in home laundering equipment by using it more frequently for a larger variety of "washables." With the advent of permanent press those who had been using home laundry equipment regularly found added use for their equipment; and those who formerly could not justify the expense of such equipment now found good reasons for buying it. The most concentrated sales of home laundry equipment in history attest to this development.

The Steel Industry. The impact of a new development in one industry on the economy and advertising practices of a distantly related one is exemplified by the nationwide promotion sponsored primarily by U.S. Steel through their "Waltz Through Wash Day" programs. These programs feature promotions in cities throughout the country that feature in some cases meetings where those in attendance are eligible for prizes ranging anywhere from automobiles to home laundry equipment, as well as minor prizes. At these meetings, that have the active backing of both the manufacturers and retailers, detergent manufacturers, clothing retailers, power and light utilities and local newspapers, the audiences are briefed on the latest developments in permanent press and home laundry equipment.

---

*This article first appeared in the April 1968 issue of the *Textile Marketing Letter*.

These promotions are accompanied by concentrated local newspaper advertising.

The Laundry Industry. It is obvious that with more articles being laundered at home the laundry industry is feeling the pinch. One big item is shirts, others are sheets and pillowcases. Present laundry practice involves the pressing of shirts while damp on hot-head presses, and the finishing of sheets while damp on flat-work ironers. (Never call them "mangles"!) Permanent press does away with the necessity of pressing shirts or sheets if they are tumble-dried after laundering. The American Institute of Laundering advises that the industry is giving priority attention to processes that will take advantage of the unique properties of permanent press and, at the same time, make their costs competitive.

Coin-a-Matic Laundries. Laundromats and coin-operated drycleaning plants have had a phenomenal growth in recent years and the current upsurge in do-it-yourself laundering can be attributed in great measure to the increased volume of permanent press items. An officer of the National Automatic Laundry and Cleaning Council recently stated that more than double the volume of laundering was now being done in coin-operated laundries as in the regular commercial plants. This certainly represents a drastic change in institutional laundry practice.

The Detergent Industry. Detergent manufacturers are paying special attention toward the development of products that will have increased wetting and penetrating action on polyester fiber in order to facilitate soil removal on fabrics containing these fibers. Much progress has already been made in this direction. Improved optical brighteners incorporated in detergents that are designed to be preferentially absorbed by polyester fibers have also been developed for home laundering products resulting in the maximum brightening effect, primarily on permanent press fabrics.

Sewing Threads. Even this industry has felt the impact of permanent press. For years mercerized cotton was the standard of quality and most widely used thread in the slacks, sportswear and work clothes industries. Where post-cured garments were being made, the chemicals present in the un-cured fabric would migrate onto the cotton sewing threads during the curing operations carried out at high temperatures with the result that the threads were badly weakened. To correct this short-coming the trade has turned to sewing threads made of polyester or nylon, or to threads made with a core of polyester and a surface of cotton. The result is threads that give no problem in post-cured garments.

The Cotton Textile Industry. The first permanent press fabrics were resin treated cotton fabrics. These were excellent in "no-iron" and crease retention properties but the resin treatment weakened the cotton fibers and greatly lowered the abrasion resistance of the fabric. In most major applications, therefore, 100 percent permanent press cotton fabrics were found impractical, with the result that blends of cotton or rayon with strong, abrasion resistant thermoplastic fibers (primarily polyester but with some nylon) became the standard fabrics comprising permanent press. Generally speaking, high percentages of polyester (65 percent in lightweight and 50 percent in medium weight fabrics) are necessary to insure good wearing qualities in most wearing apparel. Smaller percentages may be used in heavier weight fabrics for some end uses.

Research in the cotton industry during the past few years has been directed toward the development of processes that would allow the attainment of permanent press properties in 100 percent cotton fabrics without adversely affecting the wearing properties, but so far this goal has not been realized.

Soil Release Finishes. It is known that polyester, in common with other hydrophobic fibers, has a tendency to hold oil or grease stains more tenaciously than do hydrophilic fibers. This is true also of resin treated cotton. The result is that the cleansing of permanent press fabrics has produced some difficulties in home laundering, especially since much permanent press clothing is worn longer between launderings than regular clothing. The textile industry has met this challenge by developing soil release and anti soil-redeposition finishes that insure easier and better cleaning of permanent press fabrics.

Man-Made Fibers. The permanent press development has had its effect on the Man-Made Fibers industry also. The demand for polyester staple fiber for use in permanent press applications has been so great as to produce a temporary market shortage of the staple in the past. Increased production of the fiber is expected to alleviate this shortage in the future.

19. "EVERGLAZE—WASH LIKE WOOL"*

By John A. Cairns, Consultant

Since the *Textile Marketing Letter* is a "think-piece" and not a newspaper, we have not hesitated to recount marketing stories from the past that can have a direct bearing upon your profit story today. Such a one, we think, is the Everglaze story, and how it got started.

For those who are too young to remember, "Everglaze" permanent-glaze chintz fabrics were among the first, if not the first, of the durable synthetic resin-finished fabrics. They were put on the market in the early 1930's by Ralph McIntyre and Joseph Bancroft and Sons with some support from Tootal, Broadhurst and Lee, Rohm and Hass, and others.

---

*This article first appeared in the May 1972 issue of the *Textile Marketing Letter*.

Everglaze would have been a highly creditable achievement in today's market; it was a positive sensation when first introduced.

Treated with a reasonable modicum of tender, loving care, Everglaze fabrics would do everything expected of them, and come up smiling. They could be laundered and ironed and still retain their pristine loveliness. Trouble was, too many Everglaze products were going to commercial laundries that were really beating them to death. Things looked black for MacIntyre and for Bancroft.

Then came a pow-wow at the American Institute of Laundering in Joliet, Illinois, which led to an ultimate, triumphant solution.

It developed that most women at the sorters' desks in commercial laundries were not yet familiar with Everglaze and its virtues, and didn't know how to handle it. In many cases they were throwing Everglaze products right in with the work clothing and industrial uniforms.

Then came the solution. After appropriate laundering procedures had been established, swatches of Everglaze were cut and mounted on cards which were then hung over the sorters' desks in some 6,000 laundry-members of the American Institute of Laundering. The swatches were for identification. The signs said, "This is Everglaze. Wash Like Wool!"

That did it. Everglaze went on to become the great market success that it deserved to be. Another fine example of what can happen when marketing men and technical men collaborate on their mutual interests.

Chapter Five

The Textile Machinery Industry

OVERVIEW

By Jean L. Woodruff

Industry Overview*

The textile machinery industry dates back to the invention of the spinning wheel in 16th century Germany. Today it is a multi-billion dollar industry involved with producing many and varied machines— cleaning and opening machines, winding machines, yarn preparing machines, spinning frames, twisting frames, carding and combing machines, knitting machines, drawing and roving frames—and in the production of parts and attachments for these machines. The industry consists of about 640 establishments. Only about one-third of these firms have more than 20 employees and manufacture original equipment. The more numerous smaller companies are primarily engaged in furnishing parts and accessories for the original equipment the larger U.S. and

*Adapted from "The Textile Machiner Industry," Morton Research Corporation, 1980 and "Textile Machiner," *1981 U.S. Industrial Outlook for 200 Industries With Projections for 1985*, U.S. Department of Commerce.

overseas manufacturers produce. These small companies represent an important part of the industry, however. Their production potential is estimated to be about 40 percent of total industry shipments.

TABLE 1
1980 PROFILE
TEXTILE MACHINERY

Value of industry shipments (million $)	1,190
Value added (million $)	675
Total employment (000)	26
Number of establishments, total (1977)	638
Number of establishments with 20 employees or more (1977)	217
Exports as a percent of product shipments	34.9
Imports as a percent of apparent consumption*	46.9
Compound annual rate of change, 1975—80:	
Value of product shipments**	4.2
Value of exports**	3.1
Value of imports**	13.3
Total employment	-2.2

Major producing regions: Southeast and Northeast
*Imports divided by product shipments plus imports minus exports.
**Rates of change based on current dollars.
Source: 1981 U.S. Industrial Outlook, U.S. Department of Commerce.

The world market for textile machinery is estimated to be in excess of $7 billion annually. The U.S. market alone is estimated to be worth 1.4 million in 1981. Because of the size of the U.S. market, during the past several years a rapidly growing number of foreign manufacturers have established sales, service, and manufacturing facilities in the United States to serve the domestic market and for export to South and Central America.

The loss of domestic markets as well as the decline in market share of world markets has been a major concern of U.S. industry leaders. Reflecting this, the Economic Development Administration funded a major study designed to assess the industry's competitive technological and marketing position in both domestic and foreign markets. This study, conducted by the Morton Research Corporation, identified several factors which influence performance of the domestic textile industry. These include a sensitivity to the production of textiles, investment activity on the part of textile mills, intense foreign competition, a growing overseas market, and a changing product mix.

The demand for textile machinery, as might be expected, is closely tied to demand for textile products. The decade of the seventies was a sluggish period for the consumption of textile products and this was reflected in the apparent consumption of textile machinery. A review of U.S. textile machinery shipments from 1975-1980 reveals a disturbing growth pattern. Current dollar shipments grew at a compound average rate of only 4.6 percent. This is unsettling enough, but when these figures are adjusted for inflation, they show that industry shipments have actually *declined* at a compound average rate of 2.7 percent during the last five years. This trend is expected to be reversed in 1981, however, when real growth is expected to be a modest two percent.

The production of specific textile products will be of significance to the machinery manufacturer. The synthetic fiber market has shown rapid growth over the long term, and is expected to continue to expand faster than the overall textile industry. Other potentially lucrative areas are in fabric finishing, knit goods, and yarn segments. U.S. textile machinery manufacturers should channel their energies toward serving these growing markets.

Until recently, capital investment by textile mills has been a fairly reliable indicator of textile machinery sales. However, increasing governmental regulation has forced the textile industry to allocate a growing portion of their capital budgets for non-productive pollution control equipment in order to meet Federal regulatory standards on dust control and noise levels. Energy consumption is also a problem. The requirements established by governmental agencies will serve to restrict the amount of funds available for expanding productive capacity and/or the replacement of obsolete and inefficient machinery. However, on the positive side, it should be noted that, in 1980, the textile industry joined the Department of Energy in conducting a series of studies on energy consumption by textile equipment. These studies could lead to the development of equipment that will measurably decrease energy consumption per unit of output and will enhance the acceptability of U.S. manufactured equipment in world markets.

The sluggish growth of the American textile machinery industry in the last decade can largely be attributed to increasing foreign competition. Between 1963 and 1978, relative to the total domestic market for textile machinery, imports grew from nine percent to nearly 50 percent. Imports are expected to rise about eight percent in 1981, to $660 million. West Germany and Switzerland are the major foreign competitors, but significant inroads have also been made by France and Japan, with Italy emerging as a potentially significant future importer. The United Kingdom also represents an important supplier.

All types of textile machinery are imported to some degree. The largest

segments of imported machinery, representing almost 45 percent of the
total, are weaving, winding, and spinning equipment. The resulting loss
of technological parity explains our high level of imports. This trend is
expected to continue through 1981.

While many foreign firms have been clamouring for the lucrative U.S.
market, domestic companies, in turn, have been experiencing growth in
overseas markets. Parts and attachments account for the majority of foreign
shipments, although textile printing machinery and yarn preparing
equipment are growing in terms of the total export market. The overseas
market for textile machinery is quite widespread, with Canada the leading
market for exports of American textile machinery. Other major markets
include Mexico, United Kingdom, West Germany, South America and the
Far East. Increased U.S. participation in these markets is dependent upon a
number of factors, including the ability to offer technologically advanced,
competitively proven equipment; to develop a sound marketing base,
including sales and service facilities; and to furnish competitive financing
packages.

The U.S. textile machinery industry has experienced significant
changes in its makeup in the past several years (see Table 2). The parts and
attachments segment of the industry has grown immensely in the past
decade, and domestic sales are expected to be the major source of growth
for the industry in the 1980's. Parts to adapt production machinery to
current style patterns, replacement parts, and parts to modernize machinery appear to be among the most lucrative opportunities for this
segment of the industry. The outlook for the machinery segment is not
quite as bright. During the same period that parts and attachments were
enjoying a healthy growth rate, the machinery segment experienced not
only a decline in market share, but a decline in sales as well. The
substantial increase in imported textile machinery has served to erode this
once dominant submarket. And Morton Research analysts are predicting
this erosion to continue. They are anticipating machinery product sales to
rise by slightly over four percent per year through 1987, but see the segment
as continuing to lose market share, shrinking below 40 percent.

Selling Textile Machinery*

The textile machinery industry is a very competitive industry. Price
plays an important factor in a sale, but many other factors come into play
as well. Customers are concerned with energy efficiency, noise level, cleanliness in operation, machine size and durability, and a company's
reputation for service and the ability to provide replacement and repair
parts.

Machine manufacturers' customers are technically knowledgeable

---

*Adapted from an interview with Ernest Graf of Platt, Saco, Lowell (Easley,
South Carolina).

TABLE 2
THE TEXTILE MACHINERY MARKET

	Textile Machinery	Parts & Attachments	Miscellaneous Products
1947	62.8%	36.1%	1.1%
1958	44.6	52.4	3.0
1962	53.2	41.0	5.8
1967	53.4	41.0	5.6
1972	50.6	41.4	7.9
1977	42.5	47.6	9.9
1987 (F)	39.8	55.0	5.2

F—Forecast

Sources: U.S. Dept. of Commerce,
          Morton Research Corporation

about the product and have the ability to discern differences between the machines of different producers. Machines are typically built to the specifications of the buyer, because their needs vary significantly. This is particularly true as you move into international markets. For example, let's say that two manufacturers, one in the U.S. and one in Europe, want to buy a spinning machine to spin a certain yarn count. Theoretically, the machines could be identical. However, Europeans tend to prefer longer machines, say 464 spindles, while U.S. firms prefer much shorter machines, with 312 to 340 spindles. The reason? When a machine is stopped because all bobbins are full, it has to be doffed manually. The more spindles a machine has, the longer it takes to doff the machine; and consequently, the greater the machine down-time. The U.S. company, where labor costs are high and efficiency is of paramount importance, prefers the shorter machine. But in foreign markets, where labor costs are lower and the few extra minutes of down-time not so important, the longer machine is preferred since it lowers the price of each spindle. Therefore, machine specifications will vary depending on the market you are selling to, making it extremely important for salesmen to know individual market conditions.

To assist in the sale of a particular machine, demonstrator models are often used. A demonstrator in the textile machine market is typically a smaller version of the normal machine, which is given, free of charge, to the customer for a specified period. The only cost to the mill is the cost of transportation. These machines are used, however, only if an order appears imminent and a salesman wants to make şure the company is convinced his machine is superior. In fact, many salesmen use demonstrators only as a last resort. Rather than offer the machine, they prefer to wait to see if the customer asks for one. If a sale can be consummated without the. demonstrator, it is in the company's best interest to do so.

Trade shows are another important sales vehicle. Not only are potentially new customers contacted and courted at these shows, but existing customers can be brought up to date on new machinery as well. Trade shows also provide the opportunity of seeing competitors' machinery and allows a company to make firsthand comparisons with their own machines.

Outlook to 1985

The outlook for the U.S. textile machinery market through 1985, according to the U.S. Department of Commerce, Bureau of Industrial Economics' forecast is as follows:

"Uncertainty about the general economic outlook and the cost and availability of energy are expected to have an adverse effect on the sales of textile machinery during the next five years. As a result, real growth in world markets is expected to be no more than two to three percent on a compound average basis.

"U.S. machinery manufacturers are concentrating on improving market knowledge, marketing strategies, and equipment technology in an effort to maintain or increase their shares of world markets. Assuming success in these efforts, growth in U.S. production should be able to keep up with the world rate of two to three percent.

"The use of electronics in a wide variety of textile processes continues to proliferate. This trend is expected to continue during the next five years. Presently, for example, electronic controls are used for monitoring production; patterning in both weaving and knitting; controlling water temperatures in slashing, dyeing, and finishing; and for many other uses.

"As predicted several years ago, additional foreign manufacturers are establishing maufacturing facilities in the United States. A major loan manufacturer is in the process of building a large plant in the South. When this plant goes onstream in 1981, our imports will decline and possibly our exports of weaving equipment will increase in future years. It is logical to expect that other foreign manufacturers will follow in order to get closer to the world's largest single market—the U.S. textile industry.

"Even though the U.S. has lost its technological advantage in some segments of the industry, U.S. manufacturers still have the reputation for building reliable, quality products that will give an excellent return on investment over the life of the equipment. This reputation, coupled with the manufacturers' increased marketing efforts, is expected to improve the industry's competitive position in the next five years."

20. THE BUYING CROWD AT A
TEXTILE MACHINERY SHOW*

By John A. Cairns, Consultant

Five years ago we asked the editorial question, "Where were the Marketing Men at the Textile Machinery Show?" In 1978 they were at the show in substantial numbers.

We attended the show on May 3, 1978 and were very much interested in what we saw and what we heard.

The new machinery, from makers all over the world, was breathtaking in both price and performance. Better and more exciting textile products are certain to be the result. Equally important, however, were the comments of the exhibitors we chatted with. All hands agreed that the industry's Top Brass were at the show in large numbers. All agreed that this was an audience of decision-makers in a buying mood. And buy they did.

Over the years we have talked about the desirability of having textile marketing men exposed to the new machinery, the new chemicals, the new fibers, the new manufacturing processes. It is our feeling that no marketing man or woman can do a first-rate marketing job unless he or she knows what the mill machinery can do and is in a position to market that potential to the best possible advantage. Furthermore, the man or woman who knows "what's coming" can start laying out new fabrics and making new marketing plans well ahead of competition. The marketing organization that is "firstest with the mostest" is almost certain to skim the cream off the top of the bottle long before less well informed competition appreciates what's going on. We've seen it happen time after time.

Likewise, we're all for seeing that a mill man gets exposed to practical marketing problems at some time during the course of his career. You can tell a production executive everything you may know about the idiosyncrasies of the cutter, wholesaler, or retailer but he'll never fully understand what you are talking about until he meets these remarkable people head on in a buying transaction. Neither will he ever be able to fully understand the influence of trade paper editors, editors of fashion magazines and home service books, industrial purchasing agents, government buyers and all the rest until he fully understands their psychology, buying habits, and trade preferences.

We have another pet concern. We have often wished that the marketing forces of the textile and related industries were not quite so departmentalized. Some men spend their entire careers marketing gray goods. Others stick to finished fabrics. Some never get away from their starting jobs in textile chemicals, fibers, or machinery. Some spend a lifetime in women's

---

*This article first appeared in the September 1978 issue of the *Textile Marketing Letter*.

wear fabrics, while others devote their careers to home furnishing fabrics, boys' wear or men's wear. Others live a lifetime in the rarified atmosphere of fine imported fabrics and never get down to the volume levels of the market. Having been privileged to work with firms at every level and in every segment of the market over the years, we can attest to the fact that each has something to contribute to the marketing techniques of the other.

So we're glad that more marketing men and more top executives are now attending the machinery show. And we hope to see them out in equal numbers at meetings of AATCC, AATT, and other technical organizations. You don't have to build a Rolls-Royce to be pretty effective at running one. But it sure helps to know what that Rolls-Royce can do when you're behind the wheel and caught in an emergency situation!

21. MORE ON MACHINERY MAKERS IN THE MARKETPLACE*

By The Editorial Staff, Textile Marketing Letter

In one issue of *The Textile Marketing Letter* it was suggested that manufacturers of textile machinery should have sales offices in New York, this comment brought some interesting reactions.

These reactions may best be summed up by the comments of one machinery manufacturer, who prefers for obvious reasons to remain anonymous.

He summarizes the history of a typical order for, say spinning frames, in the following order:

1. A sales call is made to the superintendent of spinning and the salesman learns that this particular plant—one of the plants of perhaps a large chain of mills—is interested in new spinning frames.

2. Later, when the superintendent of spinning is putting together his capital budget request for the coming year, he remembers that X, Y, Z company among others offers for sale an acceptable spinning frame with features which the salesman has described to him.

3. When his budget has been accepted, the superintendent of spinning describes the technical features of this frame to his engineering people who review the specifications.

---

*This article first appeared in the July 1968 issue of the *Textile Marketing Letter*.

4. The X, Y, Z company is then contacted again by the engineering group to come and discuss the technical points of his spinning frames. They submit quotations, estimated return on investment, etc.

5. Keeping in close touch with the situation, the X, Y, Z company is contacted by the purchasing agent with the news that his equipment has been recommended but that he must meet price competition.

6. He competes.

7. Now the X, Y, Z company is contacted by the purchasing agent with the news that his company is thinking about buying some spinning frames and what is his best price?

8. The X, Y, Z company submits its best price for the second time.

9. The purchasing agent says the price is too high and bickering goes on until a price is finally arrived at.

Daily News Record did a study of how textile mills buy capital equipment. The conclusion of this survey was that while most such purchases originated at the plant level, usually on the recommendation of the General Manager, Plant Manager or Superintendent, divisional or corporate management may frequently initiate buying projects. Certainly, with a purchase as huge as new machinery often is, corporate management is involved in final approval.

Therefore, we repeat our suggestion that textile machinery manufacturers would be well advised to maintain important "listening posts" close to the corporate headquarters of the major textile firms.

22. TEXTILE MACHINERY: MAJOR MARKETING TOOL*

By The Editorial Staff, Textile Marketing Letter

If there remained any doubt in your mind about the role of good machinery as a *marketing force*, it must certainly have been dispelled by attendance at one of the Textile Machinery Shows in Greenville, S.C.

Almost every display offered an opportunity for someone to:

---

*This article first appeared in the December 1966 issue of the *Textile Marketing Letter*.

- Remain competitive in the marketplace by reducing costs.

- Gain a competitive advantage by improving quality.

- Enter attractive new fields.

- Diversify styling.

- Gain a larger share of the market.

- Get away from price competition.

- Develop domestic and export markets.

Machinery men are inclined to sell themselves short by discussing "payout" solely in terms of speed and increased efficiency. Nothing could be less realistic. Machinery that may take years to pay for itself in a matter of months when all of the marketing factors are taken into consideration. Witness the great success of stretch and textured yarns in recent years, the exploding development of durable press, the success of Pak-Nit, and the worldwide progress of the Chatham "Fiberwoven" process.

These are machinery successes, but they are even more important as marketing successes.

Our advice to machinery men: always have textile marketing and market research men on your sales team.

Our advice to mill men and other producers: never be without competent marketing men on your machinery buying committee. It works both ways!

Chapter Six

The Yarn Mills and Their Market Impact

OVERVIEW

By Jim H. Conner

Of all segments of the gigantic United States textile industry, one of the least understood is the sales yarn segment. To identify the sales yarn sector, it is appropriate to look briefly at the overall textile/apparel industry in terms of the degree of integration. From this viewpoint, there are two separate and distinct segments. One is the integrated manufacturers who produce and consume yarn in their own weaving, knitting, and tufting operations. The other is the smaller, non-integrated manufacturer who has no yarn production and must rely on outside sources of supply. This second category consists primarily of knitting mills, carpet and rug mills, and a large number of specialty product manufacturers.

A relatively small portion of total sales yarn production is sold to integrated manufacturers, and this is primarily yarn which they either do not produce, or do not produce in sufficient quantity to balance yarn requirements with their own weaving, knitting, or tufting operations. The end product of the large integrated manufacturers is concentrated in woven fabrics for the apparel industry and for drapery, upholstery and home furnishings' markets, particularly towels and bedding.

By contrast, the knitting and carpet and rug sectors developed as small, non-integrated, style oriented entities, requiring a much greater variety of yarns than could be efficiently produced internally. The sales yarn industry developed as a separate segment to supply this need. In the early stages, the development of the sales yarn segment was primarily in spun yarns, but later expanded into textured filament yarns, principally of nylon and polyester.

There is a grey area between the sales yarn industry and the integrated manufacturers. When integrated mills find excess capacity in yarn production, they sometimes move into the sales yarn market until their yarn and fabric production is in balance. Likewise, integrated mills will enter the market as yarn purchasers when internal production does not meet yarn requirements. Generally speaking, this swing in and out of the sales yarn market occurs in the commodity type yarns.

The sales yarn market has increased in size over the last decade because of the increased demand for knit goods in the apparel industry and the increased demand for floor coverings. Most of the growth in the 1970's was in textured polyester filament for the double-knit market and in spun and BCF nylon face yarns for the carpet and rug trades.

Toward the end of the 1970's, many of the traditional markets for sales yarn appeared to be reaching maturity. Nonetheless, three developments occurred which sustained growth for sales yarn producers. The first was a change in lifestyle of the American consumer which increased the demand for leisure and sportswear. Such apparel was a natural for knit fabrics which provided a high degree of comfort, stretch, and ease of care. Since most knitters depend on outside sources of yarn supply, the sales yarn sector was well positioned to supply this new market.

Secondly, the relative weakness of the dollar in international money markets, coupled with the installation of advanced technology, made United States-produced yarn competitive in many overseas markets. The sales yarn sector was quick to capitalize on these developments and entered the export market seriously in the late 1970's.

Finally, the introduction of high speed looms created a demand for yarn qualities which opened the door for sales yarn producers to become a larger supplier to the vertical weaving sector, particularly in textured filament yarns.

Of total U.S. yarn production, more than 40 percent is produced for sale, with the remainder produced and consumed by integrated manufacturers. Sales yarn production is divided almost equally between yarns spun from tow or staple fibers and textured filament yarns. A summary of total U.S. production versus sales yarn production by end use appears in Figure I and illustrates the importance of the machine knitting and carpet and rug markets to the sales yarn sector.

Ownership units in the sales yarn sector have traditionally been

Figure 1
Summary of U.S. Yarn Production in 1979*
(Pounds in millions)

TOTAL YARN PRODUCTION	U.S. Total	For Sale	Percent Of Total
Spun Yarns	6,006	1,838	31%
Textured Filament	2,227	1,647	74%
Total	8,233	3,485	42%
SPUN YARNS (By end use)			
Weaving	3,741	330	9%
Knitting	1,177	889	76%
Carpet and Rugs	794	419	53%
Other	294	200	68%
Total	6,006	1,838	31%
FILAMENT YARNS (By end use)			
Weaving	448	92	21%
Knitting	763	615	81%
Carpet and Rugs	1,002	927	93%
Other	13	13	100%
Total	2,226	1,647	74%

*SOURCE: U.S. Bureau of Census.

characterized as small family controlled firms specializing in a narrow range of yarns. However, the trend in recent years has been toward consolidation of the industry into fewer, more efficient management units, but still retaining a fairly high degree of product specialization. Although sharing certain technology with integrated manufacturers, the sales yarn producer is more of a custom manufacturer, designing and producing products for very specific end-uses. Whether in specialty yarns or commodity type yarns, a high degree of quality control is essential. In years gone by, much of the marketing of yarn was done by independent sales agents representing one or more manufacturers. With the trend toward consolidation into larger ownership units, more and more firms have developed their own internal marketing organizations. In doing so, management has become more marketing oriented and, consequently, more flexible in shifting to new fibers and blends. As an intermediate processor, a typical sales yarn marketing program involves coordination between fiber supplier, yarn production, and the end-user. For this reason, the successful yarn salesman needs to be familiar with the characteristics of fibers, his own yarn production capability, and the technology of his customer. In essence, he must put together a package that fits the needs of his customer and the end-use product for which his yarn is the basic component.

Looking to the future, most observers view the outlook for the sales yarn market optimistically. Continued consolidation of the industry to take advantage of both managerial and technological efficiencies is likely. Future emphasis will be improved productivity and even greater consciousness of yarn quality. Companies with vision will keep a constant eye on foreign, as well as domestic, opportunities for future growth. Management style will become increasingly more professional and marketing strategies will require a high degree of sophistication. Building on the strong base established during the 70's, the sales yarn industry is well positioned to meet the challenges and opportunities of the future.

23. A FIBER COMPANY'S PROGRAM FOR MARKETING KNITTED FABRICS*

By F. R. Longenecker, Hoechst Fibers, Inc.

As you probably know, Hoechst Fibers, Inc. produces and markets fibers, not fabrics. But we have found that we not only have to be knowledgeable and expert at marketing fiber, but also in marketing at every level of the textile industry right down to and through the retail level.

In fact, our whole marketing philosophy is based on serving as business consultants to our direct and indirect customers and to assist them in utilizing and marketing fabrics of Trevira. In the past, fiber companies have had a reputation for being sugar daddies, or bottomless pits of promotional money. Today, however, advertising dollars are short-lived, as money alone is not the answer to a successful marketing program.

Hoechst Fibers, Inc., relies far more heavily on its technology and marketing expertise than on support money. There is infinitely more knowledge and creativity available that is effective, than there is money to be all things to all people. Creativity, ingenuity, quality and service are just a few of the major factors that have helped us achieve, in just five years, the ranking of the fourth largest polyester producer in the United States.

Hoechst Fibers has more than doubled its sales each year for the past five years, and we expect to keep up this torrid pace in the future. This can only be achieved, however, by intelligent marketing.

There are any number of definitions of marketing I could give you, but the most memorable are usually those based on working analogies. A friend of mine recently said, "Finding a girl, working out the time to propose, finding the right place and selecting the right moment—that's marketing. Realizing you were wrong, getting the ring back, and giving it to another girl—that's selling."

---

*This article first appeared in the April 1972 issue of the *Textile Marketing Letter*.

Strategy of Marketing Knits. What I'm talking about now is the strategy of marketing knits. Finding out there are disappointments in the marketplace and having to work them out is selling, but the basic strategy one develops and employs is what marketing is all about.

Just to give you some perspective on our subject, I'd like to give you some figures on how far knits have come, and what some of the prospects are.

Knits, for men's and women's wear, consumed some 148 million pounds of polyester fibers in 1969. Mind you, that figure is only for polyester; not for other man-made, natural or cellulosic fibers. When the 1971 figures are in, we expect them to reach 460 million pounds. By 1976, we expect polyester fiber producers to devote 975 million pounds of their total output to knitwear.

All those figures seem pretty encouraging, and they are. A tremendous potential for knits exists today and for the future. Along with the knit boom has come just what we might expect—people moving out to form what I'll call "knit enterprises," all relating themselves to this growth market.

The sage old law of economics prevails. When there is a greater demand in a market than supply, new capital and investment will enter that market until it is unprofitable to do so. As we have seen time and time again in similar situations, the pendulum swings back too fast, and the supply becomes greater than the market demand can absorb. The outcome is disaster for the opportunist, and success only for those with a strong marketing approach to the industry.

Danger in the Knits Situation. The red flags are flying today in the knit field. A growth market is here with many small knit enterprises, yet verticalization of large textile conglomerates is growing at an unprecedented rate. In the rush to meet demand, companies have been grinding out single knits and double knits with little regard for even the simplest basics of marketing. Knitting companies, former commission knitters, have sprung up over night with 20 to 50 machines turning out fabric. Few of the new-found knitting enterprises have any feel for how big the market actually is, what the fashion trends are, what demand will be for certain patterns, coloration, or types of knits, or have a formalized marketing approach.

Finally, there has been precious little regard given to quality. Today, the buying public is more quality conscious than ever before. People have been willing to pay the price for knits to date, but repeat sales and market growth are going to be based on how the fabrics and garments perform in wearing. Every element of knit production must come under close scrutiny by all people in our business, because every one of those elements contributes to the end result—a fabric that will satisfy the consumer in terms of aesthetics, performance and fashion. The consumer is the ultimate judge in determining the success or failure of us all.

If it seems I'm casting a pall of gloom over the knitwear business, let me hasten to say this is incorrect. I am, however, trying to sound warnings about the importance of quality and long-term marketing of knitted fabrics for the welfare of all our respective businesses.

Warp knits or circular knits are no panacea. They are products which have made a magnificent contribution to the future of the textile industry, but the people who have made their careers in woven goods have not been sitting idle at their looms. The introduction of stretch wovens—wovens that perform like knits—is a clear indication that knits are due for competition. And, looking further ahead, just as knits came along, so will technology bring us another fabrication to create another boom and whet the consumer's interest and fickle appetite for fashion.

The Hoechst Marketing Approach. I don't want to be accused of posing all the problems and leaving you with no solutions. So I'd like to discuss one approach, if I may, to the marketing of knitted fabrics. At Hoechst we have a basic marketing philosophy which sets the stage for virtually everything we do. I'll try to express it as briefly as possible.

First, we know we have to deliver a quality product; fibers which meet every standard for their end use. As a result we engineer fibers to meet specific end uses, resulting in about 20 different types with various characteristics.

There are many people who are not aware that when that polyester fiber leaves our plant in Spartanburg, S.C. it is not called Trevira. It is Hoechst polyester. The name Trevira is licensed for customer use only after the customer's fabric or garment has been returned to us for an extensive battery of tests against standards we have set for that particular end usage.

Another part of our marketing philosophy is that for us to be successful, our customers must make a profit on our products. So our technical services people bring their know-how to our customers in terms of fabrication techniques and handling of fabrics properly in garment manufacture, to make sure quality is married to production economics.

Our next task is to arm ourselves with all we can get on one of the basics of marketing—to know the market itself. It's here that we employ the services of market research people for facts and figures, as well as the talents of our fashion directors who are continually searching out the latest intelligence on fashion developments here and abroad.

The final step is to bring into play the promotional expertise which will help to sell knitted fabrics at the retail level. We have separate marketing groups for women's wear, men's wear and home furnishings.

Over-the-Counter Piece Goods. But one area I'd like to concentrate on is the area of retail fashion fabrics, or what used to be called over-the-counter yard goods.

Just as there has been a boom in knits, so has there been a tremendous surge in the field of home sewing. The result is that there lies before us a major area for marketing knitted fabrics.

Let's identify the market. The most recent figures available tell us that sales of retail fabrics rose to $1.4 billion in 1970. That compares with $1 billion in 1967. Add to that about $400 million in sewing machine sales and another $650 million in patterns and notions, and you come up with a retail home sewing market of a least $2½ billion. Projections are for the market to continue to grow fast, if not faster.

In order to know our market further, we need a profile of our customer. Of the 87½ million women over the age of 10 in 1970, it is estimated that about 45 million were sewing at home. A few years ago the majority of home sewers were in the 40 to 50 age group; today they are between 18 and 30.

The customer's economic profile has changed, too. While the mainstay of the market used to be basic cottons in the dollar per yard price range, today's home sewer will pay from $5 to $15 per yard for polyester double knits. While she is interested in saving money by sewing at home, she also is interested in quality, fashion and creativity. And today she is proud to proclaim that she made the garment herself.

Now where do knits fit into this market? Recently, knits have posted an increase of 160 percent of total over-the-counter yardage. In 1969, knits represented about 10 percent of over-the-counter sales. In 1971 they represented about 25 percent, and by 1976 knits occupied about 45 percent of the retail fabric market.

We are as hungry for that kind of potential as anyone. We knew that for the long term, particularly when women would be identifying themselves so closely with our product, that we had to work out a strategy based on quality fabrics. It included an exciting promotional program for the retailer.

The Promotional Program. To launch our program, we went back and started with the quality mills and knitters.

Then we made sure that a sufficient variety of fabrics would be available for the home sewer. These included single knits, double knits, and warp knits, both raschel and tricot, all in yarn-dye and piece-dye, and in fabric weights from four to 18 ounces. The end uses include men's, women's, and children's wear and home furnishings.

Third, we developed a promotional theme for our retail fashion fabric program. We started using the slogan: "The girls who make it, make it in Trevira." This theme permits identification for fabrics as well as our own fibers.

Fourth, we spelled out a retail promotional program to zero in on the consumer, in terms of all fabrics, and particularly in terms of generating interest in knits of Trevira.

This program for retailers was built around a National Home Sewing Contest. To give you an indication of how successful such a contest can be, the National Grange contest of which we are one of the sponsors, drew more than 49,000 entries last year, and that involved making a garment. You can imagine the judges looking at 49,000 garment entries!

We learned from this that, while knits have been around for some time, there's little information available for women to use in learning how to sew knits. So we developed a film on "How to Sew a Knit" with Francine Coffey, fashion director of the Singer Company. Francine is well known to home sewers from her weekly appearances on Dinah Shore's TV show in teaching Dinah to sew. She also edited a booklet for us which gives tips on sewing knits.

Retailers participating in the promotion have the use of the film and the opportunity to give away the booklet to their customers. In addition, they are given window posters promoting the contest, to help build store traffic and sell their fabrics in Trevira.

Obviously, all this helps our direct customer sell fabric, helps us sell fiber, and helps the retailer sell to the consumer.

As an incentive to the consumer to buy Trevira fabrics and participate in the contest, we posted a variety of prizes. We related the top prize to fashion by offering American Motors' New Sportabout station wagon with an interior designed by Gucci. In addition, there are other prizes for a variety of classes, including color TV's and stereo radios.

We also included incentives for the retailer, with cash awards going to the store employees who sell the contest winners fabrics of Trevira. The retailer is expected to advertise locally, at his own expense, in local newspapers or on radio using ad mats and radio tapes which we supply to him.

Summary. While that gives you in longhand a case history of a particular marketing effort, it includes the basics of a sound marketing philosphy. In shorthand, here are the key points:

1. Assure yourself that your product or process is of the highest quality possible.

2. Maintain that quality through quality-control programs and a basic philosophy of integrity.

3. Know your market in terms of past and present performance and future expectations. Determine your marketing strategy and sales techniques accordingly.

4. Evaluate your market in terms of direct customers and end users. Associate yourself with customers whose product integrity and quality approach match yours. Sometimes this may mean turning away short term business.

5. Develop a sound package, using the tools of advertising, promotion, publicity and merchandising to communicate in a meaningful way to all who will help sell your product.

6. Deliver what you promised.

We have similar programs for all our end-use areas. All, I assure you are based on a firm commitment to marketing for the long term.

By preserving quality, the market for knitted fabrics can be encouraged to grow. By using the best talents available to us all, we can all share in the potential that knits hold.

24. THE THREAD OF THE STORY IS LUREX

How Those "Amateurs" From Cleveland Did A Great Job In a Most Unlikely Market*

By John A. Cairns, Consultant

No one told the President and Sales Manager of the Dobeckmun Company that it couldn't be done when they had the temerity to invade the textile markets with their new metallic yarn, Lurex, in the early 1950's. (For those of you who are too young to remember, the Dobeckmun Company wasn't in the textile business at all. It was a producer of "flexible laminated films and foils" for packaging and for other industrial, medical and military uses.) Not knowing that it had two strikes against it before it ever got up to bat, therefore, the Dobeckmun Company charged right ahead. And, lo and behold, just a few years later it found itself sponsoring one of the fanciest fashion shows of all time as a prelude to grabbing off one of the ripest and juiciest plums you can possibly imagine.

A few background remarks may be helpful if you don't already know the story.

Lurex metallic yarns started off as a bit of new surface interest in decorative fabrics of all kinds—drapery fabrics, curtain materials, upholstery fabrics, even a few floor covering materials. It then invaded portions of the ready-to-wear market, such as cocktail and evening dresses, where its obvious glamour lent a lot of new eye appeal. It had one big advantage over popular contemporary fibers such as nylon and the acrylics: you could

---

*This article first appeared in the October 1974 issue of the *Textile Marketing Letter*.

see the difference. After having made big inroads into the choicer decorative and apparel fabrics, Lurex was soon found in a whole host of knitted and woven goods at almost every price range. One huge prize remained to be won—the automobile upholstery market. And that was a tough one, not only because of the intense competititon but also because of the extremely complex marketing set-up for all fabrics going to the automotive trades. You almost had to be a member of the "Club" to get anywhere at all.

So a complex and elaborate marketing program was evolved, with the President and Sales Manager of Dobeckmun and the advertising agency in full agreement on strategy. Instead of going straight through the line, Lurex decided to try to make an end run of it. It had one big thing in its favor. Within two or three years' time its acceptance in the United States had brought an active demand from literally all world markets. It now had producing and distributing facilities abroad with access to markets in Europe and the Far East. So it was decided to stage a big International Lurex Fashion Show at the old Ambassador Hotel on Park Avenue in New York. The garments to be modeled were to be something very special indeed. They were to be top creations of the best known designers in all of the world's most important fashion centers—Paris, New York, London, Dublin, Rome, Tokyo, Montreal and elsewhere. Supplementing these glamorous apparel items was to be a large selection of decorative fabrics from all over the world. The decorative fabrics were to be used to line the walls in the lobby and reception rooms leading to the Grand Ballroom on the first floor where the fashion show was to be staged. It is entirely possible that there has never been another show just like it. And, of course, it was a smash hit.

Now the real marketing strategy began to unfold. The great Lurex International Fashion Show went to London where it received fantastic press coverage. In America, it went on the road to major markets, where influential mill men and their wives and customers could be found, including Philadelphia, Greensboro, Greenville, and Atlanta, with a final stop in Detroit which culminated in J. L. Hudson's party. Hudson's sent out invitations to all of the top names on their charge account list; an unprecedented step was to invite the wives of the automobile executives. It was an evening show and they all came, bringing their husbands with them. Their reaction was all that could be hoped for. When the executives' wives saw these glamorous garments against the background of those sparkling decorative fabrics, they said to their executive husbands, "Why can't we have some of those beautiful Lurex fabrics in our automobiles?"

The answer must have been decidedly positive because within the space of a very few weeks Lurex had signed up Lincoln and Mercury. And other orders started pouring in. The first step toward color in automobile bodies has always been attributed to the women in the Ford family, even before the Women's Movement brought its impact into our lives. So it wasn't long before those "inexperienced" packaging fellows from Cleveland, Ohio, had literally wrapped up the entire automobile industry.

As the *Ladies Home Journal* used to say, "Never underestimate the power of a woman." To this we might add, "Never underestimate the influence of a powerful store like Hudson's in whom the top women in the community have confidence!"

Postscript. No Lurex story would be quite complete without a few words about some of the people who were on the Dobeckmun team when this Horatio Alger story took place. The first, of course, was Thomas F. Dolan, President, who had started the business in a Cleveland garage with the aid of two partners a few years earlier. They got their start by making cellophane cigar wrappers. Second was Ennis P. Whitley, Vice-President and General Sales Manager. Before joining Dobeckmun, Mr. Whitley had been Sales Manager of a company that provided seating facilities for theaters and other places of public assembly. He had no contacts in the textile field but knew how to pick people who did. It was he who chose the late Dorothy Liebes to design yarns and fabrics made of Lurex to be used as selling samples. And it was he, with a little coaching from Dorothy, who hired Lynn Given to act as a one-person fashion department and who retained an advertising agency that knew its way around the textile and apparel markets.

Three agency people who contributed enormously to the success of Lurex were the late T. Hart Anderson, Jr., an authority in the home furnishings and automotive markets; Robert Pliskin, Art Director, who went on to become creative head of one of the country's largest advertising agencies; and Julia Morse, later Vice-President of the New York Fashion Group, whose record is known to most of the readers of the *Textile Marketing Letter*. These people were supported by Karl Prindle, Director of Research and Development for Dobeckmun, who was not only something of a genius at sticking flexible films and foils together, but who became very much a genius at coloring them and slitting them apart into textile filaments. And then, of course, there was Art Gould who worked on sales for Whitley and who was not the least bit embarrassed by the fact that he could probably not have told a worsted from a combed cotton when it all started.

So great was the success of Lurex that it was bought, along with the rest of Dobeckmun Company, by the Dow Chemical Company just a relatively short time after the Lurex Show played to wildly enthusiastic audiences in England.

We might add one further comment: Up to the time of the Lurex Show, Mr. Dolan wasn't quite certain whether or not he had a real business on his hands. I attended that show with him and his conclusion was this: "At last I'm convinced!"

25. HOW THE FMC CORPORATION MARKETS ITS AVLIN PRODUCTS*

By James C. Cumming, Consultant

Only a couple of years ago it looked as though what was then the American Viscose Division of the FMC Corporation might have been knocked completely out of the business of producing polyester yarn. The plant in Lewiston, Pennsylvania, which had been producing Avlin polyester since 1966 was ravaged by floods in 1972 and its future looked hopeless. The Juniata River crested at 43 feet and the plant was, for a time, under 10 feet of water.

"We went around in boats for a couple of days," one worker recalls. In fact, it was only the relatively new polyester plant that could be salvaged at all. The 70-year-old rayon plant was damaged beyond repair and was donated to the county for use as an industrial park. But today the polyester plant is back in business, with 870 workers spinning polyester yarn which is drawn, textured, and beamed at another FMC plant in Radford, Virginia. This plant has been described as employing the most advanced technology in the fiber industry.

But this is a marketing story as well as a maunfacturing story. So successful has the marketing been that the Radford mill is now shipping Avlin polyester at capacity and a new 100 percent plant expansion is well underway.

It's the demand for polyester double knits and warp knits that underlies the current boom in polyester sales and the expansion of the Radford mill is solid evidence of the success FMC has had in carving out a substantial share of the market for its Avlin polyester.

"We become the total marketing partners of our customers, helping them in every way we can to promote fabrics and later fashions made from them" explains John Luke, warp knit sales and marketing manager. "We follow them dowstream all the way."

Following the customer downstream all the way may be said to be the basic marketing policy behind the success of Avlin polyester. As a recent issue of *FMC Progress* described its implementation:

A complex process with no real beginning or end, the FMC sales and merchandising effort concentrates most of its effort on key mills that knit and weave. The majority of FMC mill customers make the fabric as well as print and dye on high-speed machines that can imprint as many as 14 colors. A few greige mills make the fabric and then turn it over to converters who print and dye for the cutters.

A FMC fashion staff collects information from world fashion centers, sifts it, predicts major fashion, fabric and color trends, and then works

---

*This article first appeared in the February 1975 issue of the *Textile Marketing Letter*.

directly with the technical staff to develop particular fabrics for potential end uses.

Each mill designs the prints, knits and stripes it believes will sell during the spring or fall fashion season. FMC sales people and merchandisers are in close touch, providing their own ideas on what they think will sell—and technical help on how to produce new fabrics most efficiently.

When the mills introduce their spring or fall lines of fabrics to potential garment manufacturer customers, FMC provides help by staging more than 40 shows in the garment centers in New York, Los Angeles, San Francisco, Dallas and Miami to show cutters what fabrics are available and which mills they can buy it from.

FMC merchandising representatives are also in direct touch with the garment trade, showing the new lines that are available. Still others are calling on buyers for the nation's largest retailers, showing them actual garments and fabrics that began as FMC fibers.

This marketing effort also extends to advertising and publicity. FMC advertisements designed to reach retail buyers picture the latest fashions made by the division's customer's customers—cutters who buy fabric from FMC-supplied mills. News stories on the latest fashion trends, illustrated with photographs of models wearing those same garments, are sent to hundreds of newspapers.

Do the mills like this kind of marketing support? Said one good mill customer recently, "One of the most rewarding experiences I've ever had has come from working with the FMC team."

It's that kind of reaction, as well as the expansion of the Radford plant, that indicates the success of FMC's policy of following the customer downstream all the way.

Chapter Seven

The Fabric Mills: Their Markets and Marketing Techniques

OVERVIEW

By Robert F. Eisen

The Goal

In 1979 the United States textile industry sold $46.9 billion worth of products, and in so doing consumed 12.773 billion lbs. of fiber (9.585 billion lbs. of man-made fiber or 75 percent; 3.077 billion lbs. of cotton or 24 percent; and 111 million lbs. of wool or one percent). To handle this volume of product, the marketing division of each textile mill organization has a common goal, namely, to sell their company's products at prices generating sufficient profits to have adequate sums of money for capital expenditures to keep their plants modern and to expand when prudent, and also to pay stockholders a reasonable dividend. In addition, they must sell a large enough volume to keep their machinery operating full and consistent with proper inventory control.

To achieve this goal, the industry must be alert to its customers' needs, so that adjustments can be made in production schedules and product lines as required. It must also be innovative and with the help of the manufacturing division, produce better fabrics and/or new fabrics that through styling, performance or price will attain the desired share of market at satisfactory profits.

Markets change and sometimes these changes take place over a period of time. In 1793 when Samuel Slater introduced power machinery in an American textile mill, the largest end use for cotton canvas was sails for ships. In 1830 when the Baltimore-built clipper ships were at their peak, each ship carried two sets of sails, each of which required about 7,000 linear yards of cotton canvas. As steam power gradually replaced sails on ships, the use of cotton canvas declined. However, by 1855 the western areas of the United States were under development and prairie schooner wagon trains were used to transport the settlers. Each wagon was covered by cotton canvas. This end use replaced sails as the largest user of cotton canvas.

The market division also has to be alert to profit opportunities in areas of the market other than their own and will constantly scrutinize competitor's product lines to evaluate their profit potentials. Capital expenditures usually follow profits and if a competitor is spending substantial sums of money in specific product areas, obviously he is doing so with the expectation that the money invested will earn an adequate return.

Personnel of the Marketing Division

THE SALES FORCE is a vital part of a textile mill organization in that it generates the orders that keeps the machinery running. It is usually, but not always, headquartered in New York City. Industrial fabrics, due to the nature of customer location, may have marketing division head-quarters at the manufacturing plant or adjacent to it.

Sales personnel must know their product line, current prices, and the delivery of each of their fabrics or products. They must call upon all active and potential customers in their territory and must forward promptly to headquarters, any market information that will help the product managers and management in making decisions.

Sales personnel are compensated in various ways, ranging from the extremes of straight salary at one end to a straight commission with no draw at the other end. Variations between the two extremes are common, with salary plus bonus being one of them. *Qualified sales personnel receive excellent compensation!*

Who supervises the sales force? In large organizations there is usually a national sales manager in addition to regional sales managers in such places as New York City, the West Coast, the Midwest, Europe, Hong Kong, etc. and also specialized sales managers in charge of chain and mail order sales.

When a sales person is assigned a territory or a list of accounts, the company through the sales manager will assign a large enough territory or a sufficient number of accounts so that the sales person with due diligence will be able to generate enough sales of reasonable volume and be paid accordingly.

Mill organizations selling apparel fabrics or home furnishing fabrics, usually have large staffs calling upon customers in New York City and the surrounding area. In addition important out of town markets are covered by sales personnel located in branch offices, who keep in contact with the New York headquarters through mail, telephone, and teletype. *It is necessary to have good communications to have an effective out of town sales force!* To assist branch office sales personnel, New York-based product managers and their assistants will call upon customers in the out of town sales territories with the sales person assigned to the account.

Specialized Selling

If a department's sales volume is sufficiently large, it may have its own sales force, not only in New York City but also in the larger out of town markets. Specialized selling is used by many large mills. For example, a sales person is assigned to a gray goods department and will sell only gray cloth, calling upon customers such as converters and industrial accounts who purchase cloth in the gray. Or a sales person may be assigned to a finished goods department that markets specialized cloths such as corduroy and indigo denim. In this instance the sales person will call upon those garment manufacturers and those buyers at the chain and mail order companies who purchase these cloths.

There are advantages and disadvantages to specialized selling. From the product manager's standpoint, he knows that certain sales personnel are working solely to sell his fabrics and he is not competing for their time with another department. However, it is an unusual product line that remains in strong demand year after year. When the products from that department are in slack demand, sales personnel assigned to that department go through a difficult period. On the other hand when sales personnel handle fabrics from several departments, if sales from one department slow down, usually, but not always, fabrics from another department are wanted. This gives the sales person a more balanced demand for his products, which in turn leads to better stability within the sales force.

If a textile mill has an opening in their sales force, they have a choice of either hiring an experienced person from the outside or of promoting from within through a sales training program. Large mills use both methods to keep their sales staff at full strength.

If a customer agrees to purchase a specific quantity of cloth at a specific price for a specific delivery, and the sales person has checked out all the details with his sales manager or the product manager and knows that the cloth is available, an oral commitment is made that is binding for both parties. The mill then sends out a written contract in duplicate confirming all the details and asks the customer to sign and return one copy. Oral commitments for orders in excess of one million dollars are not uncommon.

In the event of a dispute between a customer and a fabric mill, if it cannot be settled between the two parties, it may be presented, with the consent of both parties, to an impartial third party, namely, the American Arbitration Council, who will assign impartial skilled arbitrators to listen to both sides and to decide upon a fair settlement.

The Export Market

In recent years the weakness of the U.S. dollar in relation to other key currencies in the world have made U.S. prices on textile products attractive in foreign markets. In 1979 the United States exported 620 million lbs. of fabric, 240 million lbs. of made-up items, and 82 million lbs. of yarn.

Most of the larger textile mill organizations have opened sales offices abroad to supervise sales activities, which are usually done through agents or representatives. However, some of the American mills have established not only their own sales forces in some of the more important foreign markets but have also established plants to supply these markets.

When soliciting business from foreign customers, various aspects have to be considered, such as:

1. To use agents or to use your own sales personnel.

2. Do you check your own credit or do you use foreign factors who are based in each country? Or do you use a more secured basis such as letter of credit or sight draft?

3. Do you quote f.o.b. (freight on board) mill as to price and delivery? Or do you quote C.I.F. (cost, insurance, and freight) foreign port and ex mill as to delivery date? A C.I.F. price quote means the seller will deliver the cloth to the foreign port and all charges to that point are included in the price. The buyer pays the local duty or tariff. The delivery date, however, is the date the shipment leaves the mill. Do you quote in U.S. dollars or do you quote in the local currency of the customer? If the latter method is used, there is a risk to the seller if the foreign currency is devalued in the interim between the date of order and the date of payment. This risk can be overcome by hedging in the future market of the foreign currency, but this is an additional expense.

4. What kind of packing is required for the market? Are container shipments acceptable?

5. Is the customer buying in the metric system or yards? Do you bill in yards or in meters? How must the containers be marked as to weight and yards (meters)?

6. What arrangements have been made to handle quality complaints after a shipment has arrived abroad and it is not to the customer's satisfaction?

7. What legal responsibility do you incur when you hire an agent? (A study of the laws of that foreign country are necessary.)

To adequately cover foreign markets, participation in foreign fabric trade shows is sometimes desirable. Also, visits by New York-based personnel to foreign markets is necessary to indicate to the customers a strong commitment on the part of the American mill to service their market.

Over the years the handling of export shipments has changed. Many years ago it was standard practice to stamp in ink on the outside fold of a piece of cloth that was being exported, a trademark or symbol of the specific quality of that fabric. Many of the consumers in the foreign markets were illiterate and the only way they could recognize a particular mill-make or quality was through the trademark or "chopmark" as it was called in the Oriental markets. One of the New England mills in the early 1800's in catering to the Orient, used a symbol of a "duck" on their heavy cotton canvas. This symbol became so well known that in time all heavy cotton canvas was called duck. Another famous "chopmark" was the Flying Dragon of Pepperell Mfg. Co. About 1850 B.B. & R. Knight of Providence, Rhode Island substituted a printed paper label on the outside fold of each piece of cloth. This replaced the "chopmark." The label was in color and it pictured a bowl of fruit. It became one of the most famous trademarks in the American textile mill industry, namely, "Fruit of the Loom." They used this mark on their 80 x 92 gray count cotton print cloth made with 30/1 warp and 40/1 filling. Other mills copied the practice of using printed paper labels in color. Some of the printers who catered to mills exporting cloth, stocked a large selection of different printed labels and these labels were used to identify certain qualities and/or makes of cloth.

The Product Manager

THE PRODUCT MANAGER (also called the merchandise manager) is a key person in the marketing division. It is his or her responsibility to put together a product line that will generate sufficient volume to keep the assigned machinery running full, and to price these products to generate an adequate profit. In addition it is the responsibility of the product manager to keep inventories under proper controls.

The textile industry, particularly on fabrics, trades on price and sometimes prices change from order to order. The product manager must decide which bids from customers he will accept from the sales person presenting them, and which he will reject as being too low. The product manager is usually someone who has graduated from the sales force and has years of experience.

Some product managers have an assistant who is designated as assistant product manager, whereas other companies may designate co-managers for a department, or may designate one person as the product manager and the other as the sales manager.

IN GRAY GOODS MARKETING the product manager usually handles a specific mill unit or units. However, sometimes it is more advantageous to have a gray goods product manager handle specific type cloths regardless of the plant or plants where they are made.

IN FINISHED GOODS MARKETING it is usually handled by assigning a product manager either *by end use* or *by fabric type.* Each method has its advantages and disadvantages. It is also possible to have a further refinement if that cloth can be marketed by fabric type and then subdivided by end use. Some examples of the three types:

> **Marketing by End Use.** A product manager is assigned the outerwear/rainwear trade. He may have twenty cloths in his line of varying types, such as spun yarn polyester/cotton blend poplins, flat filament yarn nylon taffetas, textured filament polyester woven cloths, etc. The garment manufacturer finds this method the best for him, as he deals with only one department for all of his needs and in time a strong relationship is built up between the product manager and his customers.

> **Marketing by Fabric.** A product manager is assigned corduroy fabrics for all end uses, such as pants, outerwear, sport jackets, shirts, ladies skirts, children's wear, furniture, pillows, etc. The product manager is an expert in the specific fabric type that he handles and is able to keep himself better posted on competitive market pricing. However, he is usually less conscious of a shift away from his fabric type to another cloth, by one of his customers. In a large mill organization a customer may have to deal with a number of different departments and it is difficult to build up the same strong relationship as when marketing by end use.

> **Marketing by Fabric and Subdividing into End Use.** If the department's volume is sufficiently large, a

mill may set up a department by fabric type, such as
corduroy, and then within the department have
product managers for specific end use areas, such as
women's and children's wear, men's and boy's wear,
home furnishings, etc.

Staff Personnel

Besides sales personnel and product managers, staff personnel are
needed for a properly functioning marketing division. Stylists, fabric
technicians, quality control personnel, credit personnel, production
control personnel, and last but not least, management are required.
Management makes sure the relationships between the various departments are functioning properly and that the marketing division is
accomplishing its goal.

STYLISTS are skilled persons who create original designs for prints,
or yarn dyed patterns, or they may be skilled at putting together a line of
fabrics with the wanted colors for the next season. New product ideas are
the lifeblood of the marketing division. Sometimes they are the result of the
combined skills of the customer, the sales force, the product manager, the
stylist, the fabric technician, and manufacturing personnel. If it is
successful, all can share in the glory of having created something new and
different.

Profit margins on new fabrics are usually rewarding as the first mill in
the market sets the price. However, the machinery from mill to mill is
usually similar and therefore, a mill introducing a new fabric will not have
it exclusively for long. Most fabrics are not protected by copyrights or
patents and therefore can be duplicated.

In the early 1970's textured polyester yarn double knits were introduced into the market. This required the installation of special equipment.
Mill after mill entered this rapidly expanding and profitable market.
Eventually supply exceeded demand and only after fierce competition
lowered fabric prices and profit margins did some mills drop out of this
market. Mills enter new markets with enthusiasm but are slow to admit
mistakes and withdraw, particularly where expensive specialized machinery has been purchased.

FABRIC TECHNICIANS are the technical experts who can take the
ideas of the stylists, sales personnel, and customers, and put them down on
paper so that the necessary technical information can be transmitted to the
manufacturing units.

QUALITY CONTROL PEOPLE are skilled personnel who set up
cloth specifications for fabrics to prevent future problems. They also
investigate quality problems that arise after fabric has been shipped to a
customer. When checking out complaints of this type, they have to be dip-
lomatic in ascertaining whether the mill is at fault or whether the customer
is being unfair and is expecting more than he purchased. The best quality

control department is one that has strong standards or specifications that prevent problems from occurring before the fabric is shipped to the customer.

THE CREDIT DEPARTMENT is made up of specialists who have to reach a decision as to whether to approve an order or to reject it. They have to use their skills prudently. If they are too tough, they can make it difficult for the sales force to book orders. If they are too lenient, it will eventually show up in increased write-offs for bad debts.

Sales personnel are trained to quickly pass along to the credit department any information that indicates that a customer may be in financial difficulty.

With advances in data processing equipment, the credit departments from all facets of the market are moving into the 21st Century in that all of the information needed to reach a credit decision is available at their fingertips.

PRODUCTION CONTROL is usually handled by an executive in the marketing division. It is his or her responsibility to link the production facilities with the marketing division's requirements. Each mill organization handles this just a little bit differently and in their own way. The goal, of course, is to fully operate all of the machinery on fabrics producing adequate profits and not to pile up unwanted inventory.

The question of what is "operating full" is an interesting one. Since the late 1920's (with the exception of the depression years when the operating hours on looms and spindles were controlled by the Federal Government under the N.R.A.) most mills considered that they were operating "full" when their plants were running 144 hours per week (three shifts for six days), stopping only for Sundays. Production schedules were adjusted downward to 120 hours per week (three shifts for five days) depending upon market demand. Starting in 1976 as textile machinery became more sophisticated and accordingly more expensive, the 168 hours per week (four shifts spread over seven days) was introduced into the textile mill industry. Twenty years ago the cost per employee for the capital investment in a new spinning and weaving mill was about $50,000 per employee. By 1976 this cost had ballooned upward to about $250,000 per employee. The 168 hours per week schedule permitted spreading the depreciation costs over the greatest number of production units, and by so doing to make the purchase of more expensive equipment more easily justified from a standpoint of payback within a specified period of time. However, to operate textile plants on a four shift basis requires $1/3$ more labor, and when the labor market is "tight", sufficient skilled labor is scarce, which affects the operating efficiency.

In recent years the textile mill industry has undergone not only substantial changes in machinery but also in operating philosophies. Prior to 1975, even in periods of slack demand with softening prices, curtailment below 120 hours per week was looked upon as undesirable. Mills continued to operate 120 hours per week resulting in increased inventory which further depressed prices. However, in the recession of 1974/1975 for the first time in the memory of those still active in the industry, textile mills sharply curtailed production schedules and as a result inventories were kept under reasonable control. When market demand picked up, normal production schedules were resumed.

A Look at Some of the Fabric Markets

If a mill is marketing by fabric type, some of the larger markets are as follows:
(In linear yards for 1979 unless otherwise noted)

Broadwovens

COTTON TOBACCO AND CHEESE CLOTH—897 million yards. Although the yardage figure is large, it is deceptive inasmuch as these fabrics are very lightweight. The number of pounds of cloth is relatively modest. Some of the weavers supply their own internal needs, and the balance is sold primarily in the gray. It is a declining market that is being taken over by synthetic non-wovens.

SPUN YARN POLYESTER/COTTON BEDSHEETING—747 million yards. This yardage is primarily sold fabricated in the form of bedsheets (16 million dozen per year) and pillowcases (14 million dozen per year).

INDIGO DENIM—658 million square yards. In late 1977/early 1978 after seven straight years of increasing production and increasing demand, supply finally caught up with demand and the market went through a severe curtailment. However, the subsequent popularity of designer label women's and children's jeans at higher price points, stimulated the market and gave it a strong upward thrust that has persisted for the past 18 months.

TERRY TOWELS AND TOWELLING—430 million yards. This is sold primarily as a fabricated product (towels and wash cloths—50 million dozen per year) and to a much lesser extent as an apparel fabric for robes and beach jackets.

PRINT CLOTHS—1.025 billion yards. This large market is primarily sold in the gray to converters who bleach it, dye it, and print it and sell it finished.

TEXTURED FILAMENT POLYESTERS—392 million yards. In recent years this relatively new fabric type has grown rapidly with the advent of higher speed extrusion of polyester filament yarn, higher speed texturing, air jet commingling, and water jet loom weaving, all of which when combined led to the competitive price development of bottom-weight twills and sharkskins for men's and ladies' apparel, and topweights in crepes and pongees for blouses, dresses and shirts.

FLAT FILAMENT ACETATE TAFFETAS, TWILLS AND SATINS —350 million yards. These fabrics are sold in the gray for conversion into finished fabrics for linings, home furnishings, and bridal gowns, etc.

GLASS FIBER FABRICS—338 million yards. These cloths are used almost exclusively for industrial uses such as molded boat hulls, insulation, data processing circuit boards in computers, etc. They are produced on air jet looms and sold finished. Curtain and drapery cloths had been made from fiberglass but consumer dissatisfaction with the product gradually eliminated this market.

SPUN YARN POLYESTER/COTTON BROADCLOTHS—307 million yards. This fabric type is used for shirts, dresses, blouses, curtains, bedspreads, etc. It is sold by mills both finished and in the gray.

SPUN YARN CORDUROY—282 million yards. This cloth used to be made of 100 percent cotton, but in recent years the introduction of polyester was made in a mini-blend of 84 percent cotton/16 percent polyester for better stability, and in a blend of 50 percent polyester/50 percent cotton for crease retention in apparel. Today very little 100 percent cotton corduroy is made in the U.S.A. It is sold primarily finished and to a lesser extent in the gray.

FLAT FILAMENT NYLON TAFFETAS AND NINONS—255 million yards. The taffetas are sold for linings and outerwear shells. The ninons are sold for curtains. These cloths are primarily sold in the gray.

SPUN YARN RAYON/ACETATE BLENDS AND SPUN YARN RAYON/COTTON BLENDS—206 million yards. These blend descriptions cover a broad range of fabric weaves used in sportswear, dresses, tablecloths, etc. It is sold in the gray and also finished. It is made by a number of mills who specialize in short runs for confined styles sold to converters.

SPUN YARN POLYESTER/COTTON TWILLS AND GABARDINES—196 million yards. This fabric type is used in men's and ladies' slacks, jeans, uniforms, etc. It is sold both in the gray and finished.

SPUN YARN-DYED POLYESTER/COTTON BLENDS—166 million yards. These cloths are made in both topweights and bottomweights and are used for dresses, shirts, blouses in topweights, and for slacks, walk shorts, swimwear, jeans, etc. in bottomweights. It is sold primarily finished and to a lesser extent in the gray.

SPUN YARN POLYESTER/COTTON BATISTE—151 million yards. This cloth is used in shirts, blouses, dresses, sleepwear, etc. It is sold both gray and finished.

SPUN YARN POLYESTER/COTTON POPLINS—147 million yards. This fabric type is primarily made in mediumweights for slacks, walk shorts, rainwear, outerwear, and in lightweights for uniform shirts. It is sold primarily finished and to a lesser extent in the gray.

FLAT FILAMENT NYLON OXFORDS, TWILLS AND PLAIN WEAVES—147 million yards. These cloths are used for industrial end uses such as computer ribbons in fine deniers, and in coarse deniers for boat and truck tarpaulins, backpacks, luggage, etc.

FILAMENT POLYESTER WARP/SPUN FILLING—143 million

yards. This fabric description covers a broad range of individual cloths such as lightweights made with a flat filament warp and a spun polyester/cotton filling for curtains. Also heavier weights made with textured polyester warps and spun polyester fillings for men's and ladies' sportswear. These cloths are sold in the gray and finished.

Knit Fabrics

Circular Knits.

SINGLE KNITS—917 million lbs. in 1978. A large percentage of this production involves spun yarns. The machine cuts are primarily from 18 to 28. The fabrics go into a broad range of end uses, such as:

- **Apparel—men's and boys':** dress shirts, sport shirts, sweat shirts, underwear including T-shirts, nightwear, athletic wear, linings, etc.
  —women's, girls', and infants': blouses, shirts, T- and sweat shirts, dresses, nightwear, loungewear, play and athletic wear, pants, underwear, linings, etc.

- **Retail—Over-the-Counter**

- **Household Use**—slipcovers, etc.

- **Industrial**

Velours and terry knits have been popular in recent years, although in recent months the demand for terry has slackened somewhat.

SLIVER KNIT PILE—168 million lbs. in 1978. These are specialized single knit fabrics that are made on special machines designed to incorporate a heavy sliver to make a high pile fabric. These cloths are sold finished for linings in cold weather garments, such as liners in all-weather coats, outerwear, children's snow suits, bath mats, plush toys, etc.

DOUBLE KNITS—460 million lbs. in 1978. The preceding figure includes the production of interlock machines. Although there has been a contraction in the number of double knit machines from an estimated 20,000 during the peak in the mid 1970's, to an estimated 11,000 machines today, it is still the largest user of textured polyester yarn. Machine cuts from 18 to 28 are the most common. The fabrics go into slacks, suits, skirts, shirts, uniforms, children's wear, retail-over-the-counter, etc. It is sold finished.

Warp Knits (flat knits).

TRICOT (INCLUDING SIMPLEX AD MILANESE)—335 million lbs. in 1978. These fabrics are made almost exclusively from flat filament and textured filament yarn, primarily nylon, acetate, and polyester. The fabrics are used for underwear, sleepwear, shirts, linings in apparel, as a laminate with foam for insulation in outerwear, in industrial end uses such as headlinings in automobiles, etc.

RASCHEL (INCUDING RASCHEL-CROCHET)—59 million lbs. in 1978. The raschel machine is a very versatile machine and can use almost any yarn. However, textured polyester has captured a good share of this market for slacks, uniform fabrics, skirts, etc. Raschel fabrics are also used for bath mats, upholstery fabrics, etc.

Carpets

In 1979, 1.217 billion square yards of carpets were produced in the U.S.A. of which 96 percent or 1.168 billion square yards were tufted, 1.7 percent or 21.3 million square yards were wovens, and 2.3 percent or 27.6 million square yards were produced by other methods, primarily knits.

Nonwovens

This is a highly specialized area of the textile market. The traditional textile mills have been relatively unsuccessful in marketing products in nonwovens. The estimated usage in 1977 was 641 million lbs. going into the following end uses: diaper covers, interlinings and interfacings, carpet backing, filtration, wipes and roll towels, coated laminated fabrics, mattress pads and bedspreads, sanitary napkins, surgical gowns and surgical packs, packaging, and durable papers.

Nonwovens are made by different processes including spun bonded and spun laced, wet laid, dry processes including carded and air laid, and also composites. It is an interesting area where the fiber companies, paper mills, and textile mills have challenged each other.

Nonwovens have made a steady penetration into the fabric market, primarily in household and industrial end uses. There has been little penetration into the massive apparel shell fabric market primarily because of shortcomings of appearance, hand, flame retardant characteristics, and permanence. About ten years ago low priced printed house dresses and low priced ladies panties were marketed, but were unsuccessful.

Merchandising by End Use

The three broad end use categories for textiles are apparel, household products, and industrial. For statistical purposes any end use which does not fit into one of the first two categories is considered industrial.

The estimated size of the markets listed below are based on 1979 data and *include* foreign fabrics and foreign yarn imported into the U.S.

Apparel—10.48 billion square yards, of which wovens were 5.73 billion square yards and knits were 4.75 billion square yards, as follows:

> • *women's, girls' and infants'*—5.06 billion square
> yards, of which 2.63 billion square yards are knits
> and 2.43 billion square yards are wovens.

• *men's and boy's*—5.42 billion square yards, of which 3.30 billion square yards are wovens and 2.12 billion square yards are knits.

When merchandising by end use to apparel manufacturers, it is done by catering to specific areas within the above broad groups. For example: departments may be set up to handle fabrics for:

1. ladies dresses

2. ladies blouses and shirts

3. men's and boys' dress shirts

4. men's and boys' sport shirts

5. men's slacks

6. men's and boys' jeans

7. infants' and children's wear

8. uniforms

9. outerwear/rainwear

10. lingerie

11. men's work clothing

When a department is set up it is necessary for management to make the necessary commitment to have a broad enough product line so that the customer is convinced that the mill resource is an important one to him and thus a relationship is built with the customers.

Retail—Over-the-Counter—1.12 billion square yards. In 1978 this market was 1.32 billion square yards which would seem to indicate that this market is declining. As an indication of its lessening importance one of the major retail chains dropped fabric sales from their stores because the square footage of selling space was not producing adequate sales.

A department catering to retail-over-the-counter sales requires a different put-up of fabric as the retail store customer requires small pieces so that the cloth can be easily handled in the store. Also because the size of the orders is generally much smaller than those handled by other departments, it is necessary to have special systems for handling credit as well as from a processing standpoint. Also usually a special sales force is needed to call on retail accounts.

Industrial—5.738 billion square yards, of which 5.651 billion square yards are wovens and 87 million square yards are knits. Because of the vast number of different specific end uses, most industrial fabrics are marked by fabric types rather than end use.

Household Products—8.67 billion square yards, of which wovens were 8.041 billion square yards and knits were 628 million square yards.

Fabric departments can be set up to cater by end use to:

1. curtains and bedspreads

2. draperies

3. upholstery fabrics

However, when fabricated products such as bedsheets and pillow cases, blankets, terry towels and face cloths, bedspreads, draperies, etc. are sold, the products are merchandised by product.

Military

The United States Government can be an important customer of the American textile mill industry. The latest data available (1976) indicates that this market was 11.7 million lbs. Obviously it can be a highly volatile market depending upon the needs of the U.S. Government. Government purchasing is done by specification and the specifications are worked out by Government personnel working closely with industry personnel to insure that the specifications are practical and within the capability of the industry. Most Government purchases are handled on a "bid" basis, whereby those companies interested in supplying the needed fabric will hand in a sealed bid. At a specified time all bids are opened and the award is made to the lowest priced qualified bidder. Those textile mills which cater to the U.S. Government usually have special departments to handle the bidding.

26. MARKETING TO A DYING INDUSTRY*

By Lawrence Washer, Vice President—Sales,
Cheney Brothers

Five years ago I assumed the duties of vice president in charge of sales for Cheney Brothers. Cheney Brothers are producers of a full range of velvet fabrics. One of the trades that uses velvets is the casket industry.

Cheney Brothers had been selling to this industry for many years and perhaps there are reservations in some people's minds on "selling to a dying industry." To me, this was a marketing problem the same as if I were selling to the dress or any other industry.

Surprisingly enough, the funeral industry does have seasons and style changes. Recognizing this fact we dye up new shade and color cards in time for each season.

The funeral industry is quite specialized so we found that we could achieve best results by continuing to sell through two exclusive distribu-

---

*This article first appeared in the February 1974 issue of the *Textile Marketing Letter*.

tors. Our distributors have salesmen that regularly call on all facets of the industry. The two distributors are Theo Tiedemann and Baxter, Kelly & Faust. Both of them distribute nationally and are well known and respected by the trade.

Cheney Brothers is an old established textile company. They have been making velvets since the late 1800's. Our problem was to utilize the fine Cheney name in juxtaposition with the proper recognition with our distributors.

Our agency, Lewis Advertising Company, elected to conduct an extensive advertising program in all the major casket publications. Our theme was "Cheney Velvet—the Beauty of America." This program of advertising was being directed to the casket makers and funeral directors.

We used full color bleed pages in all our ads. Each ad was timely to the season of the year. For example, last spring we showed a typical pictur-esque New England scene of the babbling brook in the foreground with the New England church spire and town in the background. Inlayed in the lower right side were velvet casket shades draped together illustrating how well they blended with the colors of nature. The fall ad illustrated the blazing beauty of autumn in New England. The winter scene was a small Midwest town blanketed in snow with the church spire and roof tops glistening in the sun, and in the background were the hills of firs and evergreens. The summer scene was the Arizona desert bursting forth after the spring rain. Each of these ads was inlayed with various draped velvet shades that blended with nature.

Our copy was kept simple: "Cheney's skilled craftsmen have been weaving velvets of quiet beauty since 1838. They are available in many grades and more than one hundred selected shades, perfectly consistent from order to order." By these ads the trade was able to recognize the good name of Cheney as well as the availability of purchasing nationally through our distributors.

The casket industry has stringent requirements on shade matching. We wanted to stress our long experience in handling these requirements. Velvets are used on the interior of the casket to blend with the exterior wood or metal shell. A fine velvet interior makes a fine casket. An average velvet casket costs from five hundred to ten thousand dollars, so velvet is like the icing on the cake.

Reprints of our ads were sent to all casket makers and funeral directors. Everyone enjoys the beauty of nature and since these ads were so timely depending on the season of the year, they were very well received. We also directed a mail campaign to build up the reliance of our customers with our distributors. Our grand motif was: "Sometimes a casket maker needs a friend and mine is my Cheney distributor." Inside these folders were reprints of previous ads and additional features why our going the route of distributors was the best for the customer. We stressed: "My distributor comes through with the kind of frequent service that lets me keep my inventory costs down to a minimum, without ever letting me get caught short. I know that he knows me and my operation, what I'm looking for in my interior finishing, and how he can help me make a better casket."

Cheney Brothers makes a full range of grades in velvets that are woven exclusively for the casket industry. We dye them in over a hundred shades running from white to a deep dark wine. At the mill level, our standards are most exacting. The greige goods are carefully inspected and the finished goods must be consistent in shade and hand from dye lot to dye lot.

I personally worked with our distributors and visited casket makers so I was informed of their specialized needs and requirements. A number of manufacturers were invited to our mill in Manchester, Connecticut to see our operation and meet our company president, John Robinson, and our plant superintendent, John Rukus. This was an aid in our selling as they were always impressed with the cleanliness of the plant and the fine spirit of all mill personnel in doing a conscientious job. Our permanent display at the mill shows other fabrics that Cheney produces besides velvet that could also be used by casket makers.

We have achieved our marketing objective due to close cooperation between the sales department in New York, the mill, our distributors and advertising company. We have one purpose in mind: to continue to present to the casket industry the finest velvets.

27. THE SCHUMACHER APPROACH TO FABRIC MARKETING*

By James C. Cumming, Consultant

"Traditionally Schumacher has introduced fabrics in such a manner that they are irresistible to the designer," says Robert Herring, Schumacher's Director of Public Relations and Advertising. "It's this concept of irresistibility, coupled with a Total Promotional Program, that has built Schumacher to its present preeminent position."

That's a good summary of Schumacher's basic policy in the marketing of decorative fabrics, but it needs explaining.

First of all, how does Schumacher make its fabrics irresistible to the designer?

This is a matter of top-notch fabric design with each design keyed to a promotable theme. As individual prints, each of these designs is attractive but one by one they can't possibly have the selling strength that they gain when they are grouped together and tied to a single theme.

The Wedgwood collection is an example—a line of a dozen current and traditional prints, all in the Wedgwood tradition. As individual prints, no interior designer would have given them much attention but tied together with the Wedgwood theme and promoted as a group, they became one of the season's most important decorative elements. With the Wedg-

---

*This article first appeared in the November 1973 issue of the *Textile Marketing Letter.*

wood fabrics the decorator was in a position to design an entire room or series of rooms starting with the many products of the prolific Wedgwood firm.

You can imagine this for yourself. He could start with Wedgwood product accessories in the dining room, the living room, the study, or almost anywhere. He could then carry the theme through with any of the Schumacher Wedgwood fabric prints. Then he could complete his work with one of the Wedgwood patterns in wall-coverings which Schumacher also produces.

"The artistry and tradition of Wedgwood is presented in unique adaptation by Schumacher under license from Josiah Wedgwood & Sons, Inc.," is the way the firm describes the collection in color advertising in such magazines as *House Beautiful*. "The delightful designs of screen printed linen and cotton fabrics with companion wall coverings of Tyvek by DuPont are available through interior designers and in the finest stores."

You will notice that Schumacher doesn't hesitate to take advantage of the promotional support that is available from most of the fiber and finish suppliers. Tyvek is named. So is the fact that the fabric is "available with DuPont Zepel Stain Repeller."

DuPont's help is wisely welcomed in other theme promotions, too. Aepel gets important mention in the advertising of Sleepy Hollow Restoration Fabrics. The rest of the story: Schumacher, in collaboration with the curators of Sleepy Hollow Restorations, has reproduced an exclusive group of decorative fabrics and wall-coverings. They have been carefully culled from documents and antique fragments of cloth representing authentic styles of this historic area. The collection includes printed cottons, linens, embroideries and figured wovens."

Again the "where to buy it" line is "through interior designers and the finest stores." Practically irresistible to a practical designer!

Another current thematic group is the Designer's Choice Fabric Collection. "Schumacher presents the third prestigious Designer's Choice Collection. Eight illustrious interior designers, geographically dispersed across the country, were invited to choose a pattern from Schumacher's museum of documents and interpret it as a print for today's distinctive interiors. Each in turn has styled an exciting design that will enhance the beauty of either traditional or contemporary decoration."

The eight designers who contributed their talents to the creation of this collection were Blanche Morgan, Seattle; Jack Slenker, Memphis; Richard Plumer, Miami; James Hewlett, New Orleans; Olga Gordon, Philadelphia; Walter B. Broderick, San Diego; Kitty Mercer Stanley, Minneapolis; and Richard Himmel, Chicago—a group as prestigious as the designs they created.

Perhaps the best known and most widely used of the Schumacher thematic promotions is the Williamsburg collection. This is a continuing group with new fabrics being added to it at intervals.

About this group, Schumacher said in a recent message to consumers: "Under the close supervision of the Craft Advisory Committee of Colonial Williamsburg, additional fabric reproductions are being introduced by Schumacher. The collection is presented in a bright color palette that will allow a great variety of decorative uses either in 18th century period rooms or contemporary interiors."

Ideas for similar "irresistible" groups come from everywhere. An example of this was the handcrafted heritage group designed around documents in the Brooklyn Museum. The publicity plan for this group called for making the initial presentation to the press at a sit-down dinner in the museum itself. This was followed by cocktail parties with presentations to wider groups including interior designers and retail buyers. Following the introduction, the entire collection and the artifacts that inspired the designs were on view at the museum for eight weeks.

In this way publicity is injected into the firm's Total Promotional Program. For some of the groups, publicity is developed simply by sending photographs to publications. For the Wedgwood group, for example, Ed Motyka, A. I. D. (American Institute of Interior Designers), did a series of model rooms. Schumacher photographed the rooms and distributed the photographs with excellent publicity results.

Similarly, to develop retail window displays, Schumacher uses its own Third Avenue windows at the New York showroom, as a source of ideas. These windows are photographed and the pictures are sent to decorative fabric retailers who adapt them to their own use.

Finally, a very important item in decorative fabric promotion is the sample book which is one of the strongest elements in Schumacher promotion. "Since the consumer spends so much time with the sample book in making her final selections," says Mr. Herring, "we go out of our way to make it as attractive as possible. These books are among the largest items in our promotional budget."

So there you have the Schumacher marketing formula: Beautifully designed fabrics plus the strength of a total promotional program, adding up to products that are irresistible to the designer and the consumer.

28. WHAT EVERY MILL MAN SHOULD KNOW ABOUT THE HOME SEWING MARKET*

By James C. Cumming, Consultant

Textile marketers sometimes comment on the difficulty of promoting fabrics to consumers. "Ours is not an end product," they complain, "and the brand identity of the fabric is lost in the product manufactured from it."

---

*This article first appeared in the June 1975 issue of the *Textile Marketing Letter.*

But home sewers constitute an important piece goods market where identity is not lost and where fabrics are sold, to all intents and purposes, like packaged goods in a supermarket. Many mills and converters are active in this market and do very well in it while others, for one reason or another, pass it up.

It's a huge market. Irene Kleeberg, writing in *Homesewing Trade News,* the monthly publication of the industry, recently gave 60 million as a reasonably accurate estimate of the number of women who sew, but hastened to point out that this figure is an understatement. By definition, a "women who sews" is a woman who makes at least one garment a month. There are, in addition, many women who produce one or two garments a year. This would add another 15 million women to the size of the market.

Nor should we limit the market to women, although the number of men and boys who may be involved in it is too small to consider. Still, the educational programs in the secondary schools cover not only practically every female teenager but also many male teenagers. Older women, too, are enrolled in sewing classes which means an ever-enlarging market.

This growth is important in providing a direct market for the fabric of any mill. At the same time, it is an important avenue for educating women on the advantage of your fabric or your fibers when those same women are buying ready-to-wear garments. In packaged goods terms, you might call your over-the-counter sales to home sewers a great self-liquidating sampling campaign.

From a dollars-and-cents standpoint, how big is the home sewing market? In total annual sales it's at least $4 billion but this includes notions, patterns, trimmings and such. We could even peg the total volume at about $6 billion if we were to include yarns and sewing machines. If we break out these other items that may not interest you, we still have an over-the-counter piece goods sales volume of $2.6 billion— and any mill's share of that is certainly worth going after.

Tapping the home sewing market isn't as easy as selling the ready-to-wear trade, which is the main reason so many mills stay away from it. On the other hand, it's not all that difficult!

Small independent stores, often referred to as "Ma, Pa and Rosie" stores, are the backbone of distribution to home sewers. There are more than 15,000 of them and they do about 40 percent of all over-the-counter fabric business from a standpoint of dollar sales and yardage. Obviously, the best way to reach these small units is through wholesalers. This reduces the number of people you have to work with to manageable proportions and brings the number of contacts for you more nearly in line with your present ready-to-wear contacts.

In addition to these small stores, another 30 percent or so of home sewing business is done by the big national chains—Sears, Roebuck, Montgomery Ward, J. C. Penney, and the like. Another 20 percent is done by fabric chains and some stores with only two or three branches are included in this figure. The rest of the business is done by variety chains, general merchandise and department stores. The most significant market change in recent years has been the weakness of the department store in this field. The mill that wants to sell piece goods over-the-counter, however, should not overlook the department store. It's still very much alive and many stores are preparing plans to recapture what once was, for them, a very profitable business.

Why do women sew? A number of surveys have been aimed at an accurate answer to this question. One such survey, conducted some years ago, determined that sewing is the foremost hobby among adult women. Today there are other reasons. Leisure time is on the increase and most women like to use their increased leisure constructively. More than that, home sewing is a creative hobby as many women even go so far as to design their own patterns.

Today, with the average woman waging a vigorous battle against inflation, the factor of cost saving becomes very important. Equally important is the element of better quality. The dress made at home is almost invariably better than its factory-produced counterpart.

Certainly any mill that is not now marketing doubled and rolled fabrics in this field, for whatever reason, should give the home sewing market another look. It's a way to add substantially to your present volume.

Chapter Eight

The Textile Converter

OVERVIEW

By John A. Cairns

The converter is the man or organization who stands in the middle of the textile marketing picture, halfway between the fabric mill and/or the garment manufacturing (cutting-up) trades and the retail merchant. The dyeing, printing and finishing plants are probably his closest allies, and almost everyone in the textile and related industries can be his customer, at one time or another. The industry would be a rather dull, colorless place without him.

What does the converter do? He takes fabrics as they come off the loom (usually known as "gray goods," the English equivalent of the French word, "greige"), styles them up for various segments of the cutting-up and retail trades, then sends them out to print works and finishing plants to be put in their final finished form for marketing. Some mills and converters maintain large staffs of fabric designers in this country and abroad; nearly everyone in the business buys original designs from the many design studios that abound in the trade, to supplement their own creative efforts.

A recent letter from a top executive in one of the fiber companies has this to say: "One of the most interesting elements in the relationship between the mills and the converters is the influence which the converters exercise on the styling of mills' lines. In many cases, the converter acts as the eyes and ears of the mill in determining what the garment manufacturing trade will want next. This is particularly true of the higher priced fabrics going into the upper echelons of the cutting-up trade, especially the dress trade." In another quote, a highly regarded female marketing consultant points out that "some of the better converters frequently make contacts with various weaving and knitting mills to produce specific quantities of fabrics according to the converter's own original design. Some designers will blend as many as a half a dozen fibers to get an effect." The converter accounts for literally billions of yards of goods sold each year. His special genius, of course, is his ability to foretell fashion trends, and to design goods to meet those trends.

The converter can be a single individual who "carries his business around under his hat," so to speak, and who places his orders for gray goods after he has taken a safe number of orders for finished good. Or, he can be a giant organization like M. Lowenstein and Sons, Milliken and Company, Dan River, Inc. or J. P. Stevens who own their own gray goods mills and finishing plants. The converter may design and produce fabrics for many areas in the market or he may prefer to specialize in creating fabrics for such purposes as shirting materials, dress goods, drapery and upholstery fabrics, industrial uniforms, or what have you.

In former years, the textile business was a lot more rigidly segmented than it is today. The traditional flow of goods was from the mill to the converter, to the finishing plant, to the converter's customers. Not too many goods, with the exception of colored yarn shirtings and dress goods, and some of the work clothing fabrics like twills, drills, chambrays and denims were sold by the mills direct to the garment manufacturers and retailers.

Today, many mill organizations have their own converting departments and some of them now own print works and finishing plants. Likewise, the better known finishing plants have opened their own converting subsidiaries, some of which do an international business. Many mills will buy very large quantities of gray goods from their competitors while competing vigorously with these same competitors for orders of finished goods from cutters and retailers. This would appear to be the inevitable result of the severe day-to-day competition which exists in every basic industry in this country. And that competition is by no means limited to domestic operations. Huge quantities of gray and finished goods are now coming into this country from Japan, the People's Republic of China, from Hong Kong and other Oriental sources.

You might ask "what kinds of people are in the converting business these days?" and the answer is "almost everybody." It can be a large chain retailer like Penney or Sears, or a group of fine department stores working through a centrally owned buying organization such as the Associated Merchandising Corporation. It can be any one of a number of men's or women's garment manufacturers that leaves a standard order for a specific type of gray goods with his favorite mills and then sends it off to be dyed in a range of staple solid colors each month. Or it can be almost any large retail organization which adopts the "converter" method of acquiring a substantial portion of his piece goods requirements for over-the-counter selling. A rather unusual bit of marketing strategy was exhibited not long ago by one of the fiber companies working in collaboration with a large manufacturer of popular-priced women's dresses. The fiber company first tried to introduce its new fiber by taking it to the converting division of one of the larger mill organizations, with the offer to confine its sale to that organization until it had been well and safely launched. When the mill's request for promotional support exceeded the entire budget of the fiber producer, the latter took the new fiber to a friend in the dress business, with the suggestion that it be launched, in a new 50/50 blend of cotton and the new fiber. This was done, and the dress manufacturer arranged for the dyeing and finishing. He then pre-sold the dresses in one large order to Sears, Roebuck and backed the whole thing up with a half-page ad in the Sears catalogue at a fraction of the cost that would have been involved if he had worked directly with the mill, as originally planned. Everyone was happy with the results.

The moral of the story is this: "Just set up your marketing plan that you provide every organization in your marketing program with a pre-sold customer, and you're pretty sure to come out ahead!"

29. CONVERTER: TARGET OF CRANSTON COMPANY*

By James C. Cumming, Consultant

The Cranston Print Works Company was founded in 1825, and its distribution program in the 147 years since then has included about everything that can be done in textile marketing.

In some ways Cranston is an upstart. Certainly it is younger than J. P. Stevens & Co. But although the company has added plants in Webster,

---

*This article first appeared in the November 1972 issue of the *Textile Marketing Letter*.

Mass., and in Fletcher, N.C., it still manufactures in the old original buildings in Cranston, Rhode Island.

One fairly recent change: the old home of Governor Sprague, adjacent to the Cranston plant, and for years the residence of the plant manager, is now a Rhode Island historical monument.

What makes Cranston different is the fact that marketing textile printing is so very different from marketing finished fabrics such as yarn-dyed woven goods. The company's inventory consists mainly of copper rollers. It owns no yardage. Its work is done to the order of the converter who buys the greige goods, prepares the patterns, specifies the finish and orders the delivery. Cranston may be said merely to enhance the fabric.

This poses unique marketing problems as the converter is the primary customer, with the cutter secondary, the retailer tertiary, and the consumer fourth on the totem pole. Cranston has never lost sight of the fact that its program should be aimed first at the converter, although there were times back when attempts were made to establish the Cranston name with cutters, retailers and even consumers.

With these problems, and with all this experience under its belt, what does Cranston do today?

"Our entire marketing program is based on service," says Vincent McManus, Cranston Sales Manager. "We are regarded as the Tiffany of textile printing, and we take great pains to protect and maintain that reputation."

McManus points out that in order to deliver the best quality and service, Cranston works with a limited number of top-notch independent converters. They include such firms as Henry Glass, Springs Mills, Avondale, Concord, Free Associates, and E. F. Leveen.

In addition, in the course of time, Cranston has acquired four converters of its own: Qualitex, V.I.P., Schwartz-Liebman, and Crantex. These four do not step on each other's toes; each specializes in men's wear fabrics, in over-the-counter piece goods, or in different areas of sportswear fabrics.

For that matter, it's a tribute to the integrity of Cranston management that none of the converters, owned or independent, get in each other's hair. Some market loungewear, some children's wear fabrics, some shirtings, or dress goods, or slacks fabrics and some sell to sportswear cutters. With some of the patterns it's the wilder the better, but they don't collide.

Cranston advertising today is in trade publications only and is targeted solely at converters. Its message is simply that Cranston does great printing. No cutters are featured in it; no converters' fabrics are mentioned —just the theme all the way through: "Cranston—the first in prints."

"How the converters do their marketing is up to them," says Mr. McManus. "Sometimes they feature cutters, or patterns, or they tie in with fiber producers. Our message to them is loud and clear—the best service with the very best printing in the textile business."

30. THE GRAY GOODS AND
PIECE GOODS JOBBER

**A Few Words About Their Current Contributions
to Textile Marketing***

*By Robert F. Eisen,
Greenwood Mills Marketing Company*

We recently asked our long-time friend, Robert F. Eisen, at the Greenwood Mills Marketing Company, how he felt about the present-day contributions which textile brokers and jobbers are making to the marketing of basic textile products. His very interesting response follows:

"GRAY GOODS BROKERS perform a necessary function in the marketplace by making readily available to converters and to other gray goods users a 'second-hand' market where excess gray goods can be disposed of quickly and efficiently. The brokers are perhaps less important today on direct sales from domestic mills.

"A number of mills have sales forces which are sufficiently large as to enable them to maintain adequate sales customers. As a general rule, these mills do not sell any substantial portion of their production through brokers. There are, however, many mills which do not choose to maintain large sales forces and these mills will normally sell through brokers.

"It should be kept in mind that the broker is working for the buyer and will carefully shop the market to get the best price for his customer. However, it is the seller and not the buyer who pays the brokerage fee. This is one reason why some mills prefer not to sell through brokers.

"Gray goods brokers also fulfill a significant function in the marketplace by handling imported gray goods. In some instances, they act solely as brokers; in other cases, they will act as principals, buying and selling for their own accounts.

"JOBBERS AND WHOLESALERS: There are, as you know, many different types of jobbers and wholesalers who are active in various segments of the market. Some specialize in buying off-price cloth which can be seconds, pound-goods or closeouts. In the case of closeouts, they serve the market by getting rid of the mistakes made by the mills.

"Other jobbers specialize in purchasing first-quality goods at regular prices which they then distribute to retail stores for over-the-counter distribution as yard goods. This business has grown tremendously in recent years and shows no sign of abating. There are also the so-called 'Institutional Jobbers' who specialize in supplying home furnishings products (such as sheets, towels, bedspreads, tablecloths, drapes, etc.) to motels, hotels, city and state departments, hospitals, prisons, etc.

"Greenwood Mills does not produce floor coverings, but it is my understanding that the floor covering jobber is as big and important as

---

*This article first appeared in the March 1977 issue of the *Textile Marketing Letter.*

ever in the distribution of both hard and soft floor coverings. As to the fine goods jobbers who cater to the custom tailoring trade, I am sure that they still perform many useful functions in this area of the textile and apparel markets. I would assume, however, that they are today somewhat less important than they were a few years back, due to the fact that the woolen and worsted business itself has declined in recent years."

31. EXPLOSION IN PRINTS: THE STONEHENGE STORY*

By The Editorial Staff, Textile Marketing Letter

Business was barely beginning to climb out of the depression when, in 1937, C. D. Hardy left F. Schumacher & Co. to form his own converting firm of Old Deerfield Fabrics. It was a small beginning for a business that has since become one of the leaders in decorative fabrics.

The business grew steadily as a source of decorative fabrics for Schumacher, Everfast and other top line textile fabric houses. However, it did not really "take off" until the invention, in Switzerland, of a new automatic screen printer.

In 1944, Fritz Buser, of the Buser Engineering Works in Wiler, near Bern, began the construction of a fully automatic screen printing machine. Four years and 300,000 yards of fabrics later, he felt that the machine was ready for commercial use. It was, by far, the most advanced machine of its type.

Doug Hardy heard about it and went to Wiler to see it in 1949. He liked what he saw and bought the eleventh machine produced by Buser, the first automatic machine to come to the United States. With this machine under his belt, he formed the Stonehenge Processing Corporation and put up a building to house the machine in Cedar Grove, New Jersey. This was the beginning of his textile printing business.

At the same time, recognizing the vast superiority of the Buser machine and the fact that sooner or later most decorative fabric printers in this country would want it, he formed a subsidiary, Jungfrau, Inc., to act as sales representative for Buser Automatic Screen Printers in North America.

His first instinct was to attempt to slow down the sale of the machines in order to avoid building competition for Stonehenge. He quickly sensed, however, that screen prints would gain more acceptance if more screen printed fabrics were available on the market, and that with this increased acceptance Stonehenge business would be the first to profit.

Accordingly, he began the active promotion of Buser machines to other printing and finishing plants. His main selling problem at that time was that screen printers felt that it would be impossible to print one wet

---

*This article fist appeared in the April 1968 issue of the *Textile Marketing Letter.*

color on another without waiting for the first to dry. By taking prospects to the Stonehenge plant and using it as a model, he was quickly able to prove the practicality of this type of printing.

Three positive points which favored the use of the automatic screen printer were:

1. Roller print machines, which were then in use for decorative fabrics, required such long runs that converters frequently had "indigestion." They had trouble in selling so many yards of a pattern and color with the result that sharp markdowns often had to be taken.

2. Decorators and consumers want frequent changes in their decorating patterns. Most of these changes are entirely practical with the Buser machine, but are more difficult if not impossible to deliver with roller printing.

3. Decorators and consumers like the "loft" of screen prints on decorative fabrics.

As the Buser machine proved itself and the marketing demand for screen prints increased, more and more printers such as Castle Creek Prints, Inc., the Cranston Print Works Co., Colonial Print Works Ltd., California Hand Prints, Inc. and Textile Printing and Finishing Co., installed the machines.

Soon firms that were not basically printers such as J.P. Stevens & Co., Inc., Pepperell Manufacturing Co. and Springs Cotton Mills started using the automatic-screen printers. Cone Mills Corp. and Riegel Textile Corp. added Buser machines to their roller printing operations.

Economics of the Buser Machine. The southern printers discovered that the Buser gave them definite production economies. They could run as fast as 1,000 yards per hour. While the most efficient use of the machine is to produce a minimum of 1,500 yards of color, it could deliver a high quality short order business in as little as 500 yards of a pattern economically.

The increasingly widespread use of screen printers such as the Buser is generally credited with today's explosion in prints, especially since today's fashions call for large, complicated patterns "made to order" for screen printing. It may be compared with the explosion in book production that followed the invention of the linotype machine. The demand for prints from all plants and mills had increased sharply, and with this increased demand, Stonehenge business has multiplied over and over again. Nor is this business confined to decorative fabrics. Today about 25 percent of the fabrics produced on screen printers go into dress goods, with men's wear fabrics a developing market.

The Buser machine in use today is a far cry from the original machine that Stonehenge brought to this country in 1949. In addition to improvements made in Switzerland, many new features have been added at Stonehenge in order to make it suitable for use in American printing plants and mills. In addition, the machine has been adapted for another use.

Application to Wallpaper. In 1941, Doug Hardy had established Provincetown Printers for the production of wallpaper. This was done to meet the demand from various decorative jobbers for wallpapers that would harmonize with the decorative fabrics they were selling. After many experiments, Provincetown found that they could adapt the Buser machine for the screen printing of wallpaper, including scenics. This has resulted in the production of "block printed" wallpaper with automatic screens far more economically than it could be done with hand screens, and with a resulting increase in the availability of matching wallpaper and fabric patterns. Today 40 percent of the fabrics produced by Stonehenge are also available in matching wallpaper.

Evidence that research and development at Stonehenge are not confined to machine improvements alone is shown in current laboratory work on abrasion resistance in union cloth, so generally used by furniture manufacturers. One of these fabrics, with its linen fill and cotton warp, formerly would not exceed 2,800 to 3,000 runs on the Wyzenbeek Tester. With a new finish developed by Stonehenge the fabric is getting 15,000 runs on the tester.

The most interesting part of the Stonehenge story, however, remains the improvements introduced into the Buser machine and the willingness to see the machine operating in the plants of competitors across the country. The result is the explosive expansion of screen printed decorative fabrics and dress goods, and the sharp expansion of Stonehenge's own business.

Chapter Nine

The Mills' Customers

INTRODUCTION

Customers of textile mills are many and varied and can be broken down into many subdivisions. In apparel, for instance, we have business clothes, party clothes, work clothes, out-of-doors clothing, professional uniforms, rentals for men,women, misses, juniors, boys, girls, infants, etc., uniforms for the military, protective uniforms for firemen and policemen, etc. Likewise, in the domestics and home furnishings fields we have sheets and pillowcases, blankets, bedspreads, towels and wash cloths, curtains, drapes and floor coverings. Since the markets for the textile mills are so diverse, we have chosen in this chapter to highlight, in particular, the home furnishings market so that the reader might get an in-depth look at this segment. Following this brief introduction is an account of this industry segment by Kay Corinth, a leading consultant in the field. Following her article are several from past issues of the *Textile Marketing Letter* concerning not only the home furnishings industry, but other mills' customers as well.

OVERVIEW: INSIDE THE HOME FURNISHINGS TEXTILE MARKET

By Kay Corinth

"Mid pleasures and palaces though we may roam, be it ever so humble, there's no place like home," wrote John Howard Payne in the 19th Century. With the wealth of beautiful fabrics created and supplied for the home by American mills and converters at affordable prices today, home need never be humble.

Someone else wrote, "Home is where the heart is." Home is also where the family is grouping more and more, turning inward from outside economic and other major problems and threats of the times:

- Inflation, making the cost of going out for entertainment or dining prohibitive.

- The price of gasoline cutting driving to a minimum.

- Crime rampant in the streets, especially after-dark, rendering the securely locked home a snug cocoon of safety, a refuge.

These negatives add up to a positive new lifestyle, bringing families together under the shelter of one roof, with the environment a primary concern. Home becomes the focal point for living, eating, sleeping, exercising, reading, and other individual pursuits. It serves as a setting for the family alone or for gatherings of friends, as well as a home electronics center for partying on a grand scale. It demands an attractive, comfortable and compatible ambience.

Beauty, color and pattern become key considerations and must relate to the lifestyle, economic status, and geographical locale of the family. In furniture, case goods which may be available in varied styles, woods and colors cannot satisfy these goals. Only fabric offers the diversity, softness and compatibility to make a house a home that reflects today's needs and accommodates individual preferences. From diaphanous sheers to sturdy upholstery, the array of choices in textures, designs, weights, colorations, coordinations and finishes is endless.

To provide this wealth of home fabric choices, priced at around $4.00-5.00 up to $12.00 a yard retail in general, and at times climbing to over $100, both mill and converter have a much more difficult manufacturing and marketing task than their apparel fabric counterparts.

Home Fabrics Versus Apparel Fabrics. Major differences divide the home furnishings fabrics and markets from those intended for apparel.

Apparel fabrics are slaves to fashion, are quixotic and emotional, they change every season. No designer will use a print he or she used the preceding season. If it's a basic such as crepe or linen, the colors must be different. Ms. Consumer, out to buy a new outfit, doesn't want to buy what she saw her neighbor wear or what she saw in the stores last season.

On the other hand, the average life of a home furnishings fabric is seven to 10 years. The oldest known print design in the industry is Cyrus Clark's "Persian," a traditional, medium-sized allover floral on all-cotton Everglaze chintz, now running for about 50 years with new color variations added periodically in tune with changing interior color trends.

Rivaling "Persian" are Cohama/Riverdale's 38-year-old "Windemere" and Waverly's 26-year-old "Darlington."

Spectrum's "Monarch" butterfly design on glazed cotton chintz is in its tenth year, with 10 colorways always in print. Upholstery velvet has been in top demand for years, with beiges and naturals perennial favorites.

Fashion designers strongly influence apparel fabrics although they generally don't design them except for an occasional request to a converter for an exclusive color or print. Someone like Karl Lagerfeld or Kenzo in Paris may base a collection on a weave and start a trend. In the latter part of the Seventies several Paris designers, including Yves Saint Laurent, revived printed challis and it swept the American market like wildfire, almost to the exclusion of all else.

Another classic example of how a designer may make a fashion fabric is Halston and Ultrasuede. The Skinner division of Springs Mills imported this luxury suede-like fabric from Japan in 1971 and confined it to Halston. The rest is history. It remains a perennial status symbol.

But fashion designer names have meant little in decorative fabrics. One exception is the collection designed for Torrands by noted Irish designer Sybil Connelly in 1980.

Well known interior designers are retained from time to time, but this has been minimal and sporadic. An outstanding exception is Bob Van Allen who designs a number of lines for the home including an annual collection for Cohama/Riverdale. Recent groups were his "Paper Bag" collection inspired by a tan grocery bag, with the paper bag color the leitmotif threading through every one of the coordinated patterns. A later one was "Snapshots" spinning off from his own photographs taken around New York.

Another timely and successful interior designer group was "New Country Gear" by Raymond Waites. This became the basis for an entire shop concept by a group of manufacturers as their marketing strategy, including wall coverings, sheets and towels, bedroom, bathroom and kitchen gear, rugs, pillows, table accents, and even soap and paint. This first "Gear" coordination of eight patterns came out in 1980. A second group of eight was added in 1981, making this the biggest thematic group in the market.

A departure from designer names, but with a big name, was the major collection of eight coordinated designs in 1981 by Barbara Cartland, the queen of romantic paperback novels. This octogenarian English writer turns out two books a month and totes up 50 million readers in the U.S.

Feminine, pretty, and well designed, the eight coordinated patterns in this "Decorating With Love" group were named for Cartland's book titles, such as "Song of Love" and "Passion and the Flower." Her favorite blush pink colored one combination, virgin white another.

What a perfect scenario for a provocative marketing plan that would sweep in these millions of Cartland fans and also pique the interest of millions of others. So a package of related merchandise came next—area rugs, bedroom ensembles, table linens, closet accessories, china dinnerware, wall coverings, pillows, desk accessories, soaps and candles.

Almost coincidentally with the launch of this whole Barbara Cartland shop concept was the fortuitous engagement and marriage of her step-granddaughter, Lady Diana Spencer, to the future King of England, Prince Charles.

These shop concepts and thematic groupings provide a retail store with a package for dramatizing and promoting the fabrics, and serve as a springboard for personal appearances and special events. They also become a service to the consumer.

Home furnishings fabrics, both upholstery and decorative, have very stringent and essential wear requirements as opposed to apparel fabrics which emphasize color and design over performance. While a woman may buy a dress for an occasion and wear it only once or twice a season or so, she wants a fabric for the home that will last. Surveys show that, on the average, a person redecorates only every five to seven years. So the fabrics have to be long wearing and durable.

- Fast colors must be able to resist light, sun and dirt damage, especially at or near windows, or on patios or terraces.

- Fabrics must resist abrasion as people sit on upholstered pieces. Children, dogs and cats romp on them.

- Fabrics must resist crocking and pilling.

- They should be soil and stain repellent as upholstered pieces, curtains, draperies, bedspreads and other large items are very expensive and troublesome to clean.

The two brand name treatments that resist soiling and stains are 3M's Scotchgard and Du Pont's Teflon. Several converters also use a finish with their own names such as Covington's Covgard or John Wolf's Wolf-Cote.

These repellents are applied during the finishing process and may be used on almost all types of home fabrics without changing them in any way. They may be cleaned and are long lasting. Stains and spills, either water or oil based, usually bead up and may be blotted off while wet. If dry, they may be removed generally with water or a household cleaner. Wear, wrinkle and shrink resistance add to the value of such finishes.

Both 3M and Du Pont spend sizable sums in premarketing their finishes so that the mill or converter has a ready-made consumer acceptance and demand. They provide promotion pieces plus labels and tags to identify the finish on fabrics or the items in which the fabrics are used.

Classifications in Home Textiles. Fabrics for the home are divided into two major types:

- **Upholstery** to cover upholstered furniture—sofas, chairs, stools, hassocks and similar pieces. It may be defined as fabrics which are applied permanently.

- **Decorative Fabrics** which are movable and are used for making items such as draperies and curtains, casements, slip covers, bedspreads, pillows and cushions, wall coverings, table coverings, shower curtains, and any other similar usage.

A third category may also be added for certain end uses, linings for draperies, curtains, bedspreads, and anything else which calls for lining.

A newer use for linings as insulation grew out of the energy shortage, filling a consumer need and providing a new marketing opportunity for mills and converters. Fabrics used at windows and layered with linings form insulation, keeping heat in during cold weather and out during hot weather, thus cutting down the amount of energy needed.

Sof-Tex Fabrics, which markets both decorative textiles and linings, seized this opportunity to promote its linings by providing a consumer service. In order to establish a standard of measurement for insulation, the company built a simulated chamber in which to create different weather conditions for both day and night. Starting at zero with only a pane of glass and no fabric, insulation was tested by adding 14 different lining materials or combinations and taking individual measurements to develop a rating scale which consumers could use to determine the most effective insulation.

In the Sof-Tex test, the best insulation proved to be the combination of a decorative drapery fabric, a felt-like interlining, and a regular lining, like a sandwich.

The Business of Home Textiles. There are actually two markets for decorative fabrics and upholstery. In New York where most showrooms are headquartered, the "decorator" market is located around East 59th Street and Third Avenue with the "D and D" (Design and Decoration) Building the hub.

These houses cater especially to interior designers and contract firms. (Contract involves major assignments and institutions on contract.) However, almost all also sell to the furniture market, retailers, upholsterers, independent makers of decorative items for the home and other qualified customers.

Weaves and prints in this "uptown" market are generally more sophisticated and more expensive, and may be specialized short runs. Very fine fabrics such as imported silks are included. Prices can soar to well over $100 a yard.

The other market is located "downtown" in New York around lower Fifth Avenue from 29th to 34th Streets, with several houses in nearby locales including the wholesale furniture buildings at 32nd-33rd Streets and Lexington Avenue. Although quality is topnotch, the fabrics average out at lower prices because of wider distribution and bigger production runs.

Converters maintain these permanent showrooms and sales staffs the year-round, peaking at the semi-annual market periods in May and November. Then they mount special promotional displays and vignettes of their new collections, and often glamorize them further with big parties for customers. They show and sell to retail stores and distributors, furniture manufacturers, catalog houses, manufacturers of home furnishings, interior designers, and various others who legitimately use textiles of this type, even fashion apparel designers.

Two converters have sizable departments which manufacture and market ready-made items in their fabrics. Bloomcraft makes decorative pillows, bedspreads, curtains, sheer window panels, draperies, table cloths and runners, place mats, napkins, kitchen accessories, and shower curtains. Waverly does bedspreads, comforters, pillow shams, ensembles, draperies, pillows, shower curtains, and even lampshades.

Cohama/Riverdale has a companion company in United Merchants and Manufacturers which makes coordinated decorative pillows.

These ancillary operations provide a second opportunity for marketing fabrics, more sales and profits. They also benefit their customers and the ultimate consumer by having made-up items to match the fabrics.

Almost every kind of weave emerges in both the decorator and the downtown markets at some time, rising and falling with the trends over long-lasting periods. Cotton represents a substantial percentage of the offerings, now sometimes blended with polyester for added performance.

Linen is a status fabric, both beautiful and durable, but limited because of price. To stretch it, or increase performance, a blend with cotton or another fiber is often used. Even silk and wool appear in home textiles at the higher priced decorator levels.

Rayon plays a part as a sturdy and attractive fiber in draperies and casements especially where its silkiness and color affinity may be used as decoration. It is also finding a place in upholstery when blended.

Nylon and polyester are especially liked for window treatments because of their durability and performance.

Although some converters are divisions of a mill complex, there is scarcely an example of one confining its line to fabrics from a single mill, even its own. Most converters contract their weaving to several greige goods mills.

John Wolf, a division of Cone Mills, uses Cone for only two corduroy items and buys the rest of its enormous line outside. Cohama/Riverdale, although a division of United Merchants and Manufacturers operates its own mill at Elberton, Georgia, and a printing plant at Arnold, Massachusetts, but also purchases from other mills. Bloomcraft has no mills, but owns its own printing plant and manufacturing facility for its ready-mades.

Waverly, a division of Schumacher which owns some mills, operates strictly on its own as a converter, purchasing outside both greige and some finished goods, such as tapestry or velvet. This company owns workrooms in Adams, Massachusetts for ready-made items.

All of the converters operate in-house studios of artists who design print patterns and work out the repeats which must not form bars horizontally or stripe off vertically unless the pattern is intended as a stripe. These studios also purchase designs from independent studios both in the U.S. and abroad. They also work out the color ranges for each solid fabric.

The fiber producers provide a major assist in marketing home furnishings fabrics where their fibers are used. Celanese is a classic example with its Celanese House. Over many years this company has leased a three or four story brownstone house in Manhattan and retained different interior designers to decorate rooms using fabrics with Celanese fibers, especially its Fortrel polyester. Customers and other pertinent groups are invited here to see the fabrics in use, a great advantage over seeing a fabric in a flat piece.

Fiber companies sometimes start the marketing progression by working with a mill and/or converter in developing a special fiber type for an end use. An example of this is "Shalimar" by Jablan Fabrics which had its origin in six years of research by Du Pont and was launched in 1980 at a champagne breakfast for the press hosted by Du Pont.

The problem attacked by Du Pont's technicians was to develop a Dacron polyester fiber type that would weave into a synthetic home furnishings fabric approximating expensive slubbed raw silk hand woven in India. The result was "Ondulé," produced by a patented process combining stable and filament Dacron to achieve a highly stable yarn with the properties of both and an affinity for taking dye.

Jablan Fabrics then developed "Shalimar" fabric which was reversible, washable, dry cleanable, completely stable yet drapable, resistant to abrasion and sunlight degradation—all at under $10 a yard retail. Its performance qualities made it appropriate for both upholstery and decorative uses.

Where the Trends Originate. Trends in fabrics for the home derive from a number of sources:

- Foreign home shows, especially in Italy which is noted for excellent modern designs.

- From interior designers who create interiors for celebrities, wealthy people and lavish executive offices.

- From major exhibitions such as the Fortuny show at Fashion Institute of Technology and Chicago Art Institute in 1981.

- From the furniture market centered in High Point, North Carolina, where major trends in case goods and upholstered pieces are crystallized.

- Shelter magazines which photograph trendy rooms and homes—*House Beautiful, House & Garden,* and *Architectural Digest. House & Garden* is famous for its annual color evaluations and projections with which many manufacturers of home furnishings tie in. This makes it easy for a customer to put together his or her own coordination, both inside and outside the house. *House & Garden* also sponsors a color service of seminars and reports for an annual fee.

- Fashion apparel colors and print styles sometimes carry over to the home, but in different values and scale.

- Areas of the country set different styles in home furnishings and fabrics. California is "laid back," warm and sunny so colors are brighter, prints more contemporary. The Sun Belt across the Southwest relates to California with a dash of traditional hanging over. New England and the South tend to the traditional with antiques calling for compatible colors and patterns. The Midwest straddles traditional and contemporary.

All of these sources are material for marketing programs or promotions, either directly with the source or indirectly. A mill or converter might officially tie in and promote colors from *House & Garden,* or may do a "California Lifestyle" collection of colors and prints. These themes provide a base for dramatizing and glamorizing fabrics to consumers.

Dominant Styles and Trends. Trends in fabrics for the home in the early Eighties continued to emphasize patterns inspired by traditional periods— English 18th Century, Early American, and French Provincial. This harking back was the result of a loud cry from Young America to want to buy 19th Century or Turn-of-the-Century houses. It represents a direction away from slick Swedish Modern and back to the warmth and security of antiques. Young people were thronging to related galleries in museums (such as the American Wing at the Metropolitan Museum in New York), exhibitions and auctions.

Documentary fabric collections, authorized and licensed by restorations and other historical places of interest are in demand as part of the traditional trend:

- Williamsburg Restoration, Historic Newport, Sleepy Hollow Restoration, and South Street Seaport at Schumacher. This company is also authorized to make adaptations from the Smithsonian Institution.

- Old Sturbridge Village documentaries at Waverly in upholstery, decorative fabrics, and ready-made decorative items.

- Savannah Restoration, Historic Fredericksburg, and Central City (Colorado) collections at Scalamandré.

- Historic Charleston patterns at P. Kaufmann.

- China Trade Collection, from artifacts at Museum of the China Trade, at Lee/Jofa.

The tie-in of longest standing is the Schumacher relationship with the Williamsburg Restoration which has been running over 50 years. The huge collection is a part of the Williamsburg Galleries in many fine stores which include reproductions of furniture and accessories for the home. There are also authorized Williamsburg paints, china, glass, silver and numerous other items.

The Charleston Foundation has also licensed furniture, silver and china in addition to the fabrics so that a consumer can buy a ready-made coordination for the home.

Working out print patterns to satisfy the very high quality standards and specifications of the licensing organization usually takes from one to three years, but the designs will sell for many years to come. The companies holding these licenses bring out new designs periodically. These range from around $10 a yard retail to well over $50.

Without tying in with a specific historical repository, Cyrus Clark prints documentaries from its own archives of thousands of fabrics, defining a documentary as a pattern which is over 100 years old. Bloomcraft also uses historical documents as inspiration for many of its traditional patterns.

The majority of the documentary patterns are actually adaptations, often because of the difference in widths used historically and today, such as 36 inches versus today's 54 inches. Base fabrics may be the same or very close to the original, but the printing method is very different because of the cost factor. Originals were engraved on copper rollers which today would run in the neighborhood of $10,000 each. The method now used is flat-bed hand screens which yield beautiful results and excellent color penetration.

When the source requires that the documentary be identical to the original, as in the Old Sturbridge collection at Waverly, even flaws must be printed and one color combination be exactly the same as the original.

Challenging the traditional is the more informal "country" direction which has become very strong and appealing. This is a freer way of using furniture, fabrics and accessories. The feeling is casual, comfortable, relaxed, informal, and inviting.

Fabrics that complement country may lean to the chintz traditional or go the other way to textured contemporary as the "New Country Gear" group on heavy cotton printed in giant, medium and small diagonal plaids, a flat floral, a blotchy small allover, tiny floral spots—mostly in monotones.

Small informal patterns of the Laura Ashley English country type are a charming part of country decor. And Barbara Cartland's "Decorating With Love" group is perfect, reflecting her own 400-acre English country estate.

Colors may be soft, bright and cheerful, or neutrals which harmonize with pine and oak antiques.

Contemporary style is growing gradually as there is a definite need and a demand for this. Many of the fabrics are used for second homes or boats where the flavor may be more playful, casual, and colorful. Others go into formal contemporary houses. Several uptown houses specialize in fine contemporary fabrics. Major downtown converters who specialize in traditionals have had success with coordinated contemporary groups such as "New Country Gear" at Cohama/Riverdale, "New West" at Covington, and "City Lights" at Waverly, all introduced in the early Eighties. Although these are outstanding, they are still minor in relation to the entire collections.

Solid color textures are a part of the contemporary style and often span traditional when in homespun or other appropriate looks. Velvet is another fabric that goes both ways depending on color.

Contemporary print patterns may follow any theme but are rendered differently, often in a two-dimensional flat look and in brighter, more unusual colors and colorways. Bold stripes, windowpane and graph checks, and dramatic plaids also express the contemporary.

Hi Tech or the "industrial" look, although considered a separate trend, is very contemporary. It is young and inexpensive, featuring such takeoffs as wire grids in furniture and baskets, chemical glass, and factory lights. The Hi Tech partners in fabrics emphasize workmanlike cloths such as natural canvas, or quilted mats used by furniture movers. A big fad has been parachute cloth in bright colors as used by Sherwood in its "Openers," which are foam rubber seating items that open into beds.

The term "eclectic" was much overused in the Sixties and Seventies to describe a mixture, which sometimes became a mish-mash. Traditional and contemporary were mixed, antiques placed side by side with new designs, sometimes spiked with camp and kitsch accessories. The term is still used and the look still acceptable, but it has subsided as a major influence as consumers assumed a more sophisticated and put-together stance.

Patterns and colors in decorative fabrics and also in upholstery run a long time and some just never die. Florals will always be there although they may vary from period to period in type, scale, and colorations. Birds are frequent and natural partners with flowers and foliage.

Oriental designs have been prominent and popular since the opening of the People's Republic of China. Chinese colors have also emerged, such as Chinese red, yellow, and jade. Flowers, birds, trellises, and beautiful fan designs are the popular subject motifs.

Abstracts and geometrics generally tend to the contemporary, often in monotones. Sometimes small allover patterns have the effect of a texture and thus serve as a coordinate for almost any style of fabric and function.

Coordinated patterns in groups from two to eight or ten are essential in today's market. The patterns are designed to be combined in colors that relate. A coordination might include two or three companion florals in different sizes, a stripe, a plaid or a windowpane, and an allover. A promotional theme ties it all together for exciting marketing.

A room may be designed with a coordinated pair and a solid, or as many as three or four patterns, even in a traditional decor.

The color story as the Eighties developed became lighter and softer, making soil and stain resistant finishes such as Scotchgard more essential than ever. Print grounds were turning softer in some cases, "sparkier" in traditionals.

Wedgwood or French blue was coming in strongly as the new color in the leading blue family, with mulberry and plum emerging as the sophisticated new dark grounds for prints.

Navy blue and black vied for first choice numerically in dark grounds, with hunter green and brown completing the dark palette.

Naturals to medium browns to rusts persisted, being easy and safe to use for the consumer who lacks self confidence in the ability to handle color. Prints in these tones were given a fresher and prettier touch with the addition of a contrasting color, such as peach, aqua, blue or green.

Upholstery Trends Parallel Decorative Fabrics. Two big trends stood out in upholstery fabrics as the Eighties got under way—country as a style and velvets as an individual fabric family. Country also split into two directions, both expressing an informal, comfortable ambience in prints and textures.

Casual country reflected simple motifs such as weathervanes or naive flowers, while its sister style took a more sophisticated stance stemming from English and French country houses, including appropriate documentaries. "Country Provincial" by Ametex and "Country Fair" by Design Resources, a West Coast converter, exemplified more sophisticated country groups.

Velvets, far from abating in popularity, fanned out from plain weaves to a variety of designs by the specialists. Examples were Collins & Aikman's printed and cut polyester "Amanda," J. B. Martin's textured cotton "Picardy," La France's cotton/rayon printed "Gamble," and Joan's Olefin cut "Keyboard." All were treated with 3M's Scotchgard to protect their luxurious piles.

Other notable trends in the upholstery market were the continuing Eastern/Oriental, often in floral prints, and contemporary textures and prints.

As in decorative fabrics, upholstery colors were trending to paler hues and mid-tones, demanding a protective finish because upholstery gets more wear and tear than any other textile in the home.

Inside the Home Furnishings Fabric World. Every profession or line of business has its own little inside world. The home textile industry is no exception. Anyone or any company involved with marketing these fabrics must relate to this world.

Specific publications, both consumer and trade, are followed faithfully by the professionals:

> • The "shelter" magazines at the high fashion level
> are trend setters—*House Beautiful, House & Garden,*
> and *Architectural Digest.* The highly successful mass
> magazine is *Better Homes & Gardens* with an
> enormous circulation and readership per issue.
> *Apartment Life* was the magazine for young adults,
> but broadened its appeal and changed its name to
> *Metropolitan Home.*

> • The "service" magazines provide editorial sections
> on subjects of interest to women—fashion and food
> and home furnishings. These are *McCall's, Ladies'
> Home Journal, Good Housekeeping, Woman's Day,*
> and *Family Circle.*

> • "Trade" publications are required reading for those
> in the industry. First and foremost is *HFD—
> Retailing Home Furnishings.* Others are *Furniture
> Today, Inside Furniture, Furniture World, Home
> Textiles Today,* and *Curtain, Drapery and
> Bedspread.*

There are specific professional organizations which are directed to fostering the betterment of the industry, to keeping members posted on trends, and to furthering the advancement of the individual members:

- American Society of Interior Designers (ASID) is the national organization to which most interior designers belong and which indicates that they are reliable and have a level of expertise.

- National Home Fashions League (NHFL) is the only organization which spans all categories of the home, including textiles. While its national membership is confined to executive women, male executives are accepted as industry colleagues.

- The Fashion Group is an international organization of executive women engaged in some aspect of the fashion industry, including women working in home furnishings. Men are not accepted as members, but may attend its luncheon meetings and shows as guests of members.

Representatives of the mills and converters visit the furniture market shows in April and October which are centered in High Point, North Carolina, and stretch from there to Morganton. They go to see how their own fabrics are developed in furniture, to learn the direction of the style trends, and to talk to their customers and the retail buyers.

32. THE FASHION ROUTE TO PROFITS IN HOME FURNISHINGS*

*By Robert B. Jennings, President,
Bigelow-Sanford, Inc.*

When we take a close look at the almost innumerable ways in which the textile industry has changed, and is still changing, I daresay none will disagree that we need all the conceptual, creative and organizational resources we can muster to face up to our challenges.

As you may know, Bigelow-Sanford has expanded its traditional role as a leading carpet and rug producer to become an even more important factor in home furnishings with a total interiors package. We were the first in our industry to take such a step into complete units of packaged rooms.

Why Should We Do This? Why should we have extended our reach beyond an industry in which we have maintained our leadership for so long,

---

*Among the challenging addresses given at the Clemson Textile Marketing Forum, was one briefed here by the chief executive officer of the nation's oldest manufacturer of rugs and carpets, Bigelow-Sanford, Inc. Over the years there has been much talk and some action in the direction of fashion in the home furnishings industry. Here Mr. Jennings tells something of what is being done today.

This article subsequently appeared in the January 1972 issue of the *Textile Marketing Letter* which is still growing and promises to grow further, into the greater complexities of the total home furnishings business where it might appear we cannot operate from a comparable base of experience?

One reason is accelerated growth. *Forbes Magazine,* in an article describing home furnishings as "the growth industry of the Seventies," noted that "not counting TV sets and other home electronics, and notwithstanding the recession, Americans will spend $45 billion in 1972 in sprucing up their homes, up from $40 billion in 1970."

"Add in home electronics and the total comes to $50 billion," the article goes on to say. "This makes home furnishings a bigger industry than home building ($30 billion this year) and probably second only to the sale and repair of new and used autos ($59 billion) as the major U.S. consumer goods industry." Sears, Roebuck is quoted as predicting that home furnishings will surpass the automotive industry by the end of the decade.

Floor coverings, a nearly $2 billion business today, will probably grow to $5 billion by 1975. Du Pont says floor coverings are on the way to reaching 12 percent of the textile business.

The conclusions I have drawn from this growth pattern are: 1. The once-segmented interiors products industries belong together, and form more of a unity than in the past. This unity creates new marketing opportunities as well as problems. 2. We must revise our marketing strategies or devise entirely new ones to make the most of these new opportunities. 3. Working effectively within this unitary framework calls for the establishment of even closer ties than in the past between manufacturers and retailers.

In determining to go after this larger scale home furnishings business, we reckoned with the likelihood of more formidable competition, and we were not disappointed. Burlington Industries, Armstrong Cork, U.S. Plywood, Georgia-Pacific, Tappan and RCA are among the giant companies in it. Each has the resources and capabilities to share effectively in its potential.

We are all aware of the increasing effort to meet the country's pressing housing needs. But while added housing units are coming along, they are increasingly of the look-alike variety, particularly in the lower price ranges.

Bigelow sees this as a boom to the home furnishings industry. We believe that the home is the last stronghold of individuality. The need and motivation to buy our products are certainly there, but no less vital is the consumer's ability to pay for this expression of individuality.

It has been reported that the family with an average disposable income of $7,000 to $10,000 spends up to 12 percent on home furnishings. When the income reaches over $10,000, the percentage goes up to 15 percent or 16 percent. It goes up to 17 percent or so at the $24,000 level.

In other words, as disposable income moves past the $10,000 level, up to 25 percent of the increment goes into home furnishings.

Fashion in Room Interiors. Now that Bigelow-Sanford is involved in manufacturing and selling the total room package, we must cultivate a sense of how fashion applies to room interiors, which combine many products into a single context. Fashion's omnipresence, and the jet-age pace of product innovation, have provided us with unparalleled opportunities. At the same time they demand a much quicker response to what's going on in the marketplace.

The shags are an example. They give warmth and a quality of vitality. We now see patterns in shags, which adds another new dimension. In the deep textures the patterns meld, making them highly palatable. Shags are also easy to care for. They don't show lint, soil and dirt as readily as some other types. So they have tremendous acceptance.

Fashion cycles in the carpet industry alone are accelerating at a rate we would not have believed possible ten years ago. Back in the fifties I recall that biege held sway as a carpet color for an entire decade. For the past five years, greens and golds have been the favorites, but with each new season even these colors are changing, becoming brighter and clearer. The carpet color palette used to lag two years behind that of the apparel trade. Modern communications have closed that gap, and today home furnishings and apparel colors emerge simultaneously.

You may have read about Sears' plans to supply the carpeting, furniture and appliances for the factory-built modular homes to be built by Levitt Building Systems in Battle Creek, Michigan. Bigelow-Sanford entered the field a few years ago with the intention of producing and marketing completely packaged rooms for hotels, motels, institutions and apartments. Our package includes carpets, furniture, draperies, bedspreads, lamps and accessories, completely coordinated in design and correlated in color and finish.

Although the concept of package marketing is not new, it is certainly in an embryonic stage at present. I expect Bigelow will offer a total room package program before long for the residential interiors market.

Optimistic Demographics. Another brief look at demographic material is in order here to underline the opportunities ahead of us. In 1980, according to market researchers, a full 20 percent of the population will change its place of residence, compared with 15 percent in 1970. Any businessman knows what a new residence can mean in creating an appetite for new furnishings.

At the rate people are getting married, it looks as if the number of households formed in this decade will increase by 20 percent, forming a group of prospects who generally spend on home furnishings eight times as much the first year as in any subsequent year. And it was predicted that by the end of the Seventies 38 percent of all married women will be in the labor force, providing additional income that can be spent on the home. Kroehler Manufacturing Company has stated, "Working women part reluctantly with their own dollars for products they consider to be mere necessities, but spend quite happily on those associated with pleasures and a better life for their families."

Conclusion. Now to sum up:

1. We have a consumer group that is younger, better educated, well traveled, increasingly mobile, fairly well primed psychologically and ready to spend money on their homes.

2. We have housing so standardized in external appearance that consumers will go to great lengths to individualize the interiors.

3. We have an array of products that meets a greater variety of needs than ever, and many of these products are less than five years old.

4. We have the pervasive effects of fashion, once thought of as having application only to what one wears, finding increasing significance in the way we "dress up" our homes.

We believe that by treating the home furnishings business as a unified entity, by capitalizing on fashion emphasis, and by working harder at communicating with and satisfying the consumer, the home furnishings industry's much-touted promise of steadily rising profits can be realized.

33. RETAILER CHALLENGES MILLS
TO PRODUCE BETTER FABRICS*
By Richard Marcus, Neiman-Marcus Company

The quality market may soon be added to man's list of vanishing species; yet paradoxically there are probably more people today who want quality in service, make and performance than ever before. Still, symptoms of starvation are present.

Neiman-Marcus has been selling to this market for nearly 65 years, and has learned that it is made up of customers who appreciate the finest service and the finest merchandise.

It's the responsibility of the retailer to deliver the finest service, but quality merchandise poses a different problem. Retailers don't control all the elements that go into making fine merchandise or even mediocre merchandise. I say mediocre because we *buy* merchandise that's mediocre in quality.

---

*This article is excerpted from Mr. Marcus' address at Clemson University's Textile Marketing Forum and appeared in the *Textile Marketing Letter* in September 1971.

Anyone who has recently shopped a junior department in any store knows what I'm talking about. Now I am not quarreling with the need of such merchandise. I simply want to distinguish between the so-called "contemporary, with-it" clothes and clothes which represent quality of fabric, of workmanship and of design.

Although our buyers may exert influence in the market, the economic pressure on most manufacturers today has diminished the assortment and quality of merchandise. Modern technology and increasing wage standards preclude handwork in meaningful quantities. As a result, better clothes have become more expensive, while moderate and lower-price merchandise has shown increased value.

We're one of the few specialty stores—if not the only store—which maintains an inspection department for all apparel merchandise. We examine every garment that enters our stock, and at random, try them on wolf forms for inspection. It is a constant source of frustration to us to see how many things are rejected—hems are uneven, fabric cut across the grain, poorly made button-holes, patterns that don't match at front and back seams—and hundreds of other reasons. And it happens at all pricelines.

Better Fabrics Needed. With respect to fine merchandise, there is another area of lackluster quality: fabrics.

I am well aware that U.S. textile manufacturers make good fabrics, but I question whether they are capable of making really fine fabrics. By that I mean fabrics that represent not only the finest in fibers and craftsmanship, but also the finest in design and fashion influence. For the specialty store customer is a discriminating one and is not interested in the prosaic or the ordinary. Rather, she searches out that which is something special, something distinctive, unique or exceptional.

It is no secret that most specialty stores are sending more buyers to Europe and the Orient. Why? It's not only because certain goods are available at better prices and are better quality, but also it has become one of the ways stores can provide their customers with merchandise they don't see up and down the street, in fabrics that are not distributed throughout the garment industry at all price ranges.

On at least two occasions, we had the identical domestic fabrics in stock in three separate locations at substantial differences in price. In both instances one manufacturer claimed to have bought exclusively. What he didn't say was whether he had it exclusively for Seventh Avenue, or just for his building, or only for dresses with long sleeves.

Recently I have discussed this subject with several of the better manufacturers on Seventh Avenue. Few of them had praise for the American fabric industry. Most were quick to admit that we produce many kinds of fabrics well, but all explained that for the truly distinctive and fine fabrics they have to go to Europe.

One very knowledgeable manufacturer commented on how ironic it is that the United States can grow the world's finest cotton, and yet cannot manufacture the finest pure cotton fabrics.

To listen to Seventh Avenue the fault lies with the mills. Statements such as "The fabrics you're talking about aren't available," or "The mills won't produce good 'transeason fabrics' anymore," are quite common, although I'm sure the fabric industry can tell a different story. But the fact remains that the consumer isn't getting what she wants and inevitably blames the retailer.

Import Quotas?* Recently there has been much publicity on fabric import quotas. Beware lest these quotas be applied indiscriminately. For it's one thing to restrict importation of ordinary goods which are priced lower than ours. It's something else to restrict fabrics which are more expensive and, even more important, provide a source for new ideas.

I am not suggesting that Europe or the Orient is a long-term solution to the problems of the specialty stores. Mass production is no stranger abroad either, and the influx of more American buyers will limit the opportunities for exclusive merchandise.

Nor am I naively suggesting that the trend in the United States can be reversed. Mass production has benefited millions, and one can argue that these benefits out-weigh any detriment to the quality market. But in so progressing and serving the needs of many more people, we have abdicated a responsibility to those who want *more* than the ordinary.

I am by no means sounding the death knell for specialty stores serving the quality market, but I am pointing out that in the future years we will be different. There will still be merchandise available for us to sell, but it will have less intrinsic value.

Someday, soon I hope, someone may invent a machine that sews buttons on coats permanently, but the coat itself won't be the quality it was 20 years ago.

Perhaps the quality market won't necessarily starve; it will simply have to change its diet.

34. IS YOUR MILL MISSING OUT ON HOME SEWING?**

By Irene Kleeberg,
Fashion Editor, Homesewing Trade News

The home sewing market in the United States is a market of at least 60 million people sewing, committed to sewing, buying fabrics, notions, and patterns to the tune of about $2.6 million a year for fabrics alone.

---

*Speaking at Clemson University's Textile Marketing Forum—he gives reasons other than price for flood of imports. (This article is excerpted from Mr. Marcus' address.)

**This article first appeared in the March 1976 issue of the *Textile Marketing Letter.*

Nevertheless, for most American mills it is a neglected market, one viewed either as a "test area" for inexperienced marketing executives or a dumping ground for fabrics from other areas.

There are, of course, exceptions—Milliken is one—companies which have remained committed to the home sewing industry through boom years (when everyone else announced involvement) and not-so-boom years (when everyone else announced closing of home sewing divisions).

Why is this the case? Why should the home sewing market be considered a stepchild of so many mills, often even as they announce, "We're not treating it as a stepchild any longer"?

There are many reasons based on economics, on questions of ego, on distribution, on ignorance. In this article we will explore some of the causes for neglect of the home sewing market in the past and at present.

The home sewing market has been as neglected by statisticians as by anyone else, as we at *Homesewing Trade News* find when we work on our annual statistical view of it. This lack of statistical information is also attested to by Wall Street firms, advertising agencies, management consultants, and fiber companies—all of whom call us begging for additional figures. This lack of statistics is probably one of the biggest causes of a lack of awareness of the importance of the market.

One of the problems in gaining information on the market is a traditional secretiveness on the part of the industry as a whole. In early January of 1976, the Women's Fashion Fabrics Association, an organization of women in executive positions in the home sewing industry, held a meeting during which Harold Cooper, president of Simplicity Patterns, Jane Evans, president of Butterick Fashion Marketing Co. (Butterick and Vogue patterns), and Earle K. Angstadt, Jr., president of McCall's Patterns, spoke. This was the first time these top executives of the top three pattern companies had appeared on the same platform. More to the point, it was the first time they had met.

This secretiveness extends to figures on total fabric sales to the market. Only a few of the major suppliers of fabrics to the home sewing market are publicly owned; those who are, bury their home sewing figures in total yardage shipments. Furthermore, a tremendous amount of fabric going to this consumer is imported, either directly from Europe and Asia or, as one executive puts it, "round the horn"—the fabric is made up in Asia for a European fabric company which subsequently ships it here.

During the 1950's, when the dollar was a great deal stronger than it is today, these imports for the home sewing business were enormous. Figures on them, however, were buried in total fabric import figures and the true size of the home sewing market was not apparent to American mills. Furthermore, because for many converters, shop owners, and consumers, imported fabric became the fabric of choice, American mills were not as affected by the increased interest in sewing during that decade as one would have anticipated.

Just as most of the suppliers to this industry are both small and privately owned, so most of the retailers are small and privately owned.

This makes the industry difficult to get a handle on for either statistics or marketing thrust. It is completely logical for a mill to prefer to sell 100,000 yards of a fabric in a color to a Seventh Avenue manufacturer than 100 yards of the same fabric to 1,000 individual shops. It can be done, and done profitably, but there's no question that it requires long-range planning and (that word again) commitment to the over-the-counter market.

One other reason for the lack of attention by major mills to this significant market area should not be overlooked—snobbery. There's a feeling among many in the market (not the consumer, however) that sewing is still a matter of economic necessity, that women only sew because they can't afford to buy ready-to-wear.

The economic aspects of home sewing should not be ignored, but they are much less important than the desire to use leisure time creatively and the desire to have clothes that are both fashionable and well-made and well-fitting.

Those American mills which have failed to do well when they have entered the home sewing industry have an almost classic pattern in attitude. Here are some of the characteristics:

1. Lack of stability in management of the over-the-counter division. Over-the-counter is considered low man on the totem pole; people who make good there are promoted to women's wear or another division.

2. An insistence that, within the same company, the over-the-counter division bid against the ready-to-wear division for most wanted fabrics. At the same time, the over-the-counter division is not allowed to buy fabrics from "outside." This means the division is out of the hottest fabrics far too early in the season; smaller operations with importing capabilities run rings around these mills in having wanted goods at the right price.

3. A tendency to "confine" certain fabrics to Seventh Avenue and let the over-the-counter division use them only after a season. We hear many times at major mills, "We designed this fabric for over-the-counter but women's ready-to-wear manufacturers liked it so well they took it for last season." This keeps the over-the-counter division at a definite disadvantage, discourages it from introducing prophetic fabrics, and perpetuates the belief that over-the-counter is a dumping ground.

4. A lack of integrity between divisions and between
   mills and distribution outlets. Too often, hot
   fabrics, over-bought by a ready-to-wear division, are
   dumped by that division for discounters to use as
   loss leaders while over-the-counter is still selling
   the fabric at the regular price. This lack of integrity applies all too often to the relationship with
   wholesalers, too. Some mills seem to feel, "We'll
   use the wholesaler for the bad accounts but once
   an account gets good we'll cut out the wholesaler."

Are all American mills guilty of these shortsighted practices? Of course
not, but enough are to make them worth discussing. It's not a veniality on
the part of the mills that do follow them, however, but a lack of knowledge
of the potential of the home sewing marketing area. And there are
psychologically valid reasons for this lack of knowledge. The Northeast,
and especially the New York area, has not taken part in the sewing boom
to the extent the rest of the country has.

From the perspective of a major mill executive in an office high over
Avenue of the Americas, the over-the-counter market appears minuscule
compared to the possibilities of Seventh Avenue. Yet this very perspective,
which in certain other respects can be of value, prevents these executives
from realizing that in the South, Southeast, Southwest, and the West,
home sewing is not only the wave of the future, it is the wave of the
present.

Chapter Ten

The Basic Tools of Textile Marketers

OVERVIEW

By John B. Russell, Jr.

It's presumptuous to say that the textile marketer has a greater need for tools than any other executive in the corporate structure, but one could make a pretty good case for the statement nonetheless. Gone are the days when what was to be sold was decided by operators of machinery who opted for what could be made most efficiently. The marketer's job then was simple—go sell the product whether there was demand for it or not. This modus operandi proved more disastrous than successful as we moved into the modern world of fashion independence and profit orientation and it became generally accepted that the destiny of a textile product had to rest in the hands of the marketer.

The textile manufacturer, the controller, the administrator each has his/her full measure of complicated problems and conditions that are helped by supportive activities but these problems and conditions are not as many-faceted or as illusive as those of the marketer. The difference is as art is to science, as intangible is to tangible. The manufacturer knows what his problem is, usually because the marketer has created it for him. The

139

same is essentially true of the controller and administrator. They know what their problems are because they were created for them. They can be clearly defined. They have identifiable solutions. This is not so with the marketer. He has to create his own problems. In the broadest sense, he has the responsibility for the product conception. He has to be reasonably sure the product has merit and appeal. He has to package the product so that it will sell. He has to see that it has exposure in the right marketplace. None of these requirements can be dealt with in the absolute. A button can't be pushed. Machines can't be operated faster. Numbers can't be added up, and nails can't be driven to get any of this accomplished. And so we get to the tools of the marketer.

The tool of primary importance is market research. It can touch on almost all aspects of a marketer's concern, starting right from the perception of a market opportunity to the attraction of the product at the point of sale. Depending on the time and money available, research can determine whether a product idea has appeal and, if so, what size market and under what conditions. It can help with requirements for the shape, color, durability of the product. It can help determine the packaging and the type of distribution. Once a product is launched, market research can track its performance and help in the forecasting of the product's life. In all these aspects, research cuts down on the risks that must be taken in the decision-making process. If there is no limit to the money available for research, there is almost no limit to the research that can be undertaken. Obviously, there is a practical limit. There is a point beyond which research becomes a luxury and/or a financial burden and cannot be justified but there is no question that it is one of the most important tools in the marketer's tool kit.

In the same family, but of slightly different character, is market intelligence. It enables the marketer to follow what's happening in the market, and it is fed to him from a variety of sources, such as:

1. Industry association bulletins and statistics that are produced periodically and are generally based on information furnished by companies active in the industry.

2. Government statistics that are available from the Commerce Department dealing with the imports, exports, and domestic industry production.

3. Consultant services including newsletters that are apt to be more analytical than points one or two.

4. Trade media which is reporting happenings and conditions of the industry.

5. Salesmen. A perceptive salesman can be an extremely helpful source of information for determining what the competition is and whether there is a market need not being satisfied.

Just as a marketer cannot get along without research these days, so he can't get along without intelligence. These two tools, then, are of primary significance. Running a business by the seat of one's pants and not bothering or not caring about competition or market need is a sure invitation to Chapter XI.

Another tool of increasing importance in recent years in strategic market planning is the process of molding what is basically an art function, marketing, into a more rigid framework. It draws a roadway for the marketer, allowing him to follow his progress against a charted program. One of the articles contained in this chapter highlights this process in its treatment of marketing audits. The audit itself could be considered a marketing tool because it's unlikely that a strategic market plan could be developed without a thorough and objective review of a company's current operations—and this review is the audit.

One of a marketer's tools that is the most visible is advertising. Little needs to be said here about this other than to point out that the effectiveness of advertising depends to a large extent on the product and the environment within which the product is to be sold. Advertising can't sell everything. There are circumstances when advertising is ineffective no matter what the audience or the amount of money spent—a good example being a commodity. It would be hard to keep a copywriter in coffee money on the total amounts spent on print cloth advertising—and justifiably so. Dan River (and competitors) sold print cloth successfully for many years without having spent a dime on advertising—and yet the company would be in the soup if it discontinued advertising its sheets.

Akin to advertising as a tool is promotion. This is much broader in scope and can be useful in calling attention to almost any product or service without directly relating to a sale. There is an almost limitless variety of promotion forums ranging from simple trade mailers to grandiose events or happenings all designed to influence a potential buyer. Perhaps the most spectacular and successful example of promotion in textiles is the Milliken breakfast that has become the equivalent of a full-scale Broadway review. Milliken doesn't sell a yard of fabric at the breakfast but they have a good many buyers thinking "Milliken" when important purchases are contemplated.

It is very helpful to a marketer to have a recognized brand name or trademark with which to work. In some instances, just the name of the company—i.e., Cannon, has sufficient awareness in the marketplace for a cadre of products to be sold under its banner. At other times, it's the product identification, i.e., ultra suede that is helpful. Good name identification can mean a great deal in opening doors of potential customers, in maintaining price stability over "no-names" which are at the mercy of supply-demand ebbs/flows, and in introducing new products. In fact, there are a hundred ways that a good name can be of help. I'm not sure that one could say a brand name is a tool in the sense that one says market research is a tool but it sure is a powerful assist if it has been well-established.

The media is definitely a tool of the marketer. Newspapers, magazines, radio, and TV all can be effective sellers and promoters of a marketer's product, provided he knows how to work with them and is willing to spend the time to communicate properly with them. One might think of the media as another sales force and it should be given as much attention as is given a salesman carrying a bag. Good relations with the media have other benefits, not the least of which is a more considerate treatment of bad news about a company or its product than might otherwise be given without it.

For certain types of textile products, trade shows can be helpful to the marketer. They have not proved to be very effective in the sale of fabric for apparel—the largest textile category produced. There isn't a major apparel fabric show scheduled regularly in the U.S. and there are only a few in the world, Interstoff being the most outstanding. But there are dozens, perhaps hundreds, of important shows for finished textile products ready for consumer use. Most of these fall in the broad category of home furnishings, including bedding, bathwear, draperies and slipcovers, and floor covering.

Many would argue that product development is a marketer's tool. It's true that a marketer would be in trouble without it, but so he would be without quality control and other service functions and so it is not included in this chapter.

There are other tools that are available to the marketer but the above cover the most important. Each has merit and should be considered. It should be mentioned, however, that the most complete tool assortment in the world in the hands of the most skillful marketer can be no more effective than what the competence of manufacturing will permit.

35. HOW TO REDUCE ADVERTISING WASTE*

By James C. Cumming, Consultant

You must have heard the classic remark about advertising that is attributed to the Philadelphia merchant, John Wanamaker. Somebody asked him, "How much of your advertising do you feel is wasted?"

"About half," answered Wanamaker. "The trouble is I can't figure out which half."

Today it's much easier than it was in Wanamaker's time to figure out what proportion of advertising may be wasted and also how to reduce that waste to a minimum. Modern research techniques, computerization, and more accurate circulation analyses by publications make possible the direction of advertising into the most productive channels.

Most important in reducing advertising waste is the preparation of the

---

*This article first appeared in the January 1975 issue of the *Textile Marketing Letter*.

message to be presented. This requires, first, a management decision as to what you want to say about your business, and, second, professional skill in saying it.

The next step is the selection of the medium to carry your message. This may be a simple letter to a selected list, it may be more elaborate direct mail, business publications, or consumer media magazines, newspapers, radio, television. The media you use will obviously depend on your objectives and your marketing plans.

Above all, it's important, especially for the smaller company, to bring in an expert to direct the advertising program. When inexperienced home talent is used, it can add up to a loss of both advertising and sales dollars. An experienced advertising manager or an advertising agency that is knowledgeable in your field can help tremendously in reducing waste and saving money.

Looming large on the list of waste eliminators is what you do when your advertising really begins to work. The best prepared advertising program will fall flat on its face if, when inquiries come in from your initial efforts, you say, "Good Grief! What do we do now?"

The story is told of Dick Sears, founder of Sears, Roebuck, that once when he was snowed under with orders from a newspaper advertisement he picked up a shovel and scooped them into the stove.

That this is not too far-fetched a story is backed up in figures from one Cleveland company that tabulated 670,000 inquiries during a single year from its trade advertising. That's terrific response. But then what happened? Salesmen called on only 18 percent of those replying to the ads and 12 percent of those inquiring never even received a follow-up by mail! And the advertising, remember, was in business publications so every inquiry could have been turned into business!

How could such terrific waste be eliminated? Here's how one company reduced it:

A questionnaire in the form of a reply card was sent immediately in answer to each inquiry. It called for information about the company, the job of the inquiring individual, required products and other company data.

If the card is returned, the inquirer is immediately qualified as to how good a sales prospect he may be. The information he supplies is punched into a data processing card and he is qualified for follow-up by mail or by a sales call.

As a result, the manufacturer has developed an excellent mailing list and has minimized cold calls by his salesmen. He reports that 75 percent of the inquiries qualified as hot leads which have resulted in sample orders. An extra dividend is the knowledge provided on marketing trends and the product needs of prospect companies.

A system like this is excellent as it eliminates what is probably the greatest single waste of advertising dollars: the unacknowledged inquiry.

But the system requires close cooperation between the advertising and sales departments. The advertising department must see to it that the reply cards go out and that they are tabulated when they come back. The sales department must check on the salesmen to be sure they call on the prospects that qualify as "hot." Then the reports from the salesmen must be tabulated and rechecked at regular intervals. This kind of systematic follow-through takes effort but it will sharply reduce the amount of waste in your advertising.

36. HOW TO GET THE MOST FROM A TRADE SHOW*

By James C. Cumming, Consultant

The textile industry is blessed with so many shows that every textile executive must be very familiar with at least one of them. They range all the way from monster events like the Textile Machinery Show and the Knitted Outerwear Exhibit to small regional affairs where goods are sold from hangers on hotel room walls.

But no matter how big or small the show, if your firm is going to exhibit, you stand to invest quite a bit of money in time, talent and display expense. All of which means that if you're going to get the most out of the show you should have a carefully plotted strategy and every individual involved should know in advance exactly what he is to do and when he is to do it. It's safe to say that most companies prepare such a plan, often in writing, before they send their people off to a trade show. Still, some don't, and it's chiefly for them that these thoughts are presented.

Your strategy should, in fact, begin with the show itself. Should you exhibit there at all? Will it be the kind of show where an elaborate display is required, or will your exhibit involve no more than a few posters and representative garments from your line hanging on racks? In either case, your cost must be divided by the number of prospects who are likely to see your exhibit—and buy from it. When you check this out carefully, you may reach the conclusion that your cost per sale may be considerably higher than in personal, eyeball-to-eyeball selling on the road or in your own regular showroom.

Certainly if you are considering a show where you haven't exhibited in the past, go first as an observer. Check the general traffic. See how your competitors are doing. Examine the way they display their products. Talk to your customers about the show. Do they do any buying there?

If, after this preliminary look, you decide that next year this show is for you, before you finally sign up look over the available locations very carefully. You won't want to be in a cul-de-sac where traffic will be

---

*This article first appeared in the June 1974 issue of the *Textile Marketing Letter.*

especially thin. Be sure you are placed where your customers will find you without having to hunt you down.

Then, after you have decided to go into the show, be sure to put your best foot forward. If a display is called for, invest enough in it to make it competitive. This may mean arranging with a professional display house to design, build and install a display for you, but if it's something you can be proud of, it will be well worth it. After all, if you're going to join the club you should dress like a member. But if, at this point, you find that your display is going to cost more than you feel you can afford, stay out of this show. It's better to be missing than to be there looking like a second-rate outfit.

Next in your strategy is the staffing of your exhibit. Will your staff be adequate? Will they be fully informed about your products? There's nothing so irritating to a prospect who may have come several thousand miles to a show than to find an exhibit staffed with people who can answer his technical questions only by referring him back to the home office.

Plan to use your people to check your competition as well as to staff your exhibit. To accomplish this thoroughly will call for careful time allotments, but remember that a trade show presents an unmatched opportunity for seeing exactly what your competition is offering and checking your own competitive advantages and disadvantages. Be sure to make the most of it!

And while we're on the subject, be sure to instruct your people to distribute themselves. Chances are you will have brought many of your staff in from the road to man your exhibit. Some of your people will be from the home office. Their tendency will be to hob-nob with each other, comparing notes and socializing. Some of this won't hurt, but they should be warned ahead of time that they're at the show to work and not for old home week. Each man should be assigned to cover, in depth, certain customers and certain competitors. He should be required to turn in a written report, copies of which can be sent to all the others.

Special attention should be given to staff distribution at luncheons and dinners. You may have seen situations where the representatives of a firm all gather at one table and talk to each other. Check to see that your people are assigned to different tables, so that one of your representatives will be present at just as many tables as possible..Later he should report the names and business affiliations of all the people he met at such affairs; each of your representatives can give your business a lot of word-of-mouth advertising in this way.

Finally, plan not to over-entertain. There will, of course, be special situations where a good customer should be taken out to dinner. But you'll be faced with markedly diminishing returns from the big, general cocktail party and the Broadway show. Keep in mind that your customers are serious businessmen. They come to shows for information they can use to show a profit, not for entertainment they could have just as well back home.

A trade show can be expensive. Choose it carefully, plan it wisely, and you're likely to get a very good return from your investment in it.

37. THINK OF IT AS MARKETING, NOT ADVERTISING*

By John A. Cairns, Consultant

There is probably no form of advertising that has been more widely misunderstood, by more knowledgeable people, for a longer period of time than textile advertising. The reason for that, I believe, is the fact that most advertising and textile professionals think of textile advertising in much the same terms as they would automobile advertising, packaged food advertising, liquor advertising, or almost any other consumer product. They think of it in terms of "Coke: It's the Real Thing," "The Pause That Refreshes," "I'd Walk a Mile For a Camel," "See the U.S.A. in Your Chevrolet," etc. etc. In other words, they think of it in terms of slogans, of pat phrases, and other parameters that gain strength with repetition rather than one of solid and substantial tools of textile marketing which textile advertising is. When I say this, I don't for one minute mean to belittle the great importance of such textile slogans as "Lean on Klopman" or "The Thread of the Story is Lurex." These have their place in the picture and can be made to perform with great effectiveness. But it takes a lot more than a slogan to sell a million yards of gray goods or to drive customers into a men's retail store to buy Palm Beach suits made of Burlington fabrics.

If I were to try to sum up the basic difference between textile advertising and other major forms of consumer advertising, I would say that the purpose of most consumer and trade advertising is to *sell goods or services,* as the case may be. In the case of textile advertising, the Number One objective is *to build a ready and profitable market for your customer's products.* If you do that successfully, the sale of your own products will in most cases follow right along. Since most textile products are ingredient products, the direct customer and the customer's customer are usually the key people in the entire equation. No one knows this better than Fruit of The Loom, the Sanforized Company, and the synthetic fiber people who have done such a great job for so long.

There are many kinds of textile advertising, just as there are many forms of textile marketing, and each has its own set of ground rules. For example:

1. There's a kind of advertising you do when you're a Martex, Wamsutta or Pequot, Cannon or Pepperell and you have a packaged consumer product with outstanding virtues which you propose to distrib-

---

*This article first appeared in the December 1974 issue of the *Textile Marketing Letter.*

ute through good retailers, chain stores, wholesalers and others. That's where most textile advertising started and those are some of the most cherished trade names in the business today.

2. Then there is the kind you do when you are selling yard goods for over-the-counter selling. The mill identification (or perhaps the identification of the converter) is nearly always preserved but you work with a different set of buyers, perhaps a wider variety of retail outlets, employ the pattern books to good advantage, work with the sewing machine companies, and all the rest to get good and lasting results.

3. And of course, there is your distribution through the cutting up trades. Here you fit your product to the right people, at the right price ranges, with the style emphasis, or lack of it, which is most congenial to your own product. And you think in terms of garment labeling, a whole new set of merchandising problems, the use of fashion and service books, fashion shows and conventions, and you gear the tone of your advertising accordingly.

4. And there's distribution through the home furnishings trades. Once again it's a new ball park with characteristics all its own. The jobbers may become more important to you; you may work with different kinds of print works and finishing plants; trade consumer advertising media will change; you may find yourself with a Fieldcrest, Burlington House, or Schumacher Department all of your own in the good department stores.

5. Or you start at the top level the way Qiana has done and the way top imported and domestic fabrics do, and you work only with the best cutters, the most prestigious retailers, the exclusive fashion magazines, and you get on the program of the Fashion Group in New York or in Boston. No advertising you have done with any other product will look or talk like the advertising you'll do now.

6. Now you are producing a great line of fabrics for industrial and military use. You no longer have the help of the cutters, retailers, fashion magazines, the well-known retail stores and all of the others who have influenced your advertising and set the pace for the distribution of the other products you are making and selling so successfully. Now your advertising talks specifications and performance and guarantees serviceability. And you had better not be kidding in your advertising copy! Your customers have laboratories just as good as your own. But they have great respect for solid resources, are more interested in performance than price, and are quite likely to be loyal to established resources for many years in a row.

7. We think we have made the point that textile merchandising and textile advertising must necessarily change with the product and with the avenues of distribution which it follows enroute to the consumer. But we'd like to add this further point: There's a right kind of advertising for gray goods, for finished goods, for expensive, high fashion fabrics and for popular priced staple fabrics; there are clear-cut standards of advertising and distribution for bulk chemical products and for those which are

backed by patent and trademark indentification: there's the kind of advertising you do when you have little but volume to talk about; quite another approach when your story is Quality, consistent Quality, with a Capital Q. Perhaps that's what makes textile marketing and textile advertising so fascinating. Both can be the subject of lifetime studies, with new things to be learned at least four times a year, and perhaps more frequently as freshly styled lines put in their appearance. With most consumer products, it's the same can of beans, the same can of beer, the same life insurance policy, the same bottle of aspirin year after year after year.

You may be able to send a boy to do a man's job in many fields of advertising. But don't ever, ever try it in the textile business. Because, as we said at the beginning, textile advertising isn't advertising; it's merchandising and marketing. There is just no room for error.

38. HOW SHOULD A TEXTILE MARKETER DETERMINE AN ADVERTISING BUDGET?*

By James C. Cumming, Consultant

The question of how much to spend for advertising is fundamental to every marketing plan. The objective has been set:

"We have a new fabric that we want to sell to the men's clothing market." Or, "We have a water repellent finish that is, naturally enough, finding its best market in rainwear fabrics." How much should you spend for advertising to meet such definite sales objectives? Most companies approach the budget problem from one of four directions.

The Percentage of Sales Budget. This is an arbitrary figure arrived at by assigning anywhere from one to five percent of gross sales as the budget for total advertising. It is a method that often works in a business where sales are approximately even from year to year, or where they are rising steadily. It has the disadvantage of failing to be flexible, to take advantage of growing markets, or to make possible rapid follow-up on especially successful advertising. Its appeal lies in the way it relates advertising to the company's ability to pay. Its weakness is that it is based on past sales, rather than on the future volume that will be produced by the advertising. This is particularly obvious when the advertising objective is the introduction of a brand new product.

---

*This article first appeared in the April 1973 issue of the *Textile Marketing Letter*.

In such cases it is often good strategy to invest 100 percent or more of total sales in advertising during the introductory period. If the product is good, increasing sales will rapidly reduce the percentage.

The "All-You-Can-Afford" Budget. This generally makes sense to management because it takes net profit into consideration. After costs and a small profit have been budgeted, anything left is set aside for advertising. It is a method sometimes used by a manufacturer of a consumer product who wants to blast his way into a new market. He may even budget no profit at all the first year or so, with the hope of building a market franchise and increasing his net profit later. But it is a method that makes no sense at all for a textile producer.

The "What's the Competition Doing?" Budget. The thinking behind a budget like this marks the company as a follower rather than a leader. It is defensive and indicates that you have been forced into advertising because of the successful advertising of a competitor, but that your heart is not in it. How do you know your competitor is investing his advertising money wisely? Are you sure of his objectives and that his advertising is really reaching those objectives? If your product is competitive, it may be that your budget should be considerably larger than that of your competition. Or, if your objectives are sharp and theirs fuzzy, you may accomplish just as much with a smaller budget.

The Task Method. By approaching your budget from the viewpoint of exactly what you want to do and how you want to do it, you overcome the negative factors in these other three approaches to budgeting.

Start with your specific objectives, then list the tools you will need to reach these objectives. Perhaps you will want to introduce your new product with a press showing. You may require a full program of follow-up publicity. Possibly you should send a series of mailings to potential customers. Advertising in business publications will probably have a place in your plans. Advertising to consumers may be desirable. Should you offer cooperative advertising to your retailers? On what basis? How much?

One great advantage in this approach is that it stimulates the thinking of all concerned in the management, the planning, and the execution of the advertising program.

When all the needed tools have been listed and their costs figured, the total cost will usually be larger than management will regard as sensible to spend. At that point, pencils must be sharpened and projects eliminated or postponed.

In the experience of many textile companies, however, the task method of determining an advertising budget has proved to be far and away the best approach to the problem. It must be tied in closely with personal selling, but as the advertising becomes more effective, the cost of personal selling will trend downward.

39. YOUR NATIONAL BRAND:
WHAT IS IT WORTH IN DOLLARS
AND CENTS?*

By John A. Cairns, Consultant

If there is any single, infallible way of measuring the exact value of a good trade name in the textile business, we haven't heard of it. It goes without saying that the value of a brand will vary with the quality and volume of the products behind it; with the marketing skill of its owners; its share of the market; the amount of money spent to keep it alive; the distribution plan for the products which it identifies; the strength of competition; degree of patent protection and exclusive selling points; and other factors.

Over the years many gray goods mills have elected to become better known in the trade without making any effort to establish their identity to the consumer. When a good job has been done, such a mill can expect that it will get the first call on the business in poor times and at least a slight premium in good times. This can make all of the difference between a highly successful operation and one that is just so-so. Furthermore, it gives the mill more control over its own destiny since an expanded reputation for quality can always put it in a position to market a portion of its production as finished goods, if it elects to do so. The converts know this, of course, and would in most cases prefer that their mill resources remain anonymous.

Over the years, also, a number of print works and finishing plants have sought wider recognition, some with great success and others with only indifferent results. In this instance, the firm's patent position appears to be the controlling factor. Patented processes like Ban-Lon, Everglaze, Sanforizing, Koratron, Milium and Pak-Knit have made a lot of money for a lot of people. The mere ability to do a superior printing and finishing job will attract more customers, but it is hardly sufficient to warrant a promotional attack on the consumer.

Many years ago we had an unforgettable opportunity to measure the value of a national brand in the field of printed and solid color cotton flannelettes. It was shortly after the famous Amoskeag Mills had closed up shop, leaving the field wide open for a new national brand. At the request of the late Herman Cone, Sr. and the late Saul Dribben, we checked trade opinion from New York to Kansas City and from Buffalo to New Orleans. The answer was the same wherever we went. Garment manufacturers and retailers alike felt the need for one or more strong national brands in this field. When asked how much such a brand would be worth to them, their answers varied from 1/2¢ to 2¢ over the market. With flannelettes selling

---

*This article first appeared in the January 1973 issue of the *Textile Marketing Letter*.

around 10¢ a yard, this was a substantial premium. Out of all this Cone's famous "Velvelette" was born.

Several years later we had another memorable opportunity to observe the exact money value of a good name. It had to do with the introduction of that famous cloth, "Tackle Twill," by William Skinner and Sons. Having finally decided to sell this fine fabric for garments other than football pants, Stewart Kilborne, then President of William Skinner and Sons, put 25¢ a yard on the cloth for national advertising. The cloth was being offered for about $1.00 a yard and the other most expensive fabric in the raincoat and jacket field was Cramerton Army Cloth which had recently been successfully introduced at a price of about 60¢ a yard. We wondered whether Mr. Kilborne would ever be able to make it stick, but the results were simply fabulous.

Not too much later than that we were exposed to another dramatic study of the value of a good name; this time with Dan River's well-known summer suiting fabric, Rivercool. The cloth had been sold and nationally advertised for several years with great success. All good slack manufacturers had it in their line, but distribution in the summer suit field was limited to four manufacturers, all in the same price range, and all very happy with being members of the team.

Along came World War II. Every inch of goods that could be produced had been sold the previous season and production could not be increased. There was no question that the mill could sell all that it could make. The decision was made, therefore, to cancel all national advertising and to ride along on an established reputation. But the manufacturers and retailers would have no part of this decision. Having spent some of their own money in promoting the name "Rivercool," it was important to them that the mill keep the name alive—so important, in fact, that they agreed to pay for the advertising themselves, the only time we have ever known a group of garment manufacturers to make such an offer. The result was that, with every yard of "Rivercool" at 65¢ a yard, there was as a separate companion bill for advertising at 10¢ a yard! Dan River continued to supervise its own national advertising and its advertising agency continued the planning, preparation and placing of that advertising, as always. And everyone was happy. The manufacturers took in every inch of Rivercool that the mills could produce; the retailers bought every summer suit the garment manufacturer could make; and, as far as we were ever able to determine, not a single Rivercool suit remained unsold that year at the retail level.

We could wish that the name "Rivercool" was still making money for Dan River just as the name Indian Head is making money for its owners and names like Fruit of the Loom and Sanforizing are still making money for theirs. We feel very strongly that the textile industry will never have enough good names like Cannon, Martex, Chatham, Pepperell, Fieldcrest, Galey and Lord, Stevens, etc. We think it unfortunate that so many fine names have been permitted to fade into obscurity or to become completely abandoned; we refer to names like Forstmann, Mallinson, Stehli, Stroock,

Wellington Sears and Skinner. Likewise, we feel it is somewhat unfortunate that in certain major fields fiber names such as Orlon and Acrilan and Dacron and Kodel have almost replaced the name of the mill in consumer marketing. It isn't that these fiber names are not great names, entirely worthy of consumer recognition, because they most certainly are. The same can be said for other great fiber names like Avril, Zantrel, Qiana, Fortrel, Arnel, Nylon, and many others. But just as long as the ultimate marketing success of a fiber depends to a large degree on the handling it gets at the mill level, the mill's contribution should be given equal time and equal credit in the marketing process. No mill should abandon its franchise of consumer recognition. No fiber manufacturer can afford to overlook the fact that in textile marketing "success is a family affair."

40. THERE'S GOLD IN MARKET RESEARCH*

By John A. Cairns, Consultant

We are all for a big increase in market research on the part of almost everybody in the textile and related industries, especially mills, converters, cutters, retailers. We will exclude the fiber producers, chemical companies, and machinery manufacturers, because most of them are already doing a first rate job.

Market research can tell you what other people think of you and your firm—what you need to become more effective. It can tell you what kind of reception you can expect for a new product or process; how you should price and distribute it; how big your potential market is likely to be; how long it will take you to get your new project in the black; and many other worthwhile things.

It can help you to reduce the substantial risks of being in a fashion business, and it can even tell you how to package and label your product. But you have to ask the right questions to get the right answers, and you have to have a substantial degree of sophistication about your own field to interpret the results properly.

Up until recent years some of the answers you got from market research in the textile business tended to be pretty discouraging. If you checked with finishing plants for their attitudes on a new dyestuff or the finishing process, you generally got the answer, "It just won't sell at a premium of X cents a yard over regular goods."

If you checked the converters (as we did on many occasions) you were likely to get the surprising answer, "We don't get a call for anything like

*This article first appeared in the April 1968 issue of the *Textile Marketing Letter.*

that, so we are not interested." (We have always wondered how they could expect to get a call for something that didn't exist!)

If you went to the cutter, interest began to pick up because he couldn't have cared less how much it cost the mill, converter, or finishing plant to produce the new project. His principal concern was, "Will it throw these goods out of my established price lines?"

When you finally got around to the retailers, the climate suddenly got warmer and in most cases it got red hot, because the retailer was not concerned about price or production problems. He thought primarily in promotional terms, in terms of news values, consumer reactions, the opportunity to get one up on local competition, etc. If the retail reaction was favorable, you could be optimistic about the final outcome of the project because the retailer was—and is—the Boss in the textile and apparel industries.

A word about interpreting results. Some years ago we had reason to check the market potential for metallic yarns. Industry opinion generally was that they were dead. Our findings in world fashion centers, however, indicated that top designers were once again becoming interested in metallics and that business would improve rapidly if imaginative styling, distribution and selling were put in back of these products. This proved to be the case.

On another occasion, we checked the market for washable woolens. We found that everyone was interested, including the police department in Springfield, Massachusetts, who were trying out uniforms made of washable woolens. Despite all the favorable responses, we recommended that the project be killed or at least postponed. Reason? The finishing process required very precise chemical controls, and very few woolen mills had technical staffs capable of handling the process.

On still another occasion we recommended that a desirable new finish be killed because it was far too costly for the purpose, and promotional support to keep it alive was amounting to $1 a yard.

We referred earlier to the fine market research work being done by the fiber companies, chemical and dyestuffs companies and machinery manufacturers. From where we sit, all the fiber companies do a good job in this respect and their findings can be relied upon by everyone in the chain of production and distribution. Similarly, the machinery firms like Leesona, Crompton & Knowles, Rodney Hunt, Scott & Williams and others, have become highly sophisticated in researching the markets for products to be produced on their equipment. Also the dyestuffs companies have done a good job in researching the potential market for prints and for the newer dyestuffs.

Finally, we take our hats off to firms like Deering Milliken, Dan River, Burlington, Indian Head, Cone, and Stevens, who have been in the forefront of most new market developments. These firms didn't grow big and prosperous by accident, but by design. Market research has been a well used management tool with all of them.

41. LOVE THAT FIBER—HOW TO MOTIVATE THE TEXTILE CONSUMER*

*By Dr. Ernest Dichter, President, Institute for
Motivational Research, Inc.*

Most developments in human life take place in at least three phases. First we use our brawn, then our brains and eventually our hearts. As far as textiles are concerned, we first had the utilitarian age. We were freezing and we had to clothe ourselves. Pretty soon we discovered that by using our brains, becoming more sophisticated, we could make many fibers ourselves and bury them in all kinds of colors and forms. We are now reaching the necessity of the gourmet age in fibers where emotions and love affection will play a more important role. We have to learn to establish a love relationship with fibers and textiles.

We recently conducted some surveys on the psychology of slacks, blouses, skirts, socks and various other types of apparel. In these studies we were not just interested in the utilitarian use of these products, but much more in what they psychologically meant to people.

People have a tremendous number of what we call "unsatisfied desires" as far as these various products are concerned. Men do not pay enough attention to slacks because they don't find them interesting enough. They would like to, however. They would like all kinds of innovations for the pockets, for the belt regions, and what is particularly important as far as the fiber and textile manufacturer is concerned—the feel of the fabric.

We talk, for example, about the way slacks feel on the inside. Very few pants are lined today. What we are dreaming about is a fiber that feels soft on the inside and is pleasant to the touch on the outside.

Similar wishes and complaints exist as far as skirts and blouses are concerned. Women dream about materials that adapt themselves to climatic conditions. "I put a blouse on in the morning when it's cool and it gets too warm during the day. I haven't got time to change. If only they could invent some kind of fiber or fabric that would adjust itself to varying temperatures."

Men want greater elasticity in the belt region. They feel that the belt (whether built-in or not) has never been given a proper study. As far as women are concerned, the bra region of the blouse plays a similar role.

Why should I need deodorants? Why can't they make fibers that are absorbent or material that make bras unnecessary in a dress or a blouse?

Concentrating to a large extent on fashion, the textile industry has overlooked the romance of the basic materials that it is making and selling. Our studies show that a vast majority of people are barely aware of what

---

*This article first appeared in the August 1969 issue of the *Textile Marketing Letter*.

materials their garments are made of and pay much more attention to the outward appearance. They seldom realize that unless the basic fabric is satisfactory, it is difficult to manufacture the correct kind of fashionable translation.

The labor saving aspects have long run their course and do not excite anybody any longer. In the meantime, there has been more and more discussion of throw-away products that may need neither ironing or even washing.

The Textile Industry Has to Get Soul Again. We find ourselves, therefore, in an entirely new situation where many of the old-fashioned appeals of fibers—the love that people had for cotton or wool—have become faded and tired. The excitement and curiosity that new fibers aroused has led to frustrated love and disappointment, since they very often have been over sold and did not live up to the promises. What is needed? What can be done?

Fashion has the Yves St. Laurents and the Diors. Architecture has Frank Lloyd Wright and many other names. But where is the exciting name as far as new discoveries and innovations in the textile field is concerned? What names come to the consumers' minds comparable to Salk or Fleming in the medical field? When we ask in our surveys what the textile industry is associated with, what we get back are mechanized factories, chemists, physicists. No story of drama like the double helix and the discovery of DNA.

What we suggest, therefore, is that one of the first major efforts be made through public relations and through individual brand advertising and merchandising to have excitement and drama reintroduced into an industry which is basically as vital as most others. Fabrics and fibers used to have a rich folklore, and exciting connotations.

- Cotton was friendly without effusiveness or ostentatiousness.

- Wool was always seen as strongly male by men and women alike.

- Silk is at the opposite pole from wool. It is as feminine as wool is masculine. Silk evokes images of palaces, kings, queens and princesses and images of graceful oriental luxury.

- There is a standard of excellence associated with linen as with no other textile. Linen is strong yet at the same time it is soft and flexible.

On the other hand, for many people synthetic fibers still represent a certain coldness removed from the real thing—from nature. People, as our studies show, have more and more rationally accepted man-made fibers as having liberated them from drudgery, but centuries of textile experience are not so quickly wiped out. There is no doubt that a very real support for natural fibers remains. In some areas, we have achieved a point where a man-made fiber is accepted almost as well as the natural one. For example, nylon is completely acceptable for stockings and underwear—although the same material is far less acceptable for outerwear such as blouses or dresses. Here a considerable amount of work is still needed, surrounding man-made fibers with the same folklore, warmth and delicacy that natural fibers have had for ages.

Typology and Individuality. There are wool lovers, silk lovers, and cotton lovers. The textile industry has talked too much about the consumer as if he were a member of an indiscriminate mass society. Instead, the same textiles mean different things to different people.

A good part of the terminology used in the fiber field is of a technological nature. It does not take into consideration psychological factors. While we do not suggest going as far as having fibers and fabrics for introverts and extroverts, there might be a sort of emotionally designed rank order of fabrics permitting people to use fibers to express their personality—speak in the newfound language to themselves and to others.

Maybe in the near future descriptions of fibers and fabrics could include more personality factors than just type and degree of weave utilized.

Starting Fiber Education. From an early age we develop a relationship to different types of materials. We work with wood, with steel, with aluminum—but we seldom have a systematic training and appreciation of fibers. Most people don't know exactly what their garments are made of. I know of no permanent textile museums. If there is one, how many times are children taken to such a museum? Very few stores exhibit the original materials used in their work, creating a feeling of direct understanding and relationship to natural and man-made fibers.

We saw in our studies that consumers have a long list of grievances and wishes. They would like to have more materials that grow with the individual, are stainproof, and are specifically designed for functions and occasions—such are garden suits, leisure time dresses, better engineered pregnancy clothes, clothes for the young mother to help her with nursing, and yes, probably even garments that are more specifically designed for courtship and romance.

Titillating the Senses. As we reach the gourmet age, we are also becoming more sensuous. There are more and more seminars on sensitivity training. We are running our own seminar in creativity, sensitivity and thinking, where we teach people to discover the unused potentialities of their sense organs. We talk a lot about appetite in advertising but we usually think more of the palate than we think of the tactile appetite.

Child psychologists are gradually discovering the necessity of developing in very young children this expertise in the tactile field. Even our language is very poor in describing exquisite smoothness, roughness, the thrills of discovery through our tactile eyes—the tips of our fingers and the rest of our bodies. Textile advertising and merchandising should make people just as hungry to satisfy their tactile desires as the food industry does when it appeals to the oral senses.

Even our visual appetite is not sufficiently stimulated. Yes, we look at the total image of a garment but how many men can tell what kinds of buttons they have on their jackets. Women may be more observant, but not much.

In some studies, we have found that children will have a strong sense for the olfactory experience of a new suit. We have suggested at various times that the textile industry discover this sense too. Give fabrics a distinctly pleasant odor. What we are really recommending is a discovery of the sensuous aspects of an important part of our modern world—the materials and fibers that we use to decorate ourselves.

Fibers in Style. In industry and certainly in the belief of the consumer, there is a feeling that the really creative person is the fashion designer. He makes use of the dead material that is available to him. The reality should be quite different.

We recently developed for an international fashion house a new kind of vacation wardrobe. It is based on the recognition that today most people really don't need physical rest during their vacations, but instead, should concern themselves much more with getting away from themselves.

Facilitate Readiness to Accept Change. This idea was translated into fashion by designing a new type of individualized vacation wardrobe, where the textile industry will have to play an important role to provide the materials that are smooth, light, adaptable, confortable in an unhurt kind of fashion—by really providing materials to wear with freedom from worries about dust and dirt and sweat. In doing so, only one of the many possibilities of the aspects of making creative fabrics rather than just technologically desirable ones would be accomplished.

We recently were involved in a study on how to get men to wear suits made out of knitted material—jersey. Some of the resistance we found started with the name itself, that jersey has a connotation that primarily applies to women's fashions.

Tailors to whom this material was given found it something new and different to work with. We often make the mistake in introducing new ideas by putting to much stress on the fact of their difference. Instead, and this is probably what we are doing as far as this problem is concerned, we accentuate the idea that this is really an answer to man's dreams. He finally has found a fabric that permits flexibility, adaption to his own body and resistance to creases and wrinkles.

We have a somewhat easier job now inasmuch as men have become more assured of themselves and are less worried about being considered effeminate when they smell nice or wear much more colorful garments. In a study for DuPont we created a term "The Peacock Revolution" which has now made major inroads—particularly among young people. What we still need is a similar kind of Peacock Revolution as far as the fabrics themselves are concerned.

The textile consumer is probably more ready to accept new ideas and changes if only he were properly stimulated and motivated by the industry itself. A fundamental mistake is for an industry to take itself for granted and to assume that all it has to do is to produce good products and the rest will take care of itself. The modern consumer is being wooed from all sides. Everybody wants his dollar, his interest. He does not respond any longer just to the promise of a greater convenience or price reduction. He has become the gourmet. He wants to be titillated. He wants to be aroused. In short, he wants to be loved.

42. THE PLACE OF COOPERATIVE ADVERTISING IN THE MARKETING OF TEXTILE FIBERS*

By Edward S. Morse, Consultant

In its essence, Cooperative Advertising is the means of converting National Advertising into Local Advertising. Its objective is to bring the textile producer one full step closer to the consumer.

Cooperative Advertising adds these elements to a national advertising campaign:

- It pinpoints where the merchandise may be purchased.
- It describes the merchandise in consumer terms such as fabric, colors, sizes, and price.
- It carries the implied endorsement of a store with a local reputation for quality merchandise.
- Its message is timed to coincide with the customers' shopping plans.
- Its appeal is instant.

Cooperative Advertising could be termed Point-of-Sale Advertising. It is the last bit of printed information a customer receives before he or she makes up his or her mind as to whether or not to purchase the merchandise.

The Last Word, of course, is a function of the salesperson. But here, too, Cooperative Advertising may well be a factor in providing the salesperson with the essential information about the product needed to

*This article first appeared in the December 1980 issue of the *Textile Marketing Letter*.

complete the sale. Most progressive stores display on the bulletin board, where it can be read by the sales force, the day's advertising of that store.

Cooperative Advertising can also activate the store's merchandising, resulting in window displays and displays within the department, of the advertiser's products. A store with its own investment in the advertising of the merchandise has a natural interest in making the promotion a success.

By the use of Cooperative Advertising, the savings in cost to a National Advertiser can be substantial. Cooperative Advertising involves the buying of space at the store's own contract rate. The store enjoys a most favorable rate, contrasted with the national rate, because of the large quantity of space it contracts for annually, often in the hundreds of thousands.

In Cooperative Advertising, this saving in space cost is generally shared with the National Advertiser, the ratio depending on the arrangement between the store and the textile manufacturer. Stores in increasing frequency are adding a percentage of overhead for their advertising department's production costs, thus more closely equalizing the store's share of the promotion.

One consideration in the use of Cooperative Advertising is that the message on your merchandise reaches the consumer in the store's own language and conforms to which he or she is used to. To some advertisers, with strict principles on the use of their trademarks, this element may present hazards. However, if the required usage of trademarks is spelled out in the letter of agreement between the textile manufacturer and the store, the danger of misuse of a national trademark is lessened. Cooperative Advertising has reached the stage where most stores recognize and respect the proper usage of a manufacturer's trademarks.

This discussion of Cooperative Advertising has concentrated on the factors that prevail in the customary, one-to-one arrangement between the textile producer and the store, but there are many variations in the use of Cooperative Advertising.

One commonly used today is for the manufacturer of fiber, fabric, or clothing to supply the store with a mat service featuring its merchandise. The store's function is to add its name and address at the bottom of the mat and arrange for placement in the newspaper at the store's own local rate. While there is a savings to the national advertiser in paying the local instead of the national rate, the general practice is for the national advertiser to pay 100 percent of the space cost.

Cooperative Advertising, in principle, is widely employed in other media, besides newspaper advertising, such as radio and television. Here the same principle is employed to relate the advertiser's message to a local store, with a rider added to the advertiser's message giving the name and address of a local outlet.

Like other tools with a sharp cutting edge, Cooperative Advertising needs careful handling. It is not a cure-all, do-all substitute for other forms of advertising. It is at its best when used as one component in the advertising campaign, providing a local emphasis to a national overview.

43. THE IMPACT OF FASHION ON MARKETING*

By Julia Morse, Consultant

Fashion is the great energizer. It has given the textile industry a vitality and dynamism that differentiate it from commodities such as soybeans. The buying and selling of apparel and home furnishings is increasingly big business. In a simpler era, men and women bought denim and khaki to wear for work or for war; woolens for protection against cold; cotton for underwear; and silk for church-going and balls.

This logical order on which the textile industry has flourished has turned to chaos. Wrenching changes have occurred. Textile mills now must plan for a world where denim is worn to the opera; woolens chosen for coolness; silks cut into T-shirts—whims replacing economic rules, production schedules of mills disrupted.

"Fashion has loused us up again" is the outcry of the mill production manager faced with the need to reassign looms from outmoded taffeta to incoming crepe. This unpredictability is now accepted. It is status quo. Late and grudgingly came recognition by management that this unmanageable force is the route to riches, if it can be harnessed. The marketing person, not the production executive, was first to comprehend that fashion writes the bottom line—that whim is where the money is.

Out of Sears into Worldwide Favor. We saw cotton denim move out of the Sears, Roebuck pages of overalls and work pants to become a worldwide fashion—a force—the symbol in all parts of the globe of the freedom of American youth. In Japan, the discarding by the young generation, after World War II, of the traditional kimona for a total commitment to blue jeans was a flaunting of independence by way of fashion.

The worldwide demand for jeans had an impact on the New York Stock Exchange. Scarcity of the indigo dye which produced the essential faded shade shot up the price of jeans, this having an impact (as reported by the *Wall Street Journal*) on the growth potential of the stocks of the giant U.S. jeans manufacturers such as Blue Bell.

The era of the farmer as America's major consumer of jeans came to an end. Levi Strauss, maker of jeans for cowboys, put the name Levi's into our vocabulary and structured a broad sportwear business around it. For J. C. Penney, a work clothes manufacturer selling to farm families, their specialty of dungarees made this firm a fashion store for both men and women, as dungarees took to cities, campuses, and country clubs.

The marketing of not only apparel but also of domestics was transformed by a fashion trend. Cotton gray goods for white sheets had rolled off the looms of New England and Southern mills in predictable

---

*This article first appeared in the September 1980 issue of the *Textile Marketing Letter*.

quantities for decades. Suddenly came the colored sheet, to be followed rapidly by flower-printed patterns for towels as well as sheets. The retail store's tradition of "White Sales" succumbed to waves of florals, geometrics, stripes; White Sales surviving in name only. Next, printed sheets signed by name designers launched a new vogue. The Halstons, Oscar de la Rentas, and Bill Blasses not only generated a new bedroom era but recharged the retail store merchandising of domestics, enormously increasing its profitability. Designer names proved a powerful lure to the consumer and their economic force quickly spread to unrelated fields such as luggage, accessories, and shoes. Even Detroit got caught in the trend, marketing motor cars designed by Bill Blass, Oscar de la Renta, and others, featuring the designers and their designs in full-page color advertisements.

What problems does this upheaval pose for textile management? Responsible executives do not enjoy floundering among trends. Companies investing major sums on the production of fiber and fabrics require specific data.

Are there guidelines? Or dependable sources of information on which to base production schedules?

There have always been clear signals. These have changed little during this century but they call increasingly for trained interpretation. Today's marketing executive needs a sharp instinct and a good eye, as well as facts.

Paris No Longer Provided the Answers. Traditionally, Paris provided the answers. The season of collections of the Haute Couture, the great January and August events, was the preview of the social and fashion scene—the key to the future of the mode or, at the very least, to the next season. Formal showings were attended by the top echelon of America's great merchants, by invitation only. The new designs were applauded, purchased on an exclusive basis, and the phrase "line for line copy" launched new and revolutionary silhouettes, many of which transformed weaving and color conceptions such as Vionnet's bias cut, Dior's sloping shoulder, and Yves St. Laurent's peasant look.

But Haute Couture ceased to be the arbiter of fashion success as elegance ceased to be the sole prerogative of the socially elect and wealthy. "Pret a Porter," the ready-to-wear collections of Paris, Italy and London, made fashion headlines and put money in retail tills. After World War II, American design came to maturity and received international acclaim, with Paris leadership challenged by Seventh Avenue, with formal presentations by name designers initiating new trends such as the "Classic Look" which became universally accepted. The rise of American designs has made fashion interpretation more accessible to the textile industry and has often formed a partnership with it by creating fabrics to fit the designer's scheme.

Enter the Fashion Press. Clear signals are given by the fashion press. It provides the forecasts. Paris fashion has always provoked media excitement —the major collections reported fully, the minors played down. Periodic waves of excitement bobbed up and down as the more innovative Italians launched dramatic ideas such as boots worn with chiffon dresses. In London, King's Road and Carnaby Street brushed aside elegance in favor of the eccentric.

Equated in influence with the Metropolitan newspapers is *Women's Wear Daily*, the required reading of the fashion world and the textile industry. The most powerful of Fairchild's publications—the world's largest fashion news-gathering organization—*Women's Wear Daily* intermeshes social, fashion, and economic news and spices it with rumors. Reporting on the collections, both abroad and in America, is accurate, thorough, and imaginative. It is perhaps the most quoted of newspapers and the most powerful in influencing buying of apparel. Often feared because of the depth and sureness of its convictions, it can make or destroy a collection—and its designer—in one review.

A Strong New Signal—People on the Streets. "Fashion is made by fashionable women" is the dictum of one of the designer greats, Oscar de la Renta, expressing the interrelationship of personal style and fashion trends. An example: the years of the ascendency of Jacqueline Onassis whose special look gave American women a fashion idol for a decade. Today, she shares the spotlight with her sister, Lee Radziwill, and a score of socialites whose personal way of dressing is regularly reported as eventful in *Women's Wear Daily* and *Vogue*: such luminaries of fashion as C. Z. Guest, Charlotte Ford, Mildred Hilson, Chessie Raynor and Mica Ertegun. The fashion preeminence of these women exploits the theory that fashion trickles down from the top. Today, fashion also rises up from the bottom, from the streets of the cities, not only Paris, London, Rome, but also from New York, San Francisco, Detroit. Leather pants, leotards, duffle coats, and military surplus clothes are people-made fashion trends. Distribution is through boutique shopping, replacing the established American habit of one-stop shopping in big stores.

Fashion signals will continue to come from the streets and the people and pose a challenge to the textile business, as the demands of consumers fluctuate between casual chic and dressing with elegance.

The Force of the Fashion Group. And what is more pertinent than the Fashion Group, the powerhouse club of the fashion and textile industry? It is an international professional association of women with approximately 5,000 members—executives who represent every phase of fashion, manufacturing, retailing, communication and education. With members in cities of the United States, Australia, Canada, England, France, Mexico, Korea, and Japan, it serves as an international clearing house for the exchange of information on trends and developments. Periodic fashion show luncheons are the one authentic and dramatic visual presentation of the major fashion collections, edited authoritatively. The clamor for tickets, available only by invitation from members, is a clue to the status of the Fashion Group in the industry. Few textile companies can afford to be without a woman executive belonging to the Fashion Group, thereby giving the firm access to authentic, advanced information and interpretations.

Fashion is not trivia, whimsy, or eccentricity, although at times it may express these, because it is all-inclusive. Fashion is how people live. It is woven into the structure of our economic, social, and political life. It involves sex and manners. Today's sophisticated marketing executive uses all sources of information to keep himself abreast of the times.

Chapter Eleven

Technical Groups and Associations as Marketing Tools

OVERVIEW

By Thomas H. Gunter

1. How many American textile-related associations exist today?

> A. Less than 10.
>
> B. 11-50
>
> C. 51-100
>
> D. 101-200
>
> E. Who cares?

2. What trend has occurred in the export of American-made textile machinery between 1977 and 1979?

> A. Decline of 25 percent or more.
>
> B. Decline of 10 to 25 percent.
>
> C. No change (+ or - 9%).

D. 10 to 25 percent increase.

E. Over 25 percent increase.

3. The largest display of costumes is in New York City. The second largest display of American costumes is located in which city?

A. Atlanta, Ga.

B. Pittsburg, Pa.

C. Spartanburg, S.C.

D. Richmond, Va.

E. Washington, D.C.

4. Which of the following associations can train your salespeople in the technical side of the textile industry?

A. AATT

B. NKOA

C. ISTDA

D. INDA

E. MFA

5. Marketers (especially textile marketers) are a self-serving group as demonstrated by their own trade association which rewards their own kind.

A. True

B. False

Over the years the *Textile Marketing Letter* has examined a number of the multitude of associations and technical groups which serve our industry. The current issue of the *Encyclopedia of Associations* lists 191 such associations, only two of which are currently inactive. This analysis is designed to provide some information which you may not have known about with regard to this rather large list of potential resources.

Technical groups usually provide one of several services to their member or client firms; public relations, lobbying, information and/or education and trade shows are the usual functions performed by these groups. In concentrated industries such as automobiles, petroleum or primary metals, the few firms involved can provide these services themselves and have the resources to do so. In lesser concentrations of economic clout, such as the textile industry, the performance of the varied services would be diluted and vastly duplicated unless some simpler method could be found. The resultant increase in American prices for goods and services would then open the doors to a flood of lower-priced foreign goods, usually from governmentally endorsed and occasionally sponsored firms.

The textile industry lacks the vast concentration of an Exxon or a General Motors since we originally relied on the farmers for our raw material, competed with the cottage industries for production facilities, and distributed to even the smallest hamlet for our retail markets. Fashion is non-existent in the extraction and refining of minerals and petroleum, and virtually so in automobile manufacturing. We, however, must contend with dramatic shifts in consumer tastes on an almost daily basis. To obtain the kind of concentration one sees in the petroleum industry a textile firm should own its own oil fields, process its synthetic fibers, own vast tracts of cotton and wool producing soil, manufacture its own machinery as does the automobile industry, and be able to process raw materials from beginning to end in one massive plant. Then we need the functions of distribution both wholesale and retail to keep it all together. A firm large enough to accomplish this would require more capital than even our friendly telephone company possesses, and would undoubtedly be so regulated that it could not exist in a competitive marketplace.

Since it is both illogical and impractical to form such a gargantuan enterprise in our industry we have elected to maintain the free enterprise solution and permit smaller firms to specialize. This same American ingenuity has promoted the growth of professional organizations and specialty firms to provide services for groups of manufacturers and distributors in the economical usage of our resources.

ATMA—American Textile Machinery Association

One of the more newsworthy events sponsored by a textile association is the ATME-I exhibition co-sponsored by ATMA, the American Textile Machinery Association. This is only one of six major programs undertaken by this association for the benefit of its members. Market development heads their list of basic programs of the ATMA followed by government affairs. Member firms need better markets for their domestic and foreign markets, and require informed and influential governmental relations. Educational and technical services round out the basic programs of the ATMA. To better inform their members several communications programs are utilized publishing a series of Market Development Memos, a semi-annual Directory of Members' Products, the ATMA Executive Report series, and its Annual Reports.

ATMA is rather exclusive in that it is the only textile machinery association in the United States. The 130 members account for some 85 percent of the textile machinery production in this country. The ATMA (and two of its member firms, Platt Saco Lowell and West Point Foundry and Machine Company) received "E Star" Awards for outstanding creative marketing and promotional services at the highest level. Between 1977 and 1979 exports by the U.S. textile machinery industry increased from a total of 26.8 percent of annual volume to 35.3 percent—an increase of some 31.5 percent in a two year period! Domestic consumption of foreign machinery appears to have stabilized and is now running at less than 50 percent of total purchases as reported by Mr. Harry W. Buzzerd, Executive Vice President and Secretary of the ATMA.

One of the new initiatives seized upon by the ATMA involves federal grant funding to enable their member firms to become more competitive in the world marketplace. Grant areas include such items as marketing information and energy utilization.

TRRC—Textile Resource and Research Center

This Richmond Virginia association and its staff of five are dedicated to promote professional training and workshops in textile techniques. Their emphasis is on embroidery and needlework, textile care and conservation. Mr. Jean DuVal Kane, Director of the Valentine Museum reports that only the Metropolitan Museum of Art in New York City has a more extensive costume collection than his TRRC showing, the Smithsonian is far behind. Over 30,000 visitors view these masterpieces during the year. Costumes, quilts, coverlets and many other items of artistic and historical value compose the 12,000 items on display here.

The TRRC also maintains an extensive library in addition to the large number of items on display. Scholarships are provided to aspiring scholars and other professionals in the needlework and embroidery field. *Silhouette* is published on a bi-monthly schedule to members and subscribers. Workshops are provided on an annual basis to the trade in the Richmond headquarters.

AATT—American Association for Textile Technology

The AATT is a fine example of an organization dedicated to the information side of associational functions. Some 30 to 40 meetings per year are held on contemporary topics in widely scattered geographic areas to better serve their members. Semi-annual seminars to provide the basics for technicians are conducted in addition to the annual technical conferences.

This is to be expected since AATT is a professional group of "textile technologists dealing with the interchange and dissemination of professional knowledge among its members, the public and other industry groups." Karen Koopman states that AATT provides the "New in Textiles—technology, techniques and machinery." From the title of their March 1981 conference to be held in Charlotte it appears that they also offer more. "Business Techniques of Survival in the 80's" as a topic is a hard act to have to follow.

One of the associational benefits for members includes giving new technical skills to marketing personnel. As a trainer myself, that feature alone might well be worth a membership!

One of the thrusts AATT plans in the future involves a wider distribution of information to outsiders—a trouble shooting service where AATT could act as a resource for the problem areas in our industry.

TSA—Textile Salesmen's Association

TSA is one of the older associations in continuous service under its founding auspices. Founded in 1916 TSA is only junior to 15 other organizations of the 191 located. The NTA (Northern Textile Association) founded in 1854 being the patriarch. Half of the older associations are in the apparel industry, the Custom Tailors and Designers Association being the second eldest (1881). The National Association of Textile Supervisors (NATS) founded in 1883 is third oldest.

TSA publishes an annual journal which provides the revenue for the four scholarships sponsored by TSA each year. Clemson University, the Fashion Institute of Technology, N.C. State and the Philadelphia College all have students presently pursuing a textile-related degree through the efforts of TSA. Two meetings are held annually for the benefit of others. An educational seminar is held in New York City at the end of January and an annual luncheon to honor the "Textile Man of the Year."

MFA—The Men's Fashion Association of America, Inc.

The MFA was founded in 1955 as a non-profit public relations arm of the male apparel/textile industries. Women's fashions had been in the forefront for many years, but the typical male dressed much like his grandfather—with a Sunday outfit, two work outfits and maybe something for casual wear. Nature usually provides the male animal with the gorgeous plumage or striking mane. Why not make men more fashion conscious? Over a decade later it was my privilege to observe the results of MFA's efforts in the use of colored shirts, matching ties and handkerchiefs, color-coordinated suits, socks and shoes. While directing Clemson's Textile Marketing Forum Series from 1968-71, one needed merely view the audience from the podium to determine who the textile executives were— they were the ones still in the white shirts and gray suits! Today one sees a change as we begin to dress to suit our perception of the way we want our customers to dress—and buy.

MFA has instituted a series of programs to aid them in serving their membership. Press kits go to the top 750 daily papers every seven to nine weeks discussing and showing men's fashion trends. Press conferences are organized to kick-off the Spring-Summer and Fall-Winter men's fashion seasons. A close liaison is held with the syndicated columnists, wire services, and network and syndicated TV shows to disseminate information on such areas as formal wear for proms, the western "boom" in fashions and other timely fashion topics.

Retailers are served by providing an annually updated library of speeches, fashion show scripts and slide and filmstrip presentations to use in the local areas. Seasonal fashion updates for sales training and selected consumer audiences are also maintained to supply retail members.

A series of "Adam" awards, custom designed by Cartier, Inc., are annually presented to the top eight fashionable men in the areas of arts, business, communications, contemporary motion pictures, sports and television, plus an annual "Hall of Fame" award presented to such personages as Douglas Fairbanks, Jr. (1976), Benny Goodman (1977), Henry Fonda (1978), and Willie Stargell (1979). The ceremonies are conducted by outstanding women in America and are videotaped and syndicated to reach 60 percent of the homes in America.

Currently the MFA is providing a series of two-minute editorials for interested member firms to supply to their local TV stations. More than two out of three stations have accepted the MFA offer. A Corporate Dress Right Program is part of another new initiative of the MFA. Branch offices as well as corporate headquarters may utilize MFA's services to present the proper packaging of their personnel who make public and private contacts in the name of the firm.

A retrospective of fashion during the past quarter century was released early in 1981. The film "A Generation of Change" will make an impact on audiences and will be used by the MFA membership to boost awareness and investment in the packaging of the man of the 80's.

As should be patently obvious, any evaluation of all the associations serving the textile industry would either demand years of work or would be so cursory that it would be meaningless. There are a great number of associations, and it appears that there is little duplication in their basic purposes. Our Federal Government should have so little duplication!

This brief analysis indicates the potential uses of an association in trade shows and governmental relations (ATMA); education and training (TRRC); informational needs (AATT); professional recognition (TSA); and public relations (MFA). These were used here as examples of how the functions can be performed in a specified area of textiles and were not intended to be applicable to all readers. The reader who wishes to obtain more information about any of the associations listed in this section may contact the persons noted at the end. In the event you wish to obtain names of specialized associations related to your own segment of the industry, check with the *Encyclopedia of Associations,* found at your local library.

Learning is only effective when the pupil is involved—so get yourself involved—find out more about your own associations. Then see to it that they continue to provide those services which our free enterprise system demands—and many of our firms alone cannot finance without a cooperative effort.

Listing of described Associations:

- American Textile Machinery Association (ATMA)
  Phone (202) 296-1460
  1730 M Street, NW   Harry W. Buzzerd
  Washington, D.C. 20036   Executive Vice President

- Textile Resource and Research Center (TRRC)
  Phone (804) 649-0711
  1015 E. Clay St.   Jean DuVal Kane
  Richmond, VA 23219   Director of Museum

- American Association for Textile Technology (AATT)
  Phone (212) 354-5188
  1040 Avenue of the Americas   Karen L. Koopman
  New York, NY 10018   Administrative Manager

- Textile Salesmen's Association (TSA)
  Phone (212) 575-8987
  1500 Broadway, Room 1904   Edna H. Kaufman
  New York, NY 10036   Office Manager

- Men's Fashion Association of America (MFA)
  Phone (212) 581-8210
  1290 Avenue of the Americas   Norman Karr
  New York, NY 10019   Executive Director

44. WHAT IS INDA?*

By Lee J. Moremen, Executive Vice President,
International Nonwovens & Disposables Association

INDA, the International Nonwovens & Disposables Association, is an international trade association of companies involved in the nonwovens and disposable soft goods industries—material suppliers, roll goods producers, converters/fabricators, machinery and equipment manufacturers and marketers of finished products.

INDA was formed in 1968 when the nonwoven fabrics industry was starting to emerge as a separate entity. Today, nonwoven fabrics are being manufactured and used all over the world. Many distinct and unique products, both durable and disposable, are rapidly gaining recognition and acceptance. Today INDA has members in Canada, Mexico, South Africa, Sweden and Japan, in addition to the United States.

INDA was founded as The Disposables Association. For the first four years the Association's interests extended only to disposable nonwoven fabrics and the disposable soft goods made from these and related materials. Today, disposable surgical drapes and gowns, disposable

*This article first appeared in the September 1973 issue of the *Textile Marketing Letter*.

diapers and disposable wiping cloths, among other products made entirely or partially from nonwovens, are in widespread use throughout the U.S. and in many other parts of the world. The nonwoven fabrics industry covers fabrics for durable applications as well as disposable. As alternatives to conventional textiles, nonwoven fabrics are used as interlinings in apparel, as carpet backing, wall coverings, quilt backings, electrical insulation, and more.

INDA began to speak for the total industry and in July 1972 officially expanded its interest to cover the durable market, along with the disposable market. The Association's name was changed to clearly reflect those interests.

INDA's Projects and Committees. In the buying and selling of products and materials, uniform test methods for ascertaining various properties of the products are needed as guidelines for use in establishing contractual specifications and judging compliance of the products. INDA's Test Methods Subcommittee, assumed responsibility for this project and in June 1971 published the first set of recommended tests—DART—applicable to nonwoven fabrics and disposable soft goods. The DART, for the most part, designate and recommend the use of proven methods published by established standards organizations such as ASTM, TAPPI, AATCC, ANSI and others. Where necessary, certain modifications and adaptations of the published methods were made to make them specifically applicable to the products of this industry.

In the spring of 1973 the subcommittee completed the first steps in its efforts to find objective means for measuring softness, hand and drape. The project has involved 12 testing laboratories and six company test panels. The current study on these properties applies only to surgical drape materials and absorbent cover stock. The statistical analysis of the data collected was handled by Dr. Edward Vaughn and his staff at Clemson University.

INDA, along with Health Industries Association and Medical-Surgical Manufacturers Association, is sponsoring and funding (on a voluntary basis) a special study to provide the National Fire Protection Association and the industry with the data needed to determine the degree of electrostatic hazard in flammable atmospheres of hospitals. INDA is an active member of the Flammable Fabrics Laboratory Accreditation Board (FFLAB). INDA members are also providing technical expertise to the technical advisory panels which are part of the FFLAB project. The result of INDA's continuing efforts in the realm of fire safety is a new level of mutual understanding between the industry and the fire protection field.

The Marketing Data Bank Program is a recently initiated industrial statistical program by INDA which is intended to cover all products represented by the Association.

INDA Meetings and Shows. Early in 1973 INDA held its first Technical Symposium which attracted more than 400 scientific, technical and marketing personnel of companies in the industry. INDA's annual meeting of members takes place each spring, usually in May. The two-and-a-half-day format provides time for evaluating and planning Association activities and programs as well as discussing those outside events and actions that affect the industry.

IDEA is the name of the Association-sponsored trade exposition and conference, the only show exclusively representing the nonwoven fabrics industry. INDA initiated IDEA shows to provide a forum where users, suppliers and manufacturers can come together to examine, study, compare and learn each other's needs and capabilities. The show and conference also serves to make the public as well as the industry more aware of the increasingly important role of nonwoven fabrics and disposable soft goods in today's society.

INDA Publications. INDA members receive the *INDA Newsletter*, published by INDA, approximately six times a year.

A new brochure entitled "This is INDA," which outlines the purpose, activities and plans of the Association, is available upon request from the INDA office.

INDA publishes a Directory for the Nonwoven Fabrics and Disposable Soft Goods Industries. It is the only comprehensive reference source for these industries, listing products and services of manufacturers in countries throughout the world. This Directory provides sources for raw materials, machinery and equipment, nonwoven fabrics, contract converters/fabricators, finished disposable products and waste handling and disposal equipment. Trademarks and brand names are also listed. The book contains advertising and has world-wide distribution.

Association Management. INDA is managed by a Board of Governors elected by and responsible to the membership. The Board acts through an Executive Committee made up of the officers of the Association, four appointed members and the immediate past president of the Association. Day-to-day work of the organizations is carried on by a professional staff at the Association's office, 10 East 40 Street, New York, N.Y. 10016.

45. THE CARPET AND RUG INSTITUTE*

By William C. Laffoday,
Executive Vice President, CRI

The Carpet and Rug Institute, better known by its famous initials, CRI, is the singular trade association representing the dynamic and rapidly expanding carpet and rug industry. The Association's membership currently consists of 125 participating manufacturers and 250 suppliers of materials and services to the industry. In aggregate, these 375 members

*This article first appeared in the April 1972 issue of the *Textile Marketing Letter.*

represent about 95 percent of the carpet and rug industry's annual volume.

The Association's program of service and work is centered around nine principal objectives, spelled out in the Institute bylaws, approved by the membership on May 26, 1970. These objectives are:

- To promote the sale and use of the Industry's products and services.

- To act as public relations counsel for the Industry.

- To maintain contact with Government agencies and be the focal point for presenting the Industry's views in regard to regulations or legislation, proposed or enacted, of particular interest to the Industry.

- To accumulate facts and figures on an organized basis in order that the Members may be apprised of the state of the Industry and its progress.

- To conduct Industry marketing research projects in order to inform Members where the Industry's products are being sold and consumed and to identify new markets that may be developed.

- To work with Members, Government agencies and other interested organizations in order to establish standards of quality and performance for the Industry's products.

- To sponsor programs for the training and inspiration of personnel at all levels within the Industry.

- To serve as a clearing house for solving problems of mutual interest and concern to the Members of this Industry.

- To promote high standards of business ethics among the Members in order to increase the prestige of the Industry in the business community as well as among those it serves.

In a purely historical vein, the Carpet and Rug Institute, now in its third year of active leadership as a major association, evolved in January, 1969, the result of a merger. Prior to that date, the carpet and rug industry in the United States was represented by two trade associations—The American Carpet Institute (ACI) headquartered in New York City and The Tufted Textile Manufacturers Association (TTMA) located in Dalton, Georgia.

A number of manufacturer members belonged to both of these Associations, paid dues to each, and provided manpower to duplicate sets of committees.

The merger, which established CRI as the single national trade association representing the carpet and rug industry, eliminated many of the redundant and superfluous activities which had hindered the progress of its two predecessors. It was clearly evident at the outset that CRI would provide competent leadership and implement a comprehensive program of services for the mutual benefit of all members of the industry from manufacturer to retailer.

The work of the Institute is under the direction of an elected Board of Directors. Each phase of industry activity is assigned to the 25 member CRI professional staff, including a president and an executive president (both elected by the Board), a vice president of governmental affairs, and directors of technical services, installation services, public relations, marketing research, manufacturing and printing services. Lending their time and expertise to assist the staff in serving the industry more effectively are personnel from member companies who work on the more than 40 committees and subcommittees of CRI.

At the present time, the Institute's bylaw's exclude carpet retailers and distributors from membership. However, much of CRI's work has a direct and indirect bearing on this extremely vital segment of the industry. Spring and fall newspaper supplements containing feature articles and four-color photographs about new innovations and adaptations of carpet as a means of achieving new dimensions in living; publications on carpet care, color coordination, selection, and installation; films about all the myriad aspects of the industry; carpet installation seminars conducted in various locations throughout the United States each year; and marketing research efforts are all programs designed to help the retailer promote and market the products of the industry.

In simplest terms, the Institute's primary function is to serve as a focal point and sounding board where problems of a general nature can be discussed and solved. CRI acts as an industry spokesman on many matters and assembles information on a wide range of subjects relating to the total industry.

To best serve its members and the interests of the general public, in relation to the carpet and rug industry, CRI moved into a beautiful new national headquarters building in Dalton, Georgia in August, 1971. This inspiring architectural masterpiece, symbolic of the progress and dynamic achievement of the Institute, houses the many and varied activities of the association as it serves a growing and more vital function.

According to the United States Department of Commerce, the carpet and rug industry is the fastest growing consumer-oriented industry in the nation.

There are profound and dramatic changes taking place daily and the familiar recital of annual sales increases, new fibers, new technologies, new styles, and new end-uses only begins to tell the story.

The industry is truly in an age of transformation and perhaps on the verge of a marketing revolution.

What the future holds in store for the industry will depend to a large extent on the guidance and leadership of the Carpet and Rug Institute.

46. COTTON INCORPORATED

The Facts Behind a Successful Manufacturers' Association*

By The Editorial Staff, Textile Marketing Letter

Cotton Incorporated is a private corporation owned and controlled by more than 300,000 cotton producers in the United States. Its constant underlying objective is to return higher profits to its owners. Cotton Incorporated is a fiber marketing company. It conducts coordinated programs of research, marketing and sales to achieve two goals; (1) to hold or expand existing markets for cotton and create new markets; and (2) to lower the cost of producing, harvesting and processing a bale of better cotton.

Where Is Cotton Incorporated? The executive offices are in New York City. But Cotton Incorporated is where the action is—in the mill, the manufacturing plant and the marketplace; on the farm, in the gin, and at points between in its own laboratories and those of contract research facilities at near and distant places. Cotton Incorporated is everywhere its people can be when their presence will help produce better quality cotton at lower cost for an ever growing market.

Cotton Incorporated is divided into two divisions. The sales and marketing division is in New York City, with the executive offices. The research and technical services center is in Raleigh, North Carolina.

"The Cottonworks," cotton fabric libraries and workshops for textile designers and manufacturers are located in Los Angeles and Dallas, in addition to New York City. The company also maintains an office in Washington, D.C. for liaison with federal regulatory agencies, the U.S. Department of Agriculture, and the U.S. Patent Office.

What Is the Sales and Marketing Division? The sales and marketing division of Cotton Incorporated is located in New York City in order to place the cotton producer at the nerve center of the U.S. textile industry, the major consumer of cotton.

There Cotton Incorporated's experts work directly with the mills that spin, weave, knit, dye, print and finish cotton. The purpose is to sell cotton to the mill, garment manufacturer, the converter, the retailer and the individual consumer.

---

*This article first appeared in the June 1972 issue of the *Textile Marketing Letter.*

The sales and marketing division is organized along lines that parallel the structure of the industries it serves. There are three departments: (1) men's and boys' wear; (2) women's and children's wear; and (3) home furnishings and industrial products.

The sales departments receive sole support from a marketing service group which functions through four departments: (1) product development; (2) advertising and public relations; (3) fashion marketing; and (4) market research.

What Is the Research and Technical Services Center? The Research and Technical Services Center of Cotton Incorporated was located at Raleigh for two reasons: One was to give it close proximity to the manufacturing facilities of major U.S. mills. The other was to allow it the benefits of the stimulating intellectual environment emanating from the Research Triangle and the three universities nearby, North Carolina State University at Raleigh, the University of North Carolina at Chapel Hill, and Duke University at Durham.

A staff of scientists and technological experts who know and understand the problems and costs involved in producing a bale of cotton dedicate their talents to solving those problems and lowering costs. Others who know and understand the problems of spinning yarns suitable for today's changing markets seek methods of producing a better cotton product.

The staff includes chemists and entomologists, agronomists and physiologists; geneticists and pathologists; and one of the country's outstanding biochemists; textile designers, engineers, machinists, experts in dyeing, sizing and finishing; spinning technologists and authorities on weaving; and one of a half-dozen men in the world who hold doctoral degrees in knitting technology.

Some research goes on in the center's own facilities. More by far is conducted on a contractual basis by state experiment stations, USDA laboratories, universities and private institutions throughout the United States and in foreign countries.

Research at Cotton Incorporated is divided into three areas: (1) agricultural research; (2) processing, handling and services research; and (3) product research. Programs in agricultural research are aimed at improving the yield and quality of cotton and at controlling the insects, diseases and weeds which annually inflict heavy losses on producers. Research on processing, handling and services is aimed at improving the system of harvesting, storing, handling and ginning seed cotton on the farm and off, and at effecting new economies in the system. Product research is aimed at determining the best ways of processing cotton fiber into yarn, and yarn into fabric, and the best ways of finishing cotton fabrics for durable press and fire retardant properties, so as to widen and increase the utilization, and consequently the consumption of cotton.

The technical services department renders immediate, practical assistance to any mill manufacturer that encounters problems in spinning, weaving, knitting, dyeing or finishing cotton.

Where Does the Money Come from for All These Programs? All activities of Cotton Incorporated are funded by cotton producers in the form of a contribution of one dollar for every bale of cotton produced. Additional funds for research come from the U.S. Department of Agriculture under provisions of the Agricultural Act of 1970. Of all agricultural self-help programs in the world, Cotton Incorporated is by far the largest.

Are Producers Required to Contribute? Producer participation is voluntary. The monies they provide are contributions, not assessments. The first buyer of a bale of cotton collects the one dollar contribution from the producer. In 1970 contributions to support the programs of Cotton Incorporated came from 97.5 percent of cotton producers in cotton producing states.

Who Determines the Activities of Cotton Incorporated? All policies and programs of Cotton Incorporated are determined by its owners, the cotton producers of America, through a 46-member board of directors. Every director is himself a producer, chosen to serve on the board by a certified cotton producer organization in the state or states he represents. Each state's representation on the board of directors is determined by the state's monetary contributions to support Cotton Incorporated. Directors are allocated among the 19 cotton producing states.

What Are the Origins of Cotton Incorporated? Cotton Incorporated was founded in 1961 as the Cotton Producers Institute (CPI). The reason for its inception was competition.

Ordinarily an expanding population means a growing market for a producer of consumer goods. In the decade from 1951 to 1960, the population of the United States increased by more than 25 million. During the same ten years, the volume of domestic cotton consumption declined slightly, from 4.5 billion pounds to 4.2 billion. But cotton's share of America's fiber market dropped sharply, from 66.3 percent to 57.5 percent.

What Was the Cause? New man-made fibers. In 1951 non-cellulosic man-made fibers, such as nylon, Dacron and Orlon, held a meager 4.6 percent share of the American fiber market. Consumption was 315 million pounds. But by 1960 non-cellulosic fibers were consumed at the rate of almost 1.4 billion pounds. And their share of the fiber market had risen to 18.7 percent.

Studies by cotton interests revealed that the manufacturers of synthetic fibers, though few in number, were spending huge amounts of money on programs of research, product development and promotion. The programs were coordinated and market-directed. Cotton interests, on the other hand, were spending less than one-tenth of one percent of the value of the cotton crop each year on research and development.

Cotton producers read the handwriting on the wall and decided to take action. In 1961 they organized CPI.

By 1965 the volume of cotton consumption still hovered at 4.6 billion pounds. But in the face of a population growth to 195 million, cotton's share of the fiber market had dropped even more sharply, to 44.3 percent. The non-cellulosic fibers in 1965 were being consumed at a volume of 3.5 billion pounds, and their share of the domestic fiber market approached 33 percent.

Testimony before the House Agriculture Committee of Congress in 1966 reflected that the concern of the cotton producers had been justified.

Synthetic fiber manufacturers in 1965 spent $125 million on research and development. The amount spent by all cotton interests, including governmental agencies, for the same purposes totaled $26.5 million. Expenditures by manufacturers of man-made fibers to promote cotton were $4 million. Our synthetic fiber company alone spent more on research than was spent for research, development and promotion by all cotton interests combined.

So cotton producers had clearly perceived the serious threat of new competition. They took realistic action to encounter it. With the formation of CPI, cotton producers recognized that the costs of research, product development and promotion are necessary.

47. INTERNATIONAL FABRICARE INSTITUTE—A GREAT NEW MARKETING FORCE*

By John A. Cairns, Consultant

When the American Institute of Laundering and the National Institute of Drycleaning merged to form the International Fabricare Institute, a marketing force of tremendous vitality and effectiveness was born; a force that can be used on a day-to-day basis by virtually everyone in the textile and apparel industries, from the producers of fibers and finishes right down the line to the mills, converters, and retailers.

Compared with almost anything else that is set up to serve these industries of ours, the International Fabricare Institute (IFI for short) is a giant, indeed. It represents some 13,500 members located in the United States, Canada, and over 50 other countries. Its members here do something like 85 percent of all the laundering and drycleaning done professionally for the American consumer, as well as for institutional and commercial accounts, a volume that is estimated to be well above six billion dollars annually.

As a marketing ally, the IFI is equipped to walk every step of the way

---

*This article first appeared in the February 1973 issue of the *Textile Marketing Letter*.

with its affiliates in the textile and apparel industries. It can work with the mill or the manufacturer at the very beginning of the marketing process by suggesting performance standards for the product that will enable it to give complete satisfaction in consumer end use. It can test that product for performance reliability before it is marketed. It can even award one of its Seals of Approval. It can also suggest the wording for permanent labels to satisfy government requirements and to assure proper care.

Nationwide Service. IFI laboratories are spotted across the country from the Atlantic to the Pacific for convenient service to IFI members and its textile industry affiliates. A new Research Center is being built in Silver Spring, Maryland where the National Institute of Drycleaning had been located since the 1920's. The Center, headed by Dr. Manfred Wentz, is especially designed and equipped to work with textile mills, fiber companies, chemical producers, garment manufacturers, and makers of home furnishings products at every level, from market evaluations of new compounds to investigations of the behavioral characteristics of textile products under conditions of laundering or drycleaning. The Center utilizes the vast laundry facilities and laboratories, as well as complete commercial dry-cleaning service, that have been centered in Joliet, Illinois, for more than 60 years, now also the administrative headquarters of IFI. A third laboratory, fully equipped for making drycleaning evaluations and investigations of damage claims, is located in Glendale, California. An office in the Empire State Building serves to accommodate and coordinate within the New York market the business and textile trade relations affairs of these activities.

IFI research facilities include the latest kinds of operating equipment employed by the nation's industry and drycleaning establishments, as well as complete facilities for establishing the most effective and efficient operating procedures for their members. It is this day-to-day, down-to-earth practicality that makes IFI service so valuable to everyone in the textile and apparel industries who seek their help.

Damage Claims Analyzed. Beyond that, IFI laboratories handle the largest volume of damage analysis work of any laboratory in the world. The service helps in pinpointing the responsibility of damage claims from consumers. In many cases the cause of damage is product failure rather than improper care treatments or some harmful condition of use that showed up only after laundering or drycleaning. The fabric may have shrunk or delaminated, or the color may have disappeared under normal conditions of use and care which would not have occurred with better materials and use of standard test procedures for quality control in the manufacturing process. Even the label can be the culprit, because of incorrect or contradictory information. Upwards of 25,000 such problems are analyzed annually for its members and others, a good percentage of which becomes restored to usefulness in the process. And millions upon millions of dollars are saved as a result of the facts these investigations reveal, especially for the producer for whom a single mistake in the choice of a material can prove extremely costly.

Several Kinds of Service. It doesn't cost an arm and a leg to do business with the International Fabricare Institute. You can become an Affiliate Member for the very modest fee of $100 a year. For this fee you receive all of the services and all the information that js regularly made available to IFI members. For research and development programs, the IFI provides the staff and facilities for solving an extremely wide range of textile maintenance problems for almost every segment of the textile industry. Fees for this service are established by mutual agreement, in line with the size of the project at hand. Testing services are another popular feature of IFI cooperation with the textile industries. Here, the IFI provides laboratory facilities plus full-scale equipment and standard procedures for compliance with various laws, rules and regulations, and with industry standards of performance. Again, costs are kept in line with the size of the job.

And finally, there are IFI's Certification Programs which have proved their value over a good many years. These are of two kinds: (1) continuing support of the highest caliber for all types of marketing programs where professional certification of performance claims is an important factor (an example is the new Bonded Fabric Council's certification program for which IFI is the administrator), and (2) the use of IFI's own CERTIFIED WASHABLE Seal or CERTIFIED DRYCLEANABLE Seal on products which have established their merit under IFI standards. Either type of certification provides an assurance of quality to the consumer, plus a guide to laundries and drycleaners for the satisfactory handling of the product in their establishments.

Annual Convention and Exhibit. Still another activity which benefited from the merger was the Annual Convention and Exhibit now representing more than ever the broad market spectrum for machinery, chemical supplies, and textile products of all kinds that go into the operation of this vast, multi-faceted textile care service industry. With an attendance of over 15,000, many from abroad, textile firms active in the uniform rental and linen supply markets are keenly interested in the exhibit. Many exhibit their lines at these conventions. Inquiries should be addressed to IFI Headquarters in Joliet, Illinois.

All textile trade relations activities for IFI are under the direct supervision of Albert E. Johnson, who was awarded the 1973 Bronze Medal of the American Association for Textile Technology for distinguished service to the textile industry. Mr. Johnson makes his headquarters in IFI's New York Office, Room 5623 of the Empire State Building. He served four terms as Director of AATT, where he had much to do with establishing the Annual Conference and the Council on Technology. He also had much to do with the establishment of American National Stand L-22, the National Fair Claims Guide for Consumer Textile Products, the Voluntary Permanent Care Label Guide developed in 1966, and the IFI Chair for Textile and Apparel Care Technology established at the Fashion Institute of Technology in 1966. Mr. Johnson is also Chairman of the AATCC Committee on Drycleaning Test Methods which has promulgated most of the drycleaning evaluation tests in current use in the textile industry.

48. THE AMERICAN TEXTILE MACHINERY ASSOCIATION*

By Howard W. Geyer, President, ATMA

From its beginnings in Washington, D.C. the American Textile Machinery Association provided a unifying force for the diverse textile machinery of the United States. Its nearly 100 members represent 90 percent of the industry's sales dollar volume. No other national trade association has as its primary objective representation of this industry.

The rich history of U.S. textile machinery dates back to the late 1700's. In succeeding years the industry took on a distinct personality and an awareness of the advantages of collective action. In 1881 many of its manufacturers gathered together in Atlanta, Georgia, to produce the first American Textile Machinery Exhibition. This exhibition has been followed by many more—even larger than the last—until, today, ATMA owns and co-sponsors, quadrennially, one of the largest capital equipment exhibitions in the United States.

ATMA was formally organized in Boston, Massachusetts, in 1933, at which time it was known as the National Association of Textile Machinery Manufacturers. The name was changed to its present form in 1952, and a short time later the headquarters office was transferred to the Washington, D.C. area.

The Association maintains a small permanent staff in its downtown Washington offices which are located in the Madison National Bank Building. Professional legal, accounting and other services as necessary are provided by consultants to the Association. Key government and private industry representatives are only a few blocks from its central location. Also, nearby are transportation and hotel facilities which make it convenient for ATMA members to visit their Washington office to discuss industry affairs or utilize the conference room provided by the organization for their use.

Membership in ATMA is available to companies which have their principal office and manufacturing plant in the United States and have as their principal business the manufacture and sale of complete machines used in textile establishments. Associate members in ATMA make parts or machine accessories which aid the products of regular members.

---

*This article first appeared in the June 1974 issue of the *Textile Marketing Letter*.

In addition to its role as exhibition owner and sponsor, ATMA has been widely recognized as the official office of the textile machinery industry. ATMA representatives maintain liaison with top legislative and administrative officials in Washington. From its Washington vantage point the Association alerts the industry to governmental activities which may affect its interests.

When necessary, ATMA coordinates the formal presentation of industry views on important subjects through testimony, briefs, position papers, etc. Textile machinery makers have spoken out in this fashion many times on matters relating to taxes, foreign trade, tariff rates and classification, industrial health and safety, as well as on a host of other important issues.

Further, the Association provides an all important vehicle through which textile machinery makers can meet each other and learn of new industry developments. ATMA conducts an annual membership meeting and smaller meetings or seminars as necessary to achieve this cross-pollination of ideas and information.

At the same time, the Association, through special projects such as a Directory, enables the industry to convey to related industries, the government, the educational community, and to the general public its dedication to progressive and reliable service to the textile industry of the world.

49. THE IMPORTANCE OF AAMA*
By John Druckenbrod, Director of Public Relations,
AAMA

The American Apparel Manufacturers Association is the largest and most representative trade association serving the giant American apparel industry.

Members produce every major item of wearing apparel for men, women and children, as well as for personnel in the armed forces and the space programs.

Associate Members—companies supplying goods and/or services to apparel manufacturers—include a major cross-section of the American industry: textile mills; manufacturers of buttons, zippers and thread; producers of sewing, knitting and other types of machinery; binding, bonding and laminating companies; computer and accounting companies; research and management consulting firms—the list is endless.

To the American public and the economy, AAMA membership represents millions of jobs, some $13 billion of annual volume at wholesale, and the largest or a key industry employer in at least 20 states. The apparel industry is the largest employer of women in the United States, one in five being so employed.

---

*This article first appeared in the February 1974 issue of the *Textile Marketing Letter.*

AAMA Members represent more than 60 percent of the annual apparel volume in the U.S. and are located in 44 states, the District of Columbia, Puerto Rico, Canada and 13 other foreign countries.

AAMA's primary purpose, simplified, is to keep its membership functioning in this vital American industry as the most profitable and most progressive apparel companies in the world.

To accomplish this goal AAMA provides members with many services: recognition within the industry, the U.S. and the world; mutually advantageous contacts and a voice in the industry through special and standing committees; information through numerous publications, research reports and audio-visual presentations; representation before government, the consuming public and important business groups; technological assistance through a wide range of seminars and meetings; insurance through our special group programs, and, most important, leadership for all these services from within the industry itself.

Recognition comes from listings in the AAMA Membership Directory, the "Bible" for all major apparel manufacturers and suppliers in the U.S. This puts a member company's name on the desk of most leading executives in the American apparel industry every single day. Recognition also comes from the dozens of news releases mailed yearly to the mass media and the trade press.

Contacts and a voice in the industry come from close participation in the 27 standing committees of AAMA, composed of more than 700 top member executives.

Every member and associate member is given the opportunity to provide personnel for these committees, giving them personal contacts with their counterparts in the industry. This participation allows a single firm to have a voice in decisions affecting the entire industry; to make inputs to methods of coping with apparel industry problems; to help formulate industry policies; and to contribute to joint technical and business advances, special reports and studies.

Information from AAMA comes in almost every possible format—special reports, newsletters, surveys, technical books, directories, individual replies to specific requests, even movie and slide presentations complete with sound.

Representation of AAMA membership in Washington, representation before the public and representation before other industry groups is a key part of the business of AAMA. During the past year this had become an even more crucial job, with tough government controls, legislation and standards accelerating their movement into our industry. Whether it's a meeting, a public hearing, Congressional action or a single government decision, AAMA is monitoring this area for its members.

The vital knowledge gained in such monitoring is forwarded to AAMA members after careful coordination with other industry groups. When appropriate, such material also is presented to the media. In the last 12 months more than 200,000 words have appeared in various consumer and trade press publications concerning, AAMA, its policies, its members and the industry it serves.

Technology on an industry-wide level is presented in the dozens of meetings and symposiums held throughout the U.S. each year by AAMA— an annual convention featuring many fine seminars, prepared carefully and professionally over a full year by AAMA committees; regional production seminars; an apparel industry economic outlook seminar; state meetings and special conferences as needed.

Insurance for member and associate member companies is available from AAMA in group life and 24-hour accidental death programs. Under these programs companies can have, depending on income, up to $50,000 group coverage over and above any existing coverage—at a special low cost! The accidental death policy is available up to $150,000, also at a special rate.

"Service Through Leadership" has long been the standard for AAMA programs and committees. It simply means that the leadership within the apparel industry is there—in AAMA. The proof is in the Association's constant and successful efforts to bring top industry people into positions of broad responsibility on the AAMA board of directors, committees and subcommittees, and for special projects.

The AAMA membership and staff are proud of the exceptional results that have been realized. Throughout AAMA's 40 year Record of Excellence and Achievement, leaders of the apparel industry have consistently and effectively served the Association and, through it, their industry, its executives and its workers.

50. AATT: MARKETING'S LINK TO TECHNOLOGY*

By The Editorial Staff, Textile Marketing Letter

Because the textile industry is large, complex and dynamic, its technical progress is unusually rapid. Individual segments of the industry are so related and dependent on the success of each other that everybody must know the problems, thinking and developments of all sections of the industry.

It was with this concept in mind that the American Association of Textile Technology was 'founded in 1934 as a professional society for textile technologists. It has remained so to this day, but in recent years its role has been expanded to reflect the growing interaction between the worlds of textile technology and textile marketing. In addition, it is expanding its activities to reflect the relationship between the textile industry and the consumer of its products.

---

*This article first appeared in the October 1972 issue of the *Textile Marketing Letter*.

Here is an organization that reflects advanced thinking at every level—from producers of chemicals, fibers and machinery, through to mills, converters, retailers and advertising-public relations agencies. AATT stands as perhaps the most important contact between marketing executives and textile technologists. As an association it is sufficiently broad in its membership and scope to cross marketing, manufacturing and technical lines at all levels. Through its various activities, members in the technical sector explore the pivotal role of marketing in textiles. Similarly, marketing men are given insight into the technical aspect of the products they sell.

The objectives of the Association are "to encourage mutual understanding in the fields of textile technology and marketing; the advancement of textile technology in all its branches; cooperation with established facilities for textile education; and the interchange and dissemination of professional knowledge among its members and with other industry groups."

Many new technical developments have been introduced to the textile marketplace at meetings of AATT. It was here that marketing executives and their technical staffs learned firsthand about:

- Properties of new synthetic fibers, such as duPont's Qiana, Monsanto's 22N nylon and WD-2 polyester.

- Impact of technical developments, machinery improvements and manufacturing advances, such as open-end spinning and Texfi's computer aided pattern design for knitting.

- Aspects of new textile finishes.

- Improving natural fibers.

AATT keeps closely in touch with all regulations and requirements of the U.S. Government and other regulatory agencies, and when appropriate they hold meetings, seminars and conferences dealing with such matters so as to keep the industry well informed.

AATT's Members and Meetings. The association's many members are truly representative of every segment of the textile industry—from fiber producer to retailer. Geographically, AATT is composed of five regional chapters—Appalachian, Gulf States, New England, New York and Piedmont. AATT is vitally concerned with the continued recruitment, preparation and development of both marketing and technical personnel for the textile industry. It takes an active role in interesting students in textile technology as a career and keeping them apprised of new technical developments which affect the industry. To carry out this program AATT maintains student chapters at eight major textile schools.

Each local chapter holds regular meetings and seminars throughout the year, featuring in-depth discussions of subjects of vital and timely interest to members. In February, an annual conference is held under the sponsorship of the national organization.

When the national organization sponsored a symposium and panel discussion on durable press, the 1,400 representatives of the textile industry, distributing trades, garment manufacturers and retailers attending the meeting claimed the papers and discussions were the most significant and comprehensive coverage of this subject.

Similar reaction has been experienced consistently at monthly chapter meetings. Many papers are held in such high regard it is not unusual for an individual firm to send as many as a dozen of its technical and executive staff members to an AATT meeting.

Council on Technology. A vital part of AATT's organization is its Council on Technology. The council consists of four major interest groups, each with specialists in an important area of textile technology or marketing. Areas of interest include textile structure—knitting, weaving, nonwoven, and tufted and carpet technology; end-use—care labeling, consumer education and legislation, end product performance, and product refurbishing; information—the storage, retrieval, and dissemination of technical information; miscellaneous—apparel technology, fabric development and style, and yarn technology.

These groups prepare reports on key trends in their fields, sponsor seminars, and serve as sources of information.

Kinds of Membership. AATT has five membership categories: regular, affiliate, junior, student, and corporate. Regular members are textile technologists qualified by professional training and/or experience. Affiliate members are persons not technically trained but who are interested in maintaining contact with recent innovations in the field of textile technology. Junior members are any persons employed as textile technologists, but without sufficient experience to qualify as a regular member. Student members are persons studying textiles and related industries interested in aiding the Association's program of expanding activities.

Further information can be obtained from the American Association for Textile Technology, 295 Fifth Avenue, New York, N.Y. 10016.

51. THE AMERICAN YARN
  SPINNERS ASSOCIATION*

By Jim H. Conner,
American Yarn Spinners Association

The American Yarn Spinners Association is the national trade association of the "short staple" sales yarn manufacturing industry. All active member companies share at least two characteristics: first, each manufactures spun yarn on the short staple, or cotton, system of spinning;

---

*This article first appeared in the January 1974 issue of the *Textile Marketing Letter*.

and, second, each has a substantial and continuing interest in producing yarn for sale.

Yarn produced for sale on the cotton system represents approximately one-fourth of the total spun yarn produced domestically. This yarn is sold to knitters, weavers, thread manufacturers and others who further process it into textile products for the apparel, household or industrial markets.

AYSA member companies produce sales yarn made of cotton and man-made fibers. Although the industry continues to be heavily involved with 100 percent cotton yarns, there is a growing market for man-made fiber yarns made of a single fiber, blends of two or more man-made fibers, and blends of cotton and man-made fiber.

AYSA was formed in 1967 through the merger of two old established yarn trade associations, the Combed Yarn Spinners Association and The Carded Yarn Association. At that time the scope of the new association was broadened to include yarns of all fibers spun on the short staple system.

Today, AYSA is comprised of some 100 active member firms who manufacture yarn, and approximately 55 associate member firms who supply and service the industry. The active members operate over three million spindles in some 200 plants scattered over a six-state southeastern area. The employment in this segment of textiles is estimated to be in the range of 70,000 people.

The Role of AYSA. The charter and bylaws of the Association give it a number of broad technical, economic, promotional, educational and social purposes. With its clearly defined functional interests, the Association has a unique ·opportunity for relevancy that is not possible in the broader based textile associations.

Several characteristics of the industry support the need of a specialized trade association devoted exclusively to sales yarn:

1. The end products of the old industry are semi-manufactured products that are sold to other segments of textiles.

2. The marketing system for sales yarn is unique and separate from other textile marketing systems.

3. Although sharing certain technology with the integrated manufacturer, the sales yarn spinner is more of a custom manufacturer, producing products that are manufactured and packaged for very specific end uses.

4. The industry has traditionally consisted of smaller management and ownership units than exist in most other textile segments.

AYSA has thus restricted its role to that of dealing with problems and opportunities that are uniquely yarn industry oriented and to delving into the broader problem areas only when it can effectively complement, or supplement, the broader based textile associations.

Organization. AYSA is governed by a board of directors who actively participate in, and guide, the Association's affairs. The board consists of the three senior officers of the Association, 12 elected directors who each serve for a three-year term, and the three chairmen of the Product Groups. In addition, the immediate past president and the treasurer serve as ex officio board members.

The president, first vice-president and second vice-president are elected by the membership each year and are charged with implementing the board's policies and program directives. A professional staff performs the actual mechanics of the programs. At its meetings during the year, the AYSA board continually reviews the policies and programs of the Association and establishes priorities according to need.

To make a number of programs even more relevant, the active members of AYSA have an opportunity to join any, or all, of three product groups: The Combed Yarn Group, The Carded Yarn Group and The Synthetics/Blends Group.

Programs. Working within the constraints of a relatively small professional staff and budget, AYSA attempts to place program emphasis on subject areas of primary interest to the sales yarn industry. Program priorities are adjusted annually to reflect changing industry needs.

Each program of the Association is examined to determine its contribution to the basic objectives of the Association itself.

- Does the program contribute to a better informed member company?

- Does the program contribute to better understanding of the industry by those not directly involved?

- Does the program increase the Association's capability to act responsibly for the industry?

Although the specific programs of AYSA change with time, some of the current ones are:

Government and Trade Liaison. Government activities have a significant impact on textile industry affairs. Working in close coordination with other national textile trade groups, AYSA strives to bring yarn expertise not only to government, but to other fiber-textile-apparel associations who regularly work with government. Our role is to supplement and complement these other groups' activities.

Specifically, AYSA has become involved, on a continuing basis, in the following subject areas: Import Controls; Export Programs; Cotton Legislation; and Government Statistical Programs.

Statistical and Economic Information. The staff collects and disseminates economic data on the sales yarn industry from a number of sources. An annual summary of production and marketing trends is published in the fall. Additionally, economic and marketing reports are published on special areas throughout the year.

Workshops. Over the few years of its existence, AYSA has developed a format for some highly successful workshops for its members. In conducting these workshops, the Association has found that the maximum interest is generated when the subject is one that is highly relevant to a sales yarn operation, when industry executives themselves participate, and when attendance is restricted to executives who are directly involved in the particular subject area.

General. Through its regular newsletter and other special mailings, AYSA strives to keep its membership informed on matters relating to government, market and economic trends, and on any other subject that is of particular interest to the sales yarn manufacturer.

A number of special projects have also been undertaken by the Association. One of particular interest is revision of the Yarn Rules, the sales yarn industry's counterpart to the Worth Street Rules. Working with legal counsel, the Association's Yarn Rules Committee has been charged not only with developing an up-to-date set of trading rules and contracts, but also of keeping these revised as conditions change.

AYSA's annual meeting, held each fall, is an important part of its total program. Through this vehicle, industry members come to know each other and additionally have time to assess industry trends in an atmosphere apart from day-to-day operations. The programs at the annual meeting draw from speakers who address themselves exclusively to this industry's problems and opportunities.

An important, but undefined, role of any effective association is to be able to respond to unanticipated needs before they become full-scaled problems. AYSA interprets its role to keep informed, to be able to respond quickly, and to call for membership responses on a number of subjects that are not part of any regular program.

Affiliates. The expenses of maintaining AYSA's professional staff and offices are shared through management service agreements with the Association of Synthetic Yarn Manufacturers, the national trade association of the textured yarn industry; the Carpet Yarn Association, with interests in woolen and worsted system machines and hand knitting yarns. Although working closely together and sharing staff and offices, the four associations are operated separately and independently. AYSA is the central administrative organization under the service agreements but each association has its own offices and governing board. The common fiber running through each of the four organizations is that they are made up of companies producing yarn for sale.

Conclusion. Membership in AYSA is a relatively low-cost item for any company. Dues are established by the board of directors and applications for membership must be approved by both a membership committee and the full board of directors. Information pertaining to membership may be obtained by writing the AYSA office.

52. CONTRIBUTIONS OF TDA TO TEXTILE INDUSTRY*

By James C. Cumming, Consultant

The Textile Distributors Association, Inc. is the recognized trade association for the converting and distributing sections of the textile industry. While other associations are more interested in technical work, TDA concentrates on marketing.

The objectives of TDA, as expressed in its own constitution, make this clear:

1. To foster the trade and commerce of its members.

2. To assist in the establishment and enforcement of trade practice rules and government regulations.

3. To collect and distribute data and information of interest and benefit to the members of the association and to the textile fabric distributing industry.

4. To advise its members of improvements being made in fibers and fabrics and of new and beneficial terms in textile fabric distribution.

5. To represent the textile fabric industry in the study and interpretation of pertinent laws, regulations and orders applicable to its members.

6. To do all things necessary to promote the best interests and welfare of the textile fabric distributing and allied industries.

Who Belongs to TDA? There are few important converters or distributors who are not currently members of TDA. Membership includes 131 regular members and 52 associate members, who produce, by rough estimate, close to two billion dollars' worth of finished goods.

The 131 regular members include virtually all the converters, printers, and finishers in the industry. Fiber producers, greige goods mills,

---

*This article first appeared in the January 1971 issue of the *Textile Marketing Letter*.

throwsters, factors and others close to the industry make up the group of associate members.

In accordance with its objectives, how does TDA serve these members and the industry?

Design, Trademark and Copyright Registration. TDA maintains a bureau for design registration, which acts as a clearing house for registering print designs.

A trademark reference library permits users to search proposed trademarks efficiently and economically. Its files contain nearly 250,000 names that are registered or in use in the industry, or in allied fields where duplication might be an infringement.

Since many of these names have not been used for as many as 20 or 30 years, the trademark bureau recently adopted a new rule designed to unfreeze thousands of them.

Under this rule, if an application is received to record a name that duplicates one that has been in the TDA file for more than three years, the Bureau will ask the original filer if he has used the name during the past three years. If he has not, the Bureau will accept the new recording. It should be noted, however, that this rule has no bearing on trademarks registered in the Patent Office in Washington.

By way of follow-through, an increasing number of companies are using TDA to take care of their copyright applications in Washington.

Employment Service. The TDA free employment service is widely known in the industry and is usually the first port of call for job-seekers with textile backgrounds. A weekly bulletin listing these people by job description goes out to members, and has resulted in placing a high percentage of applicants. Many regard the TDA employment service as one of the most useful of the association's services to the industry.

Recruitment. Another important TDA activity is bringing young people into the marketing branch of the textile industry.

The association's brochure, "Career Opportunities for You in the Fabulous World of Fabrics," has been widely distributed and closely read by students considering careers. It helps the student to see where he might fit into the various phases of the textile industry, including work in designing, printing and finishing, and marketing management.

The brochure also names technical schools specializing in training for the textile industry. Under this program the Education Committee of TDA grants marketing scholarships to students at Fashion Institute of Technology in New York, the Philadelphia College of Textiles and North Carolina State at Raleigh. The committee is interested in extending scholarship aid to any qualified students with a particular flair for textile marketing.

Traffic Bureau. TDA's Freight Rate and Traffic Bureau works with the transportation services on behalf of TDA members, and renders frequent reports on how to reduce transportation and warehousing costs and expedite shipments. Also, as a telephone service, it supplies the most economical and fastest routings for projected shipments.

Life Insurance Programs. The TDA insurance program for its members is the result of several years of investigation, study and development. The plan had hardly been announced when a sufficient number of applications were received from members to put the plan into operation, and at present almost a million dollars worth of coverage is involved.

It has provided low cost life insurance, without medical examination and on a tax-deductible basis, to companies which would not have been able to have plans of their own.

Representation in Washington. TDA's executive director, Richard S. Lowell, serves as a member of the Exporters' Textile Advisory Committee, an important group that advises the government on textile problems relating to foreign commerce.

Mr. Lowell also represents TDA members on the Industry Advisory Committee on Textile Information, which has played a key role in the development of Care Labeling provisions. The association is also represented on the Executive Committee of the General Arbitration Council, on the newly-formed Committee on Flammability Standards, and on the committee which is formulating the revised L-22 standards.

Other Activities. But these activities represent just a few of the contributions that TDA makes to textile marketing.

The Quality Control Committee, for example, provides TDA members with guides to the maintenance of quality and performance standards. It carries on a continuing campaign with its members and with finishers and dyers for improved quality.

A recently initiated project is the publication of the *TDA News* to keep members informed of the work of the organization and to pass along pertinent industry information as it comes up.

All this, plus Coffee Workshops for the exchange of information and the discussion of problems, plus social events such as an annual dinner dance and a golf convention, make participation in the work of the Textile Distributors Association highly worthwhile for its members.

This point is proved by the active participation of key figures from the industry in the work of TDA. It is, in fact, the involvement of these people that has made the association so successful and so important to the textile industry as a whole.

As one TDA member remarked, "Considering the fact that these are extremely busy executives, in many cases the top people of their respective companies, it is quite remarkable that they have shown sufficient interest to give so liberally of their time."

Chapter Twelve

The Retailer Is The Boss

OVERVIEW

By Jane Towler Smiley

The thread is long between that which nature nurtures and/or man formulates and the ultimate consumer. A majority of fiber eventually finds its way to and through the retail store. Preceding chapters have delineated the manufacturing process, but the penultimate customer is described as the "Boss". Why Boss? and who is this Boss?

We wear clothes, we sleep on sheets, we sit on fabric covered seats, our floors are carpeted, windows curtained; in effect, we are surrounded by products from the textile world. We buy them from a middle man, the Boss, the retailer.

The retailer is the boss because he has access to the market. The ability to select or reject is a powerful position, and the department, specialty or chain store, or catalog buyer is a very important key to any product manufactured for a consumer. The retailer is important as a means of getting exposure to the market, of promoting the product directly where response produces sales, of reaching the ultimate customer.

Like every multi-leveled market, retail distribution forms the same pyramidal shape. However, it is often size which controls the pyramid today, not always leadership, which influences the movement of ideas and products through the pyramid. Traditional thinking dictates that one must sell to the most influential people, the people in the know, and as a result, other people, the masses, will follow to insure success on all levels. This chain originated with the king, spread down to the court, to the burghers, and to the peasants. The concept of providing goods in quantity for the masses was a slowly evolving process which had its beginnings in the 1800's when the industrial revolution was just getting underway. Verbal communication did not instantly spread the word that "sleeves were puffed" and feet were showing under "scandalous" ankle-length hems. However, even with mass production of ready-to-wear and household products, which brought about the formation of a new system of marketing in the retail department store, the "follow-the-leader" marketing pattern prevailed until the 1960's—and is by no means totally dead.

As the middle class developed, and a rich bourgeoisie had access to the leading apparel designers; i.e., Poiret, Vionnet, Patou in France primarily during the early 1900's; Mainbocher, Schiaparelli, Chanel, etc., in the 30's; Dior, Balenciaga, Jacques Fath, etc., in the 50's; the copy-cat concept of buying was maintained in a strict pyramid. The retail outlets maintained a socio-economic structure as rigid as the designers. Couture clothes were sold at Bergdorf Goodman, Bonwit Teller, Saks Fifth Avenue, Neiman-Marcus, I. Magnin, Bullocks, Wilshire, and other very fine smaller specialty stores. Designers had access to the maximum number of wealthy customers through these fine key stores, and the ruboff of this elite clientele brought in the more average customers for the same retail label and taste level, if not for the same designer names.

Department stores did not have the same entre to the top French designers before the 1940's, and so the American designer was developed and became an established entity during World War II when retailers did not go to Europe to buy. Among the originals were Valentina, Hattie Carnegie, Charles James and Norman Norell of the very expensive names. But it was sportswear and casual clothes that developed as truly American products. Claire McCardell, Tom Brigance, Bonnie Cashin, Carolyn Schnurer, Jantzen, Rose Marie Reid, Cole of California and many others led the way. Specialty stores bought these lines, but department stores really could sell these more moderately priced clothes in quantity. Occasionally, a key retailer would introduce an idea to a manufacturer for a shop or fabric promotion, and set off a successful chain reaction. (Mary Lewis is a name in fashion history identified with such trend setting ideas.)

Following World War II, department stores began to attend the couture market for the sole reason of copying. They pay a stiff fee for permission to attend openings, and may bring garments or toiles back in bond, to copy and then return to the country of origin. Many stores do not buy originals outright as the duty to be paid to the U.S. Customs is high and makes the retail price prohibitive to all but a few customers. The department store works with its big manufacturers to reproduce an original exactly, or to copy it in another fabric, or to interpret various details; a shoulder, a collar, a skirt line—one outfit may be the inspiration for a dozen designs. Thus retailers have given the designer access to many customers through the purchasing of a few originals for the very top level, through copying exactly at a medium price, and influencing an entire market at any number of other levels, down to the broadest based chains.

European designers provide what amounts to a design laboratory for the world, but the price paid for originals hardly can pay to maintain these famous establishments. Hence the licensing of products, and the development of "pret-a-porte" or ready-to-wear lines. This has brought good design down to the pocketbook of most everyone.

The 1960's saw an inversion of the pyramid in terms of influence, and a social phenomena rearranged the flow of ideas from bottom to top. Fashion started to come from the street—Elvis Presley, the Beatles, Courreges, Cardin, the motorcyclists, the WAR—the world rebelled, fashion tumbled, and denim became king. TV reporters broadcast the news before it had time to be digested, and the fashion manufacturers and retail stores were hard pressed to follow—the youth market led. The establishment was in theory overturned, and in reality a long period of reappraisal shook the tenets of marketing. The retailer was the boss, but the customer was telling him "no" too often—the stability of continuity disappeared, ethnic was everything, and every season provided a new story. Although the turmoil of the 60's subsided, the 70's provided individualism, me-ism, and a personal search for identity. As personal income rose, people began bedecking themselves with initials, other peoples, to insure the fact that their friends and associates were aware that they had money to spend, and were in the know. "They" had arrived. Pucci, Cardin and other European designers started the trend and the department store spread this new status marked merchandise throughout the world. One may not be able to afford a St. Laurent, Givenchy or Dior original but the initials abound on ready-to-wear products, fragrances, and decorative home furnishings and fabrics. However, designer name or not, if the product is not salable, that name (or item from a line) is denied access to the market.

Much of the foregoing pertains to specialty and department stores in which the buyers have some first hand acquaintances with their customers. Large chains such as Sears, Penney, K mart, and catalog operations must access their markets more conservatively than other types of retailers. The commitment made for a dress cutting ticket or a set of sheets is so large that errors are very costly. The turn of merchandise is slower so profits must come from a shorter mark-up and fewer mark-downs. As the ordering is so far from time of delivery, much of the excitement of fashion and "hot items" does not exist. The customer is looking for value, not assortment.

Mills working with manufacturers who supply large retail and catalog operations will have a steady flow of stable goods with limited patterns and colors.

This is the broad base of the pyramid which is not affected somehow by the vagaries of the fashion world, but which is sensitive to the economy. Products must be thoroughly tested, and prices honed to specification. The retailer is boss, and his input to the manufacturer and the mill is deeper than that in the fashion world. As in our total pyramid, it is access to the customer that makes him boss.

53. A NEW DIRECTION IN RETAILING: THE SHOPPING MALL*

By Julia Morse, Consultant

A gigantic shopping complex—the Mall—is a major phenomenon not only as the new direction in retailing, but also in its sociological effects on American life. It is a shopping center plus—banks, schools, restaurants, post office, entertainment. It provides controlled environment shopping. It influences and is influenced by the energy crisis.

Take Watergate Mall in the District of Columbia. Like the Prudential complex in Boston of dwellings, office buildings, and retail stores, Watergate is an urban Mall providing concentrated shopping at the high and medium price levels, including such exclusive shops as Rive Gauche and Mark Cross as well as the expected supermarkets and drug chains.

In the development studied in this Washington area, Mall size ranged from units of 100 to 350 stores. Generally, the Mall is directed to shoppers in a broad, medium income range but recently new small Malls are being constructed, aimed at high income shoppers.

Sears Roebuck has a unit in every Mall in the area visited. In 1973, it is estimated that Sears, Ward and J. C. Penney will have built 23 million square feet of new space throughout the country. New store construction, exclusive of department stores, is reported at $488 billion for 1973.

An indication of the new direction in Mall development was provided by a real estate developer from Kansas City. In conversation, he outlined his plans for building a 310-acre development near Kansas City—where the

---

*The essentials of this article appeared originally as a December 1973 report to the Board of Directors of Chirurg and Cairns, Inc. The report was based on a November 1973 study of shopping malls in the District of Columbia and Fairfax County, Virginia. It is precisely this kind of qualitative information which all textile marketers should possess about the trends and directions in the retail segment of their industry

The article subsequently appeared in the April 1974 issue of the *Textile Marketing Letter.*

Mall concept was originated—building condominium homes simultaneously with retail stores and supermarkets, as well as schools, churches, theatres and a post office.

Sociological Aspects. With Malls creating new living styles, some characteristic urban problems are moving to the Mall.

SECURITY: Juvenile delinquency and shoplifting flourish where people and goods are concentrated. Mall condominiums and retail stores are compelled to cope with the problems.

ENERGY CRISIS: With curtailment of electricity and heating oil, stores are planning more holiday closings, few night openings, less heating and less air-conditioning. The assumption is that customers will adapt their planning to the new opening schedules and that possible loss of business will be offset by economies in operation.

ENTERTAINMENT: The appearance of a new aspect of merchandising—large Malls have "theatre marquees" at the entrance, announcing photographic exhibits, sports events and merchandise classes.

Merchandising Techniques. All price lines are now dominated by the same sales practices.

COORDINATION: With apparel lines tending toward fashion uniformity, sales are best with fully coordinated lines, displayed to sell the customer visually, aided by minimum, but adequate, personal service. Confinement of lines is giving way to this type of coordinated selling. Successful lines such as Blassport and Anne Klein, in the higher price ranges, and Act III, moderately priced, are featured by competing stores. The same coordination/display techniques work for all price lines.

In at-home apparel and lingerie, coordination also makes the sale. Van Raalte and Vanity Fair lines are seen in all lingerie departments. Bikini-and-bra coordinates are purchased by youth as swimwear, taking swimwear business away from the swim department. Spontaneous merchandising results from the initiative of young customers.

DISPLAY: While Malls tend to create a monotony of uniformity, they also provide good visual display opportunities for manufacturers, with more space for effective display than downtown stores. The best displayed lines sell the best. Quality advantages—real ones—can be stressed at the point of sale. Functional advantages—as with housewares—can be stressed by demonstration or counter activity.

Best displayed merchandise are housewares, china and coordinated bed linens; least imaginative displays noted were in small leather goods. The cosmetics department consistently is given preferred store space, immediately inside the main entrance, with Revlon up front, the first view of the entering shopper.

SALES TRAINING: Mall sales personnel were observed as better informed, more courteous and more attractive than in downtown stores. Time did not permit sales training techniques to be explored. A report, however, was heard that the success of Sears is attributed in large part to sales personnel incentive planning.

DISTRIBUTION: This major retail operation, impersonalized since the suburban shopping center years, is now expedited by computer techniques. A problem in this field referred to by Lord & Taylor has an application to International Silver or Lenox: the necessity of merchandise coverage in all branches of the patterns selected by a bride through the bridal registry of one unit, assuming availability in whatever branch or suburban store friends and relatives may shop. Uniformity, a characteristic of Mall merchandising, inevitably is governed by the requirements of computerized distribution.

The Obsolescence of Quality. Quality in the old familiar "Tiffany" concept is outmoded, so even is the word "quality." Since the concept of quality has a strong hold on retail tradition in America, it is not likely to totally disappear. But it requires redefinition.

The May Co. offers red acrylic knit suits priced at $49.95. This is "quality" to the government clerk, whether she be black or white, to whom it represents high fashion. At Garfinckel's in the same Mall, the concept "elite" serves better. Even *The New Yorker* has dropped the word "quality" from its new market study.

Mall stores are attractive, contrary to the negative impression of "asphalt jungles" suggested by *Women's Wear Daily* and *Advertising Age*. The design is pleasingly open and modern, not unlike Bloomingdale's in Chestnut Hill. The middle price Hecht Company store is distinguished by enormous Williamsburg type crystal chandeliers, making it much more attractive than Lord & Taylor's, Chevy Chase.

The simplicity of Mall store design generally is downgraded on floors displaying apparel and textiles. In the apparel divisions of The May Co. stores, the impression given by the look—and feel—of the fabrics is unappealing. A store cannot look much better than the wares it offers for sale.

The quality concept is injured by uniformity. All income levels shop in Malls, with the possible exception of the upper one percent. In the parking areas adjoining Garfinckel or Woodward & Lothrop the shoppers look no different from the customers of Saks or Lord & Taylor in the Westchester suburbs.

Another innovation in retailing is catalog shopping, with the customer purchasing the catalog in advance. Individualistic, wealthy consumers are bypassing shopping to a noteworthy extent to make their selections from catalogs of such stores as Kenton, Bergdorf, Neiman-Marcus and Gucci. *Harpers Bazaar* reports 22,000 requests to the magazine for catalogs priced at $1.00 or higher, with the Gucci catalog selling at $5.00 having the most outstanding response. The rise in prepaid catalog selling is an event in retailing.

Reappraisal of Youth. Youth is again viewed as an important marketing target. While the pendulum has swung and youth is no longer everything, new ways are developing of working ·with high school and college students. Stores are consulting with schools and colleges; teachers now confer with stores; stores are now conducting merchandising classes. College Boards are a thing of the past, with Teen Boards de-emphasized. The impression conveyed by stores is that new approaches of marketing to youth are being sought, with the emphasis on "serious" rather than "fun."

Some Conclusions. When there is interrelationship between advertising agency and client in merchandising at point of sale, the advertising has greater force.

Many of the traditional concepts of retailing—brand loyalty, quality standards, price resistance—have lost their significance, giving way to pressures created by bigness, by dispersal of population, and by new life styles.

Even the meaning of point-of-sales merchandising has changed. Once referring to the selling floor or counter, today it can mean a page in a catalog, selling by events in the store's auditorium, or by a class in the local high school.

Today, store display is less a matter of counter cards and more a matter of utilizing the store as a background for design strength or a sales message.

In creating advertising and marketing plans for clients, awareness on the part of the Agency of the new trends in retailing and the changing attitudes of the consumer should be an asset.

54. THE CHANGING RETAIL SCENE*

By Robbie Bishop, Celanese Marketing Company

For the past year or two, everybody has told me our industry was in a state of confusion, but nobody could tell me why, so I did an extensive study on merchandising and marketing at the retail level because consumer and retail activities dramatically affect every phase of the textile industry. And yes...there has been CONFUSION.

Why? We've had rapid change in the last several decades which made it difficult to get a fix on the future...so today's consumer is difficult to forecast.

Only within the past six years or so have there been any serious attempts made to develop social indicators, and you can't predict consumer

---

*This is a somewhat condensed version of a slide film address given by Ms. Robbie Bishop, Retail Marketing Manager of the Celanese Marketing Company before the Fashion Group of Boston on March 31, 1977. There can be no question whatever that cutters, mills and fiber producers will all be profoundly affected by the changes in retail merchandising practices which Ms. Bishop describes.

This article subsequently appeared in the May 1977 issue of the *Textile Marketing Letter*.

attitudes or fashion preferences on measurements in the areas of demographics and economics.

Last year, a research and marketing vice president said it was apparent that our ability to predict lifestyles and social values was contingent to a large extent on our ability to predict social, economic, technological and political forecasts along side each other, each of them being affected by and influencing the other. The vice president stated they should not be observed independently. So with economic conditions uncertain to the consumer, with breakthroughs unforseeable in areas of technology and the international situation so volatile, how can we have confidence in our ability to do social forecasting on any long-term basis?

If we are unable to accurately predict, then it is no wonder retailers have been groping for answers and ways of effective merchandising.

They have, however, made tremendous strides. The word "lifestyle" started a whole new way of thinking and everybody in the industry latched on to it. Most retailers say they are merchandising to LIFESTYLE.

I won't go into interpretations of lifestyle here, but I can tell you if you ask 50 different people what lifestyle is, you will get 50 different answers. I know, because I did.

But aside from lifestyle, most retailers are now CLASSIFYING THEIR CUSTOMERS.

Some stores say they have two types of customers, some say three, and some say four, but, generally speaking, they are merchandising to three groups—traditional, updated and contemporary. However, the word "contemporary" is now often referred to as advanced or directional. I will give you the retailers' description of the three goups:

TRADITIONAL: The conventional person who wants the understated look—not adventurous in style—buys apparel that doesn't go out of style...establishment.

UPDATED: Goes along with trends but does not want extremes... traditional with a new flair.

CONTEMPORARY: Trend-setter, avant-garde...first to try newest ...wants something different from the masses.

Though the merchandise in many departments relates specifically to one of these customer types, you will also find departments where there is a mixture of the three. As of today, approximately 75 percent of the merchandise in stores is traditional, 15 to 20 percent is updated, and between 5 and 10 percent is contemporary. However, it is the general consensus of retailers that the updated departments have the greatest growth potential.

Merchandise Presentation. Now let's talk about merchandise presentation which retailers are proving is all-important.

Back in the days when more Americans walked, the window display was a big thing. They were "a mirror of the store." After World War II, the window spectacular was gone because of shortages of basic items.

In the Sixties, concentration began on the store's interior. And today, everybody is busy re-doing those interiors. Racks and displays that used to be so high they obstructed the customers' view are no longer prevalent. Remodeled departments are now very open. Merchandise presentation is a growing art and high salaried experts have been hired to project merchandise in an effective and exciting manner. In interiors, there is new fixturing—quad racks and front hanging fixtures so you no longer see a thousand sleeves and shoulders but a visual spectrum of color and lighting—and a grouping of various items in one department for convenience (dresses, sportswear, accessories, etc.).

I'm sure merchandise presentation will be the key for some years to come.

This is where retailing is today. So, are retailers merchandising to lifestyle, to attitude, to customer type, or to customer convenience?

The word "lifestyle" was the catalyst and a great word to initiate change but I would like to obsolete the word right now because it's too nebulous as it relates to merchandising. As one retailer said, "Lifestyle is the way in which one lives one's own life and if a store really merchandised to lifestyle, it would have to be a thousand times bigger than the Boston Common and have a million departments. It's impossible to refine the many lifestyles that exist and I don't think you can look at any department in a store and distinguish its lifestyle. Look, assortment, and convenience —yes—but not lifestyle."

In my opinion, retailers are merchandising to looks and/or customer convenience. So I repeat, drop the word lifestyle, except in its true meaning; it has served its purpose for merchandising. Some people will not agree with me because it has been a "magic" word that sparked all kinds of imagination. I think in time, however, they will find another word. Now let's take a look at THE FUTURE.

The Future. There will be many factors that affect merchandising and marketing but I will use just the four mentioned by the research and marketing vice president that I spoke of in the beginning and relate them to our industry.

DEPOLARIZATION OF THE SEXES. As male and female roles merge and change, merchandise and marketing will be affected. Careers, activities, interests, finances—to name a few—will come closer together and will influence future products and shopping habits.

PLURALISTIC LIFESTYLES. Latest research conducted by Gilbert Youth Research shows that over half of today's 14 to 25 year olds consider the "opportunity to develop as an individual" life's most important goal. This will result in a multiplicity of principles, of interests and of various "groups" operating autonomously, which will increase customer types.

CONFIDENCE IN INSTITUTIONS. The Harris polls conducted during 1966-1974 show confidence has declined in major companies, 34 percent; in colleges, 21 percent; in the Executive Branch of the Government, 13 percent; and in the press, four percent. This means we must rebuild consumer confidence.

ENVIRONMENT AND NATURAL RESOURCES. People *are* concerned—with energy, pollution, food, etc.—and this is certainly going to affect products and marketing. Groups have been formed whose objectives are to reduce meat consumption in order to save grain. Will groups form that will reduce the use of the merchandise we sell?

What I'm really saying is: All phases of industry are faced with a CHALLENGE. A challenge to help our industry, and a challenge to get ahead of consumer attitudes which have actually been ahead of us for quite awhile.

We should:

REACT IMMEDIATELY TO WARNING SIGNALS. When a product is "hot" everybody jumps on the bandwagon and gluts the market. I believe in jumping on the bandwagon, but this in itself is a warning signal, a warning for communication within our industry—fiber firms, mills, manufacturers, retailers—everybody talking to each other to generate new ideas, or we lose consumer interest.

LOOK FOR AND LATCH ON TO NEGLECTED AREAS. A good example of this is the half-size or large-size market, which has been neglected since Adam and Eve. Anybody who concentrates on this hungry consumer can make anything but money.

ADJUST PROMOTIONS AND ADVERTISING TO CONSUMER HABITS OR CHANGES. How can we do this when we don't know enough about today's consumer? We can put some efforts into research and marketing and find out.

ESTABLISH THE UNITED STATES AS THE FASHION CAPITAL OF THE WORLD. Every country in the world designs for the American consumer, so why shouldn't we be the fashion leaders and form a "World Fashion Congress," a la the United Nations. It could be done and it could well increase our country's prestige and improve our balance of payments.

In conclusion, I'm sure there are many remedies but communication within the industry and catching up with the consumer will be a healthy shot in the arm.

55. RETAILING TO QUALITY MARKETS: A WARNING FOR TEXTILE MARKETERS*

By Jane Towler Smiley, Burdine's

Down through the years there have been revolts of the masses. Currently, we seem to be building up to a revolt of the classes. Little inklings keep showing up in reports from all over.

"There's a consumers' revolt against gigantism, whether it's in shopping centers or anything else in American life...the novelty of

---

*This article first appeared in the November 1973 issue of the *Textile Marketing Letter*.

shopping centers has worn thin...(they're) sick and tired (of)...fighting traffic jams, crowds, and not being able to find what they wanted in these shopping centers, with service generally lousy." So says Leonard Himmel, co-owner of The Opulent Female store in Huntington, L.I. (*WWD* 9/11/73).

Quotations from other store owners indicate that the selective customer has really had it with gigantic stores and shopping centers, except on special occasions. E. B. Weiss of Doyle, Dane, Bernbach referring to why the department store may disappear says, "Affluent shoppers—especially the nouveaux riches—tend to prefer not to rub shoulders with their less fortunate brethren. Call it snobbery, which it is—but it is also a realistic appraisal." He goes on to say, "The potent young customer exercising individual taste simply cannot be catered to in gigantic units. The image of the giant store inevitably reflects the masses. The image of the specialty store reflects the individual." (*Stores*, May 1971).

"Suburban schlock; stores sitting in endless seas of asphalt out in some vast nowhereland; quagmires of garish signs; Roy Rogers and Jr. Hot Shoppes...parking lots jammed with cruiser-sized stationwagons; middle-aged hausfraus in curlers—that's what shopping centers mean to some," Laura Longley Babb (*Washingtonian Magazine*, Summer 1973).

More and more companies are reaching for larger volume, which presupposes greater profits, but the study which *Fortune Magazine* did recently of the 500 largest corporations vs. the second 500 indicated that a greater number of the smaller ones showed a better profit picture. Bigness does not necessarily mean efficiency. We have learned through the homogenization of retailing that quality suffers when controls are spread throughout a chain and the supervision of the creative merchants and tastemakers is diluted. Our current retail princes have come not from frogs, but from bulls or bears, or legal eagles.

Eagerness to keep abreast of our supposed burgeoning population and its forthcoming need for places to shop has caused real estate operators to grab land and builders to pre-plan shopping centers for the future. Over-development may lead us to being over-stored. The cost of maintaining these excess operations and the building of too many competitive malls may tend to cause a high percentage of failures. Howard Goldfeder, president of Bullock's, recently stated in regard to retail expansion in southern California: "The square footage of these stores will have grown about four times faster than the population. I know what the retailers are going to have to do; they are going to have to start 'retailing'—running stores, not just building them. Important growth will have to come from existing stores." (*WWD* 11/10/72). Yet the *Department Store Guide* and *Sheldon's Retail Directory* both indicate a small step backward in number of stores each year. In 1972 and 1973 they have added 79 new stores and deleted 200. This means that, along with increased population, more people are shopping in each existing store. Many of the stores which have closed are in downtown areas which are being abandoned or they are older suburban stores which are forced out of business by the large centers.

What does this have to do with you and me? I suggest that it signifies two trends in marketing which will bear upon our future planning. The continuation of mass merchandising is certain and large corporations, to say nothing of the government, will provide the quantitative factor for the computers to direct the planning of these companies. The other area, far more elusive, is the assessment of quality: what it is, where it is, and how important it is in today's mode of life.

In the tiny world of *The New Yorker* Magazine (circ. 480,000) and similar operations, their markets are the affluent consumers who seek the smaller stores, the quality centers; in places like the New Canaan and Beverly Hills Malls and the Somerset Mall in Troy, Michigan, to name a few.

Where are these stores? This is what *The New Yorker's* retail consultant has been engaged in discovering since 1926. Strange as it may seem, the business heads of the magazine recognized many years ago a need for knowing where the selective markets were. They hired a woman to criss-cross the country to study them, starting in their second year of business, even though the magazine was then strictly a local, New York-oriented publication with a tiny circulation. Without today's airline network, it was a far more arduous job to travel to the major cities but, over a period of time, 60 markets were analyzed. Once the Retail Consultant had arrived on the scene, a bit of footwork did the rest. Suburbs were few and the bulk of the better stores were generally located together so that an appraisal could be made quite readily through personal visits.

In 1932 *The New Yorker* issued its first market book entitled *The 41 Primary Trade Areas—The Gateways to the National Market*. The 60 cities were refined and, along with some census figures of 1930 and other qualitative indices including the ranking of stores, this book rapidly established *The New Yorker* as a leading source of research material for manufacturers of premium merchandise. Small or large, seldom has any company had one person travel to all its major markets to obtain a total picture of its prospects. A series of women have shopped the U.S. over a period of 45 years. Their mission was, and is, solely to ascertain the nature of the major markets and to classify the stores within them as to their ability to sell various types and price levels of merchandise. With the advent of the jet, many people are now fairly familiar with the major cities, yet few really can offer comprehensive understanding of the quality aspects of the whole U.S. *The New Yorker* consultants have been invaluable in initiating the target market and store lists for many new manufacturers and for those who are seeking secondary levels of distributions.

Today, probably the most important indicator of the quality of a market is the nature of its stores. One can be pretty sure that if a Saks Fifth Avenue is located in an area there is a solid gold foundation under it. Former indices of quality, such as automobiles, may be changing their status. High family incomes, although an excellent index, do not always reflect taste. Retailers, with their flexibility and endless resources, can reflect customers' needs and desires as well as influence them. The sure sign of the deterioration of a market is the change in merchandising approach of its stores, or their removal to other locations. Recent trips around the country to look at new shopping centers only affirm the fact that it is difficult to maintain the unique assets of quality when too many fingers are in the pie. Miles of driving through suburbs testify to the destruction of our land by cement and to a way of life that, money or no money, is rapidly disappearing with the disappearance of servants. Many fine shops are hidden in side streets and by-ways, often hard to find—but therein lies much of the pleasure and fun in shopping.

In this fast food world of worn-out denims—over-stored and over-statused—there seems to be a strong current toward a new conservatism... a trend to structure, formality, manners. Apparel for Fall 1973 started pushing the refined, luxurious look of suits and formal day-wear, as well as bared evening clothes. Glittered and furred, not at-home-entertaining clothes, but go-out-dancing attire. Tweeds, grey flannel, plaids—less noisy, not I-am-me-who-am-I? clothes. Not mass produced but for a choice few—to be found in special stores. A change in attitude toward clothes indicates a change in lifestyle which will tend to change the look of stores. Everyone is out watching: press, manufacturers, stores, customers. All are pushing and pulling. It is time for something to happen—something to make the customer come into the store. Are you contributing to that something?

The New Yorker has always believed that the discriminating reader is a discriminating shopper and has maintained its quality marketing service to help its advertisers and other friends. If you would like to know more about selling to the fine stores in the U.S., we would be pleased to help you.

Chapter Thirteen

Case Histories

OVERVIEW

By Nancy C. Boiter

A *Handbook of Textile Marketing* simply wouldn't be complete without looking at the stories of some of the companies and events that lead the way in the marketing of textiles. These are case stories and histories chosen to highlight examples of effective marketing. During the years of the *Textile Marketing Letter* dozens of case histories have appeared which told of dramatic turn-arounds, courageous decisions, simple but powerful advertising campaigns, and the agonies of the firms who failed to adapt and went under. So, choosing those cases that *best* "illustrate" textile marketing is almost an impossibility. Let's just say that herein are found some stories that point out ideas that worked and some that didn't. And, while these histories are mainly about "companies" we should keep in mind the people behind the ideas and decisions...for these men and women who carried through with these ideas are not only *Homo sapiens* but also *Homo faber*, the maker, the doer. We can be thankful they were active, not passive, creative, not idle, and ever-changing in their quests to improve their businesses.

A business name long known for its importance in the industry is that of Burlington. In "Burlington's Marketing Philosophy: One Name, One Trademark, For All Products" we are shown the real advantages of a basic marketing strategy designed to develop a consumer franchise by only advertising under "one name." Burlington's success is analyzed via this philosophy of marketing under (for example) the Burlington House trademark and name as opposed to fragmented lesser brand names. While Burlington has widely known sub-brand names, its basic strategy has long been to rely on one major trademark and name...*Burlington!*

No textile marketing book would be complete without the mention of Elliott White Springs' famous 1950's ad for his sheets... "A Buck Well Spent on a Springmaid Sheet," and its effectiveness is shown to be still intact in "How Springs Has Updated Its Marketing Strategy." From the days of this ad to the present, Spring Mills has concentrated on organizing itself for a marketing orientation. This case looks at an overall picture of how Springs has adapted its marketing strategies to suit the company, its customers, and environment. In fact, Springs is not one to miss the potential in keeping an eye on what will help sell its goods. For Elliott White Springs' old ad proved so popular that it was recently updated and reused to read: "This buck may look more like 47 cents... which is what *most* bucks are worth these days. But not this 'deerslayer.' Any buck spent on a SPRINGMAID sheet gets you value of 100 cents on the dollar—as any two smart squaws know."

Springs' marketing strategies are further explained in "How Springs Markets Its Apparel Fabrics." Specifically this article points out that Springs has evolved to this concept: "Since everything sold by the Apparel Fabrics Division gets cut and made into an end product by somebody else, the basic strategy revolves around careful selection of *who* that somebody is! Over the years Springs has concentrated mainly on a broad group of customers who are staple houses (as opposed to fashion houses). Hence, Springs has now essentially a high volume, relatively staple business characterized by one Springs marketing executive as "aggressively seeking converting situations with the criterion that it meet a customer need while representing a profit opportunity."

A logical follow-up to the Spring case is "What Makes a Consumer Buy?" This article presents a practical summary of research on *what* purchase decisions apparel consumers make. Several thought provoking ideas are offered on rethinking: price, quality, color, style, care labels, material, and desirable, as well as undesirable, characteristics of apparels.

In "Dan River Does It Again" a classic marketing story is analyzed. In 1947 Dan River introduced its first all-cotton wrinkle resistant fabrics marketed under its registered trade name: "Wrinkl-Shed." "Wrinkl-Shed" was generally considered to be the first durable finish to achieve market success on a 100 percent cotton construction. These early triumphs eventually gave way to a chain of events leading up to Dan River's 1978 introduction of a whole new line of combed all-cotton shirting materials under the "Sanforset" label.

Along somewhat different lines is the success of Lowenstein in its first major consumer effort to acquaint the public with its fabrics in the early 1950's. "How Cutters' Fashions Sold Lowenstein Fabrics" points out how Lowenstein helped sell "color consciousness" to American consumers. Their basic approach was to use color presentations of cutters' garments in their advertising and to tie it into very active participation and promotion with garment manufacturers.

An unusual story, in that it shows how a small (by comparison to Springs, Dan River, et al.) company succeeded, is contained in "How One Small Blanket Mill Gets National Distribution." For the student and practitioner of textile marketing, this story should cause reconsideration of the importance of the "basics." This small mill used solid marketing techniques constrained by a limited budget. The keys to success were: concentration on a superior product, strong personal selling with national coverage, trade promotions to retailers and buying offices, good retail advertising and displays, and the education of salespeople by supplying all the selling points about each item in their line.

In "A Bigger Slice of a Bigger Pie" we see what approaches to take when the market for a firm's goods isn't as big as it has to be to keep operating at a profit... such a position has three likely choices: get out of the business entirely, break the market in the hopes of grabbing off a larger share, or take imaginative steps to *enlarge* the market. This story takes the third choice as we trace steps by which the total market for corduroys and velveteens was enlarged.

And finally, as we approach the 1980's and beyond, it might be wise to consider textile marketing and its relation to our basic armed services. "Military Textiles and the Energy Crunch" presents a very thought-provoking analysis of wartime demands for textile products. We see from this case that several potential problem areas face our preparedness: the energy crunch and petrochemical based products, dependence on imports, low profit margins, and a declining cotton-type fabrics industry segment (meeting military specifications).

These stories illustrate successes and failures. They are included as "think-type" teaching examples... designed to highlight key ideas, and designed to cause us to reflect back on: What does it take to succeed in textile marketing?

56. BURLINGTON'S MARKETING PHILOSOPHY: ONE NAME, ONE TRADEMARK, FOR ALL PRODUCTS*

By James C. Cumming, Consultant

If you've been in the habit of thinking that you had to have a different name for every product or new item in your line, it might be a good idea to have another look at the situation. Yes, General Motors has its different named and trademarked lines from Chevrolet to Cadillac, and even breaks down those lines into a number of confusing model names. But do you do the kind of promotion General Motors puts behind each of its individual

---

*This article first appeared in the February 1973 issue of the *Textile Marketing Letter*.

lines? And maybe even GM would be better off if a Buick could still just be a Buick instead of a Skylark or a Riviera or a Centurion or something else.

You'll have to admit that while Burlington Industries may not put the money into promotion that GM does, among textile firms it is still one of the biggest investors in advertising. And Jack Hanson, Burlington's advertising director, has given much hard and deep thought to this business of establishing a number of brand names in the mind of the consumer. His conclusion: forget it! Bring as many as possible into line under the Burlington name and the Burlington trademark.

You know as well as we do that Burlington has many good line names in its stable of products.

Consider Cameo hosiery, for example. Remember it? When the late Kenneth Collins directed Burlington's marketing policies he looked at all Burlington products and determined that Cameo hosiery was the company's one outstanding product on which a real consumer franchise could be built. Accordingly he put the lion's share of Burlington's promotional money behind Cameo.

Was this effort wasted? Not at all, for when management decided that Cameo hosiery should become exclusively Burlington hosiery, they engineered the change in such a way that the goodwill behind the old name carried over to the new. But change he did—to the point where a trade advertisement proclaimed simply: "Cameo (inscribed on a tombstone) Rest in Peace." Or, we might add, "Sic transit gloria mundi."

Occasionally the promotion of Burlington products is still being done under well-established former names, but in every case that former name is overshadowed by the name of Burlington. Two lines of men's socks, "Gold Cup" and "Top Brass," are examples. But "Glove" for furniture, "United" for furniture, and "Charm Tred Mills" have all been dropped in favor of the single name of "Burlington House." And new products, such as sheets, are being named simply Burlington without any confusing line names. So there are now Burlington House Carpets, area rugs, blankets and furniture as well as Burlington hosiery.

As for the "warp and woof" trademark—where Burlington goes the trademark goes. It's on everything from the letterhead to the lobby display in the company's new building, Burlington House, on New York's Avenue of the Americas; from the print advertising and television commercials to the product packaging.

It's obvious that by textile or any standards Burlington has a sizable advertising budget. It totals over $13 million, with about $3 million going for network and spot television, $4 million for magazine advertising, $1 million for newspaper promotion, $500 thousand for spot radio, $1.5 million for advertising to the trade in business papers, and the remainder for sales promotion. In other words, better than $10 million worth of advertising and promotion is directed toward building a Burlington consumer franchise, while the remainder of the advertising budget is devoted to cultivating the trade.

Is It Working? Surveys made at regular intervals since the present program started show that, with the general public, awareness of the Burlington name has risen from 40 to 74 percent. Among adults with incomes of $15,000 and over, who can be reasonably expected to do most of the buying at retail of Burlington products, awareness now stands at 87 percent.

If the single name marketing concept works so well from Burlington, shouldn't it work even better for you?

57. HOW SPRINGS HAS UPDATED ITS MARKETING STRATEGY*

By James C. Cumming, Consultant

Since the days in the early 1950's when Elliott White Springs was shaking up the textile industry with ads like the one about the buck well spent on a Springmaid sheet, a lot of progress has been made in Springs Mills' marketing. Which is only natural since the modern Springs is doing its marketing in many more areas.

Springs today is even in frozen foods, through its acquisition of Seabrook Foods, Inc. There's an International Division, too, and the Retail and Specialty Fabrics Division which sells woven and knitted fabrics for home sewing and specialty manufacturers under the Springmaid and Skinner brand names.

Every division is highly organized for marketing; each has a president who has risen to that position through sales and marketing. Each is based in New York, with responsibility for manufacturing as well as marketing, except for the Retail and Specialty Fabrics Division which is a converting operation with no manufacturing facilities of its own. It buys fabrics from many sources, including Spring's Apparel Fabrics and Knit Divisions.

There is much importance placed on Research and Development, too. The Apparel Fabrics, Consumer Products and Knit Divisions have full-time product development staffs based in New York and a corporate market research staff is based there also. Since 1927 Springs has also had a centralized R & D Department in a $3 million Center in Fort Mill. This department pursues profit-oriented applied textile research and assists the divisions in profitable product development.

But since we are interested here chiefly in domestic textiles, let's take a quick look at the way the modern Springs has reorganized for textile marketing in the U.S.A. In this field there are now four divisions.

The Apparel Fabrics Division markets woven goods for apparel and decorative home furnishings, all under the Springmaid trademark. The division has its own president and its own vice president for marketing. A vice president for merchandising and two sales vice presidents report to the

---

*This article first appeared in the April 1975 issue of the *Textile Marketing Letter.*

vice president-marketing. Then, as in all the other divisions, the division president reports to Peter C. Scotese, president* of the corporation.

The Consumer Products Division, selling sheets, pillowcases, towels, bedspreads and draperies under the Springmaid, Morgan Jones and Pequot brand names, has its own president and five vice presidents who concentrate on marketing. One of these guides sells to department stores. Working with him are six regional managers, supervising a sales force that calls on the stores.

This is important for virtually all the important retailers who sell Springmaid products. In New York, alone for example, Abraham & Strauss, Lord & Taylor, Bloomingdale's, Macy's, Gimbels and Bamberger's are all regarded as key accounts.

Another vice president of the division concentrates on selling to mass merchandisers under the Pequot trademark. These retailers include K mart, Two Guys and similar outlets, plus stamp and premium firms, and the military.

Sears, Montgomery Ward and J.C. Penney get special attention, too, all selling Springs merchandise under their own private brand labels. The importance of these private brands is shown by Department of Commerce figures for 1973. They show that Sears, Ward and Penney accounted for 25 percent of the total domestic market for sheets and pillowcases. The institutional market—hotels, motels, hospitals and such—accounted for 12 percent of the total volume, with sheets under manufacturers' brands making up the rest.

The entire market for the products of the Consumer Products Division amounts to $1.5 billion—a market well worth the effort involved in seeing that Springs gets its full share.

How does this division reach its retailers?

To begin with, there are three "market weeks" in the course of a year at which new lines are introduced and which must, of necessity, be attended by all major buyers and merchandising people. For these market weeks Springs currently prepares "collections"—specially coordinated groupings of sheets, cases, quilted bedspreads and towels around which good retail promotions can be organized. A collection designed by Bill Blass, for example, was presented at one February show. As usual, the buyers flooded in and the buyers bought.

But the object of Springs' marketing is not just to sell to the retailers. It's to help the retailers sell to *their* customers. To do this, Springs gives its retailers "Buyers' Kits" which contain ideas for displaying the collection; layouts and copy for advertising them locally; preproduction of Springs' own advertising campaign on the collections; publicity releases; and a "Fashion Newsletter" described as "A Guide to Merchandising Bed Fashions." This is full of ideas and suggestions to buyers for displaying and selling the Bill Blass collections.

---

*The current (1981) president of Springs Mills is Walter Y. Elisha.

One suggestion, for example, is on merchandising to specific markets. "It is important to bed fashions," says the newsletter, "to zero in on various market segments with a direct sales appeal." Then come specific suggestions for appealing to the men's market, apartment living, college freshmen, and young career women.

In addition, during market week, Springs stages a press party to review the new lines with representatives of the trade and consumer press. A result of the press party one year was a feature article in the "Talk of the Town" section of *The New Yorker* and a story on the Bill Blass collection by Eugenia Sheppard in her "Inside Fashion" column which appears in about 100 major newspapers across the country.

Market week, however, is just the beginning. When it's over, the retailers are followed up directly by the Springs salesmen. Also, in addition to supplying the stores with the ideas for advertising and display, Springs helps with cash on the barrel head in the form of annual contracts for cooperative advertising. Springs pays two-thirds and the retailer one-third. And Springs' own advertising reaches consumers directly through inserts in *The New York Times Magazine* and single pages in other appropriate publications.

It should be noted, too, that the impudent sparks that were fanned at Springs Mills by Elliott White Springs are still very much alive in the present marketing organization. Only recently the "Buck Well Spent" advertisement was updated and reused.

"This buck," it said, "may look more like 47 cents—which is what *most* bucks are worth these days. But not this 'deerslayer.' Any buck spent on a SPRINGMAID sheet gets you value of 100 cents on the dollar—as any two smart squaws know."

58. HOW SPRINGS MARKETS ITS APPAREL FABRICS*

By James C. Cumming, Consultant

In the April 1975 issue of the *Textile Marketing Letter* we presented a general overview of how much the modern Springs Mills has updated its marketing strategy. In that article we touched on the Apparel Fabrics Division because of its importance in the total Springs Mills picture. But we concentrated our attention on the Consumer Products Division, with its sales of sheets, pillowcases, towels, draperies and quilted bedspreads, all end products.

Now let's have a look at the way Springs markets ingredient products —woven fabrics—to the apparel industry.

---

*This article first appeared in the December 1975 issue of the *Textile Marketing Letter*.

The division is headed by its own president, James P. Kelley,* with the heads of manufacturing, marketing, financial and product development sections all reporting to him. Marketing, for example, is headed by Edward P. Harding,* although all sections contribute importantly to the marketing function.

Since everything sold by the Apparel Fabrics Division gets cut and made into an end product by somebody else, the basic strategy revolves around careful selection of who that somebody else is. Garment manufacturers make up approximately 80 percent of the market, with the remainder of both printed and plain fabrics going to the decorative market, including curtains and bedspreads.

Four Marketing Objectives. In addition to home furnishings, where Springs' objective obviously is to get its share of the potential volume, the apparel markets are broken down into four major objectives:

1. Men's shirts and sportswear. Industrial uniforms and the industrial laundry trade are included in this category.

2. Women's sportswear.

3. Children's wear.

4. Sleepwear and lingerie.

Within these groups Springs sets important standards. They don't want to be dependent on a single customer or a single outlet for too large a portion of the total volume. Consequently, a broad group of customers has been developed, selected largely on the basis of whether each is a staple house or a fashion house.

Springs is an essentially high-volume, relatively staple business. At the same time they probably run as many dobby looms as anybody in the industry and they do a substantial amount of in-house printing. The policy is to walk a chalk line, emphasizing flexibility within practical cost limits. "We don't jump on whims from texturing to tufting," says Ed Harding, "but we do our level best to stay technically innovative."

Product Development. Meanwhile, to complement any specific line, Springs aggressively seeks converting situations with the criterion that it meet a customer need while representing a profit opportunity. A typical example is a range of yarn-dyed and/or box-loom styles run for the sportswear trade.

This is where product development contributes so importantly to the marketing function at Springs.

We hardly need to point out that to reach the children's wear and

---

*The current (1981) president of the Consumer Products Division is Edward
P. Harding and Murphy L. Fontenot is the head of the Marketing Department.

sleepwear markets in recent years, the most important requirement has been flame-resistant fabrics. In this area Springs has pioneered and may safely lay claim to developing the first truly marketable flame-resistant fabric, which was named "FireFoe." This is produced in plain, printed and napped styles and has been received enthusiastically by these two large-volume sections of the apparel market.

In promoting to its target markets, Springs uses all the appropriate tools of sales promotion.

The Advertising Strategy. Advertising is concentrated on reaching manufacturers through the trade press. Such media as *Women's Wear Daily, Daily News Record* and *California Apparel News* are used to reach the market horizontally, supplemented by *Earnshaw's Clothes, Men's Wear* and similar publications that concentrate vertically on specific sections of the market. The messages are of first importance.

To blouse manufacturers, for example:

Gunga Din is fabric news.

You can make it fashion news.

Natural. Gentle. Totally at ease. Crinkle gauze. Perfect for the soft clothes, the free clothes, all the tender new blouses and floats for the summer of '76. Gunga Din...50 percent polyester and 50 percent cotton in true cotton colors: natural, of course. A wide range of solids from very pale to very dark, plus wide and skinny strip combinations done in powdery, muted colors. A variation of the theme: Lost Gauze...a thin, plain gauze in natural.

Or this message to sleepwear manufacturers:

FireFoe prints are fabric news.

You can make them fashion news.

These are the sleepwear prints kids will love because they practically tell a bedtime story all on their own. They're Puffin 100 percent Kodel polyester batiste coordinates that you can mix and match two and even three ways. There's a "Little Engine That Can" surrounded by flowers. Then there's the "Cow with the Crumpled Horn" in a barnyard story. There's even a "Just-So-story" with a dear little elephant that's all dotted and striped. And each one has coordinates especially designed to work with it. Puffin...in solids, prints and a new diamond check. But that's not Enuffin. Enuffin's our embossed batiste in solids, prints and seersucker. And this season we're introducing a yarn-dyed gingham check that mixes and matches with all our prints and plains. Springmaid FireFoe flame-resistant fabrics.

We could go on and on, but these two advertisements will give you the idea—a good basic theme with strong, playful, interesting, factual and readable copy.

Furthermore, Springs' advertising is supplemented by fiber suppliers such as Eastman, FMC and Celanese who coordinate their promotional programs to achieve continuous visibility for Springs fabrics in the trade press.

Other Promotional Tools. Fashion Shows, also directed at the trade, while not a regular pattern in Springs promotion, are presented from time to time in New York and other markets such as Dallas and Los Angeles.

Press Kits are prepared in connection with the shows and include photographs and descriptions of all the garments shown.

Trade Shows are often important in Springs' Apparel Fabrics Division promotion. Examples are the Men's Wear Retailers and Men's Fashion Association Shows, and the MAGIC and BAGIC shows, as well as TEXPO.

Hang tags that tell the story of Springmaid Fabrics are supplied to cutters for identification through to the consumer, although promotion is not directed to consumers.

"Promotion with us is a pragmatic affair," concludes Ed Harding. "In challenging years, like 1975, we will promote heavily to the large end user with specific 'hot' fabrics, whereas in sold-up periods, emphasis is put on exposure of our technical and fashion leadership."

59. WHAT MAKES A CONSUMER BUY?*

By Ursula Holahan, Associate Professor of Home Economics, Clemson University

If you are satisfied with your profits and sales, don't read on. If you are unsure or dissatisfied, here are some reflections that can stimulate your sales.

Quality vs. Price. One needs only to walk into the major chains to see that retailers are convinced the consumer wants better quality, and some say at any price. This may be true for some consumers of fashion in the higher middle income brackets, but for the middle income to lower middle income families, this usually is not true and they are the majority in the U.S.

When buying apparel, price is the strong motivating factor that influences a consumer in his final decision to buy or not to buy apparel. This has been supported in marketing studies. A Harris survey in 1978 supports the increased concern about higher prices. Of course, this is not the only factor but it is a primary influence. This assumption is made on the premise that price usually goes up as quality improves. Now the question is, "What is quality?" This is a far-reaching question and the answer will vary among ages, income levels, and lifestyles.

I am not suggesting that quality be disregarded but we need to put things into more realistic perspective in terms of what the majority can

---

*This article first appeared in the June 1979 issue of the *Textile Marketing Letter*.

afford. *The Women's Wear Daily* series on "The Customer Speaks" showed that over 59 percent said they expected to spend the same for clothing in 1978 as they spent in 1977. Another 25 percent expected to have less money available for clothing. This trend could mean more women will buy less or seek lower quality than they previously could afford.

Let us move on to what makes the consumer buy apparel. Market research shows that color and style lead a consumer to an item, but she wants more information before her final decision to buy. The *Women's Wear Daily* report on "The Customer Speaks" showed that over 70 percent of those surveyed very frequently read care labels. Claude R. Martin, Jr. of the University of Michigan supports the fact that 62 percent of their participants wanted to know the price as the first "bit" of information they received. The subsequent distribution of their choice showed that after price they ranked color and material next, in that order. This study was conducted just prior to the legislation on care labels.

Schultz & Phillips in their report on "Consumer Perception of Textiles," which appeared in the *Home Economics Research Journal*, showed desirable characteristics and problem areas that 50 respondents mentioned most often in relation to specific fabrics. The attributes are listed in their order of importance to them. The participants were in Woodland, California.

Desirable Characteristics	Problem Areas
Practical	Itchy
Easy to care for	Unpleasant smell
Washes well	Uncomfortable
Economical	Not flame resistant
Durable	Pills
For sports clothes	Coarse appearance
For traveling	Can be bleached
Easy to sew	Color fades
Clean and fresh	Shape stretches
Doesn't need lining	Appearance changes
For kids' clothes	Hard, firm feel
Enjoy wearing it	Dyes easily
Improved recently	Seams ravel
Fabric breathes	Wrinkles easily
For summer clothes	Shiny appearance
For sport or dress	
Quality differs	
Moves with body	
Summery	
No ironing	
Cool	
Absorbs moisture	
Feels feminine	
Warm	
Light and airy	

This list supports what many of us have known from personal experience. What used to be called quality in apparel—hand finishing, fully lined jackets, skirts with three inch hems, luxurious dry cleanable fabrics—has been replaced with easy care, easy wear, and durability.

Changing Trends. What makes a consumer buy? Naturally, you want to look at where the bulk of your population is—the men and women 24 to 44 years old. They are well educated and are dressing up more. Yes, they will be influenced by designers, but beyond that they are looking for practical fabrics and construction that will hold up for two or three years. The current stagflation and shortages in our economy have altered our lifestyle patterns and expectations. Buyers are modifying their behavior in view of these expectations about an uncertain future.

Travel could very well be curbed. Action clothes for sports that families can do at home could very well continue to increase. Fabrics and clothes that can be worn seven or eight months out of the year are wanted. Seasonless clothing is popular among many consumers.

Who Are the Consumers? In our growing concern for economy and holding prices, manufacturers have narrowed specifications to a standard population—emphasis on normality and averages. Perhaps manufacturers are missing important marketing fields when they neglect to look at specific consumer needs—whether it be comfort and ease of care for the aging citizen or apparel for individuals with special needs. There is much talk now about mainstreaming children and adults who have handicaps.

I have recently been working on consumer educational leaflets dealing with clothing for the handicapped. Individuals with special needs vary from those with chronic arthritis, to children who are spastic, to amputees, and to the incontinent. Obviously their needs vary, but there are some common characteristics that come through loud and clear: absorbency, stretch fabrics, soft fabrics, and sturdy fabrics. Clothing designs are needed for those with limited finger and hand dexterity, wheel chair designs, and designs to help handicapped children and adults to dress independently. They don't want to look too different from their friends and neighbors. They like to be fashionable and colorful in their clothes, but they need easy care.

The fabrics that go into action clothes might very well suit many of those with physical disabilities. Working with special schools or agencies that deal with various handicaps can provide a new market. You will be helping to provide textiles that are sorely needed, but often these consumers are not aware of what may be available.

Consumer Information. Most manufacturers are missing out on keeping consumers informed about the performance features they are building into their fabrics and apparel. The average consumer is not aware of what affects the price of textiles. Apparel manufacturers who tell their story about what goes into the production of their product, the research that is conducted to meet changing lifestyles, are appealing to that large majority of educated consumers. Many consumers want to know that you are improving the environment and working conditions, working to decrease energy consumption, and, most of all, if your product will suit their lifestyle.

Don't forget about letting cooperative extension educators and other consumer educators have slides, video tapes, and literature that will provide good consumer education. But most of all, pursue more television coverage through special features and advertising. This is an excellent way to improve your public and business image.

James C. Cumming had some excellent advice on "Publicity in Marketing Textiles" in the January 1979 issue of the *Textile Marketing Letter.* He closed this informative article with:

"For successful marketing, get your product talked about. To get your product talked about, develop a sound publicity program."

References

Balchen, Audrey S. "The Customer Speaks" *Women's Wear Daily,* June 19, 1978: 11-12

Martin, Claude R., Jr. "What Consumers of Fashion Want to Know," *Journal of Retailing,* Winter 1971-72: 65-71, 94.

"Quality Control: But Sam You Made the Pants Too Long," *Clothes. etc.* April 15, 1976: 61-65.

Schultz, Howard G. and Betty Ann Phillips. "Consumer Perceptions of Textiles," *Home Economics Research Journal,* 1976 5(1): 2-14.

60. DAN RIVER DOES IT AGAIN!*

By John A. Cairns, Consultant

Back in 1947, Dan River introduced its first all-cotton wrinkle resistant fabrics under its registered trade name, "Wrinkl-Shed**." Although Tootal, Broadhurst and Lee's "T.B.L." finish had prior market success in linens and spun rayons, Dan River's "Wrinkl-Shed" was pretty generally considered to be the first durable finish to achieve market success on 100 percent cotton constructions. But it took a full year to get "Wrinkl-Shed" properly placed in the market and successfully launched.

"Wrinkl-Shed" was first introduced in shirting fabrics at a price premium of something like 5¢ to 8¢ a yard, but the shirt trade just couldn't see it. At that time, the Arrow Trump Shirt, at a retail price of $1.95, was

---

*This article first appeared in the June 1979 issue of the *Textile Marketing Letter.*

**When Dan River's "Wrinkl-Shed" fabrics were introduced some 30 years ago, the name was derived from the fact that the editors of *Good Housekeeping* magazine liked the way these new all-cotton fabrics "shed wrinkles."

about the biggest selling branded shirt in the market and a number of other shirts were being offered at the same price. Shirt manufacturers argued that "Wrinkl-Shed," at a price premium of from 5¢ to 8¢ a yard would not fit into their established wholesale price ranges and could therefore not be offered at retail at the big selling price of $1.95. So another approach had to be made and Dan River's Dress Goods Department came to the rescue.

Under the able leadership of Bill Fullerton and his #1 assistant Jim Gardner, "Wrinkl-Shed" was soon successfully launched in a full line of ginghams for the women's wear trade. (It was necessary to stick pretty much to "square" constructions since the new finish tended to weaken unbalanced fabrics.) Suffice it to say, "Wrinkl-Shed" took off in the women's and children's trades and soon made a lasting name for itself. If memory serves properly, first year's sales amounted to some 6 million yards. This was a period of fabric and market testing. Second year's sales jumped to 19 million yards as garment manufacturers and retailers alike became impressed with the virtues of these new Dan River offerings. And third year's sales hit some 33 million yards. Sales for the fourth year were 51 million yards, the full capacity of the mill at that time for that kind of finishing.

There were some interesting sidelights to this market success. Manufacturers soon found that "Wrinkl-Shed" saved them a lot of money in their showrooms and on the road. After a busy day in the showrooms with a new line, manufacturers had always had to iron and sometimes launder the line before showing it again the following day. The same problem beset the salesmen who were showing the line on the road. It wasn't long before these manufacturers discovered that dresses made of "Wrinkl-Shed" fabrics stayed fresh on the racks much longer and saved many dollars in refinishing. The same thing, of course, applied to the sale of "Wrinkl-Shed" dresses at retail. So manufacturers and retailers took those new fabrics to their hearts and they remained big sellers until the polyester blends came along and gradually begun to replace the all-cotton constructions. It might be said in passing that housewives loved both types of fabrics because of their lasting good looks, their comfortable hand, and their easy-care qualities. So much for past history.

In 1978, Dan River did it all over again. In collaboration with Cluett, Peabody and Company, owners of the "Sanforset" patents and trademarks, Dan River introduced a whole new line of combed all-cotton shirting materials under the "Sanforset" label. According to Linwood Wright, Dan River's Director of Research and Development: "The fabric is first treated with liquid ammonia... The chemical finishing which is added to this cloth is the culmination of all the thermosetting resin research which has taken place over the past 30 years. The problem of crosslinking cotton is the same as it has always been—strength loss versus improved wrinkle resistance... We are enjoying good market success and acceptance at retail... The consumer does appear to want a minimum care properties in

a comfortable, luxurious hand, 100 percent combed cotton shirting fabric."
To all of this, we say "Amen!"

During the past several years there has been a notable revival in
consumer interest in fabrics made of natural fibers, cotton, wool and linen,
as well as silk. If the prices of these natural fibers can be more carefully
controlled so that the mills can buy with confidence and the growers can
raise them with confidence, we believe that they will enjoy steadily
increasing market success. In the meantime, our hats are off to Dan River,
Inc. and to all those other textile firms who are doing so much on a daily
basis to make this a better country in which to live and work. Research and
development programs can be expensive, and sometimes disheartening,
but they are most certainly good for everyone when they pay off as they
have in this instance with Dan River's "Sanforset" fabrics.

61. HOW CUTTERS' FASHIONS
SOLD LOWENSTEIN FABRICS*

By William W. Smith, M. Lowenstein & Sons

For many years the "House of Lowenstein" used only trade publica-
tons to introduce and promote its new fabric lines each season to the cutter
and retail trades. It depended on wholesaler and manufacturers to carry its
fabric story to the public.

Then in the early 1950s, with the introduction of *Signature* prints,
came the company's first major consumer effort to acquaint the public
with its fabrics. Consistent full-page color schedules in fashion and general
magazines directed attention to women's, misses and children's dresses,
sportswear, housecoats, outerwear and other garments made from Signature fabrics.

The success of Signature advertising induced the company to jump its
advertising and promotion investment and add established house brands
like Good Behavior, Easytime and Courtesy, among others, to its trade and
magazine schedules. Later, men's and boys' wear fabrics got similar
support—but to a lesser degree.

With rare exceptions, all Lowenstein advertising employed four-color
illustrations. At that time, Lowenstein was one of the largest printers of
cotton fabrics in this country. Its design studios in New York and Paris
together were the largest in the world. It employed over 150 staff designers,

---

*Bill Smith served M. Lowenstein & Sons for 11 years, first as Director of
Advertising and then as Vice President—Sales. He has contributed several
articles to the *Textile Marketing Letter*. In this article, he describes the results
of one of the early mill advertising campaigns featuring the garments of cutters
using the mill's fabrics. It is a technique that has proven itself as one of the
soundest advertising strategies for a mill to employ.

This article first appeared in the September 1975 issue of the *Textile
Marketing Letter*.

colorists and stylists in New York alone, creating a constant flow of patterns in a rainbow of colors for its 25 merchandise departments.

Only color presentation could truly translate the hundreds of designs produced each season in their full beauty and variation to the consumer. Experience showed that color attracted reader attention, stimulated buying interest in the items illustrated before the consumer visited a store displaying the garments advertised, and often produced sales direct..

Only cutters' garments were used in the illustrations. These had to be made completely from Lowenstein fabrics. The garments chosen were selected by the manufacturer and he, or his designer, was invited to be present when photographs were taken. Often he also participated in the selection of the models used in the photography.

The general practice was to show three garments in each advertisement. This was done to present variation in color, fabric and garment design to satisfy different tastes and to give the consumer a choice of neckline.

The manufacturer was invited to participate in this program for his benefit. He was never given an advertisement to use where and when he chose. Lowenstein controlled and paid for all advertising. It established schedules in those publications which were believed best for the presentation and sale of its fabrics as well as the garments in which they were used.

The company also invited cutter participation by garment category and in price ranges in which the fabric might normally be used in volume—dresses, sportswear, etc. The reputation of the manufacturer, his distribution of product, and its acceptance by the trade and public, were other considerations.

Since national media were employed in this program, the manufacturer had to support the advertising with a substantial original yardage order, before a specific page and date of issue were assigned to him, to assure availability of his garments in the 50 principal retail markets when the advertising appeared. There was never any problem on this score.

Another requisite was the manufacturer's purchase of Lowenstein fabric hang tags and their attachment to the garment featured. Thus, the fabric story got to the ultimate consumer with regard to color-fastness, shrinkage, wash-wear features and general care of the fabric itself. This requirement resulted in educating the clerk that sold the garment as well as the purchaser.

All copy that appeared in the advertisement highlighted the fabric illustrated and its features. It was indirectly a *fabric* story. It identified the maker of the garment and included sizes and prices. A dozen names of prominent retail outlets carrying and displaying the items were listed at the foot of the advertisement so prospects might know where the merchandise was available. Often, the participating cutter would buy an adjoining column on the facing page to add to his retail outlet listing. This column ran in black and white and sometimes included as many as a hundred names.

The advertising format was distinctly Lowenstein. The fabric brand name was prominently displayed in the logotype. It was a Lowenstein fabric advertisement.

Lowenstein mailed pre-prints of the advertisement in full color to the manufacturer's retailers with a personal letter, well in advance of the insertion date, to promote his merchandise and pre-sell his customers. Often the pre-prints produced retail orders direct by mail for the maker's line prior to a visit by his salesmen. They served as a reminder to the dealer to plan his department and window displays, as well as his local advertising, in advance of the arrival of the merchandise.

The company promoted these cutter national advertisements in its trade advertising. This effort gave added impetus to the program and sales support to the manufacturer's salesmen when they showed their lines to prospects and customers.

This program eliminated "give away" advertising. It produced earnest and sincere manufacturer cooperation that made the advertising successful and profitable. It established Lowenstein brands and fabrics solidly in the retail and public minds. It identified its product with prime, established, universally accepted fashion houses and garment lines. It carried the story of Lowenstein fabrics—their variety, features and values—to everyone who made garment buying decisions at all levels. It enhanced the reputation of the "House of Lowenstein" as a prime creator and producer of fabrics—cottons as well as blends. It sold "color consciousness" to American consumers...and it produced volume for all who participated.

62. HOW ONE SMALL BLANKET MILL GETS NATIONAL DISTRIBUTION*

By James C. Cumming, Consultant

If a mill is too small to send enough salesmen to travel the country, if its promotional budget can't provide for national advertising, if its line is too specialized to command attention from buyers who like to stock a "complete line," how can it get distribution in depth?

You might say that such a situation must be left to a solution in accordance with the "mousetrap theory**." That's an easy out, but the mousetrap theory has long since been fully discredited, so we'll give you

---

*This article first appeared in the January 1975 issue of the *Textile Marketing Letter*.

**Often ascribed to Elbert Hubbard, the mousetrap theory derives from a quotation from Ralph Waldo Emerson: "If a man has good corn, or wood, or boards, or pigs to sell, or can make better chairs or knives, crucibles or church organs than anybody else, you will find a broad hard-beaten road to his house, though it be in the woods." Hubbard made it: "If a man builds a better mousetrap," and went on from there.

the case history of just such a mill that has solved its marketing problem very satisfactorily.

Our story is about the Faribault Woolen Mill Co., Faribault, Minnesota. They weave blankets, throws, leisure blankets and Pak-a-Robes which are robe and case combinations. It's not the broad line that would be produced by a big mill like Chatham, for example, but it's a quality line. And distribution is excellent. You'll find Faribault products in such leading stores as Strawbridge & Clothier, Philadelphia; J. L. Hudson, Detroit; Frederick & Nelson, Seattle; and dozens of other important stores across the country.

Most of these carry the merchandise under the brand name of "Faribo," an excellent phonetic rendering of the mill name.

So how does Faribault get such excellent coverage of the market?

First, since they can travel no salesmen of their own, they work through manufacturer's representatives. Eight of them cover the entire country. In New York, Paul Hollenbach uses the name "Faribo Woolen Mill Company" as a listing for his office. To cover Chicago, Alex Campbell operates from Hoffman Estates, Illinois. Arne Bergren has the Minnesota territory, working from Edina, Minn. Thomas Roe has headquarters in Atlanta; John Ray in North Ridgeville, Ohio; H. W. Rossum in Whittier, California; Joseph and Kyle Robertson in Salt Lake City; and Shelton Textiles, Inc. covers the Dallas territory.

Each of these representatives is protected in his territory by Faribault but each carries other, related merchandise as well, which gives him that much more clout with retail buyers.

Second, Faribault backs its representatives with trade advertising in *Linens & Domestics* and *Daily News Record* and provides them with catalog sheets that illustrate and describe each item completely. These, in turn, are passed along to retailers by the representatives.

Third, Faribault arranges to exhibit at the Marketing Shows in the showrooms and resident buying offices in New York in November and February and at the Premium Show at the New York Coliseum in May.

Fourth, although there is no Faribo national advertising as such, the mill backs the representatives in making cooperative advertising deals with retailers, up to five percent of sales. The retailer must name Faribo in the advertisement. Usually the space cost is divided fifty-fifty but sometimes tie-ins with the Wool Bureau are arranged, in which case the cost is divided one-third, one-third, one-third.

Also, the representatives are encouraged to offer retailers certain types of exclusivity. Sometimes this may be in the form of a new pattern, originated by the retailer or by the mill, for which the retailer is permitted exclusive rights for an agreed-upon length of time. Or, in a city where Faribo may not have a retailer, an exclusive deal may be made for the entire line for a limited length of time in order to get representation.

Substantial display racks are used in most of the representatives' showrooms and are frequently bought from Faribault by retailers for their own use. A number of retailers have commented that these are by far the best blanket displays available anywhere.

You can see from all this that the representatives spend most of their time and energy in working directly with the stores. However, a great deal of work is also done with such buying offices as the Associated Merchandising Corporation, Mutual Buying Syndicate, Frederick Atkins, Associated Dry Goods, Allied Stores, Mercantile and Felix Lilienthal. This points up, also, a high degree of cooperation among the Faribault representatives, for the New York representative, because of his closeness to the buying offices, must cover them more thoroughly than is possible for the other, out-of-town representatives.

In short, Faribault's success rests on the foundation of faithful adherence, within budget limitations, to the foundation stones of sound sales promotion:

1. Concentration on a superior product.

2. Strong personal selling with national coverage.

3. Trade promotion to retailers and buying offices.

4. Good retail advertising and display.

5. Education of salespeople by supplying all the selling points about each item on the catalog sheets.

Faribault, in a nutshell, is a good laboratory study of how to market a textile product successfully.

63. A BIGGER SLICE OF A BIGGER PIE*

By John A. Cairns, Consultant

There comes a time in the life of every marketing man when the market for his goods isn't as big as it has to be to keep him operating at a profit. That leaves him with three choices: 1.) Get out of that business entirely. 2.) Break the market in the hopes of grabbing off a larger share for himself, or 3.) Take imaginative steps to *enlarge* the market.

That was the situation that faced William L. Syrop back in the late 1930's or early 1940's when he was president of Crompton Richmond. The situation on corduroys and velveteens was plenty tough. Corduroys were limited largely to boys' knickers and longies, and Hockmeyer Brothers' famous "Tweeduroy" had just about all the business worth having. No one else could break into that "Tweeduroy Club" for love or money. The garment manufacturers were happy with what they had, and so were the retailers.

*This article first appeared in the March 1972 issue of the *Textile Marketing Letter.*

Bill Syrop and his advertising agency decided to try alternative No. 3 listed above. They wanted to see what could be done to enlarge the market for everyone and hopefully get a bigger chunk of the total for Crompton Richmond.

They hired Perkins Baily, then the gifted Editor of *Men's Wear Magazine* to design a new garment each month to be made of corduroy or velveteen. These garments were then featured in full color advertisements in *Men's Wear Magazine* to stimulate the thinking of retailers and manufacturers. The new designs were offered to all manufacturers and retailers, without restriction, as Crompton Richmond's contribution to the trade. Later, the women's, misses' and children's trades were brought into the picture.

The idea caught on fast, and in very short order the new merchandise was being made available to thousands of good retailers by a fine team of good cutters. The whole affair reached its climax in a successful fashion show held in the Grand Ballroom of the Old Ritz Carlton. It was a day when Bill Syrop and his agency could really stand up and take a bow.

As a general consideration, the market for both of these fabrics has been growing ever since. Much of the follow-up work has been done by the Corduroy Council and its public relations people, one of whom was involved in the original program in which Crompton Richmond went it alone.

Others, of course, have done the same kind of thing, and others will do it again in the future. Generally, this sort of operation is considered to be more than a single firm can handle. Thus you see the very effective programs of the Denim Institute, Corduroy Council, the old Vat Dye Institute, Man-Made Fibers Association, the Print Group of T.D.A. and others, all doing a fine creative job to expand the market for all hands.

The group effort is still excellent and always will be. For the brave man or brave firm that wants to go it alone, however, the kudos are exceptional. Best of all, they establish a leadership position that doesn't have to be shared with anyone else.

64. MILITARY TEXTILES AND THE ENERGY CRUNCH*

By Stephen J. Kennedy, Former Director, Army
Research and Development on Clothing and Textiles

The experience of the American public during the energy crisis of the mild winter of 1973-74 brought home to a lot of people the hazard of depending on waterborne petroleum as a source of their heating oil and gasoline. But not many have thought of what it would be like if our energy requirements continue to grow at their present rate of doubling every 10 or 12 years.

*This article first appeared in the September 1974 issue of the *Textile Marketing Letter*.

Few people seriously believe that we can either reduce our present limited dependence upon foreign oil and liquified natural gas (LNG) by 1980 or 1985, considering the time and the capital required to open up new coal fields, build new refineries, construct new nuclear power plants (and the gaseous diffusion plants to get the enriched uranium) or even build new fossil fuel power plants; or, on the other hand, start to approach zero-growth in energy requirements.

Hence, the military hazard posed over the next decade of possible involvement in a war in which our waterborne shipments of oil would be cut off and our off-shore oil wells blown up by enemy submarines is one of major proportions to a country whose armed forces have now geared up to total dependence upon fighting from gasoline-, diesel-, or oil-fueled vehicles, planes, and ships.

Just to look at this problem in terms of what it would mean to military supply of clothing and textiles raises serious questions as to whether our textile industry could adequately support a sudden military mobilization.

The Demands of Textile Mobilization. The key factor in relating the amount of textiles required at the outbreak of war to available supply is the rate of mobilization required by the military situation. General Eisenhower in his final report as Chief of Staff said: "What we are able or not able to do within the first 60 days of another war will be decisive in the determination of our ability to carry the war to a successful conclusion." This proved literally true in Korea. From June 25, 1950, when the North Korean invasion of South Korea began, it was only by September 10, after a strategic retreat, that the United States and the allied United Nations forces could stabilize the front at the beachhead around Pusan, thereby occupying the enemy forces so as to permit the Inchon landing on September 25.

In both World Wars I and II we had ample warning time for preparation, with other powers engaging the enemy while we had time to bring to bear the long-run superiority of American potentiality for war. And yet when we look at the rate of mobilization required during both World War II and Korea, as shown in Figure 1, the doubling of our armed strengths during the first year of the war represented the maximum of what we could do. Granted that there were limiting factors in many areas, the fact is that the textile and clothing industries did not inhibit mobilization. They were able to supply all the requirements for the mobilizing forces in sufficient quantity and within the required time. The supply of wool and cotton on hand at the outbreak of the war was entirely adequate and the capacity of the industry to produce military-type textiles was in being. That situation can never be repeated in the future.

The near disaster in supply of textiles and textile fabricated products at the outbreak of the Korean War has tended to be glossed over by the favorable outcome of the war and the relative ease of meeting the requirements of the gradual mobilization which occurred in the limited objective war in Vietnam. But there is a lesson to be learned there, as is shown in Figures 2 and 3.

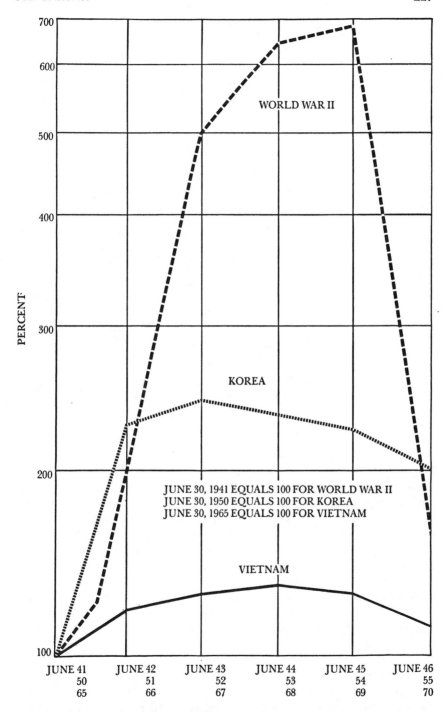

FIGURE 1 RATE OF INCREASE OF TOTAL MILITARY
STRENGTH WORLD WAR II, KOREA, VIETNAM

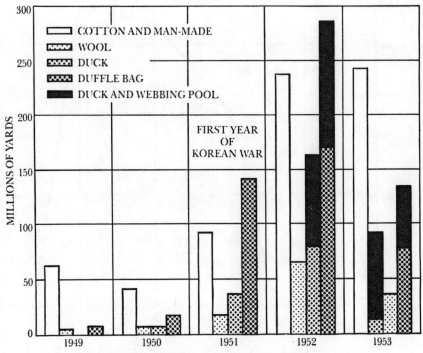

FIGURE 2 DELIVERY OF TEXTILES TO THE
QUARTERMASTER CORPS (KOREAN WAR)

It will be evident from Figure 2, which shows deliveries of textiles direct to the Quartermaster Corps of the Army for use as government furnished materials, that no supplies of any size were received during the entire year 1950, which would include the first half of the first year of the war from July to December 1950. It can also be presumed that most of what is shown to have been delivered in 1951, which was the first year in which the report is for a fiscal year ending June 30, was delivered in the second half of the year from January to June 1951. Delays in procurement and production caused a build-up in demand which was met only in fiscal years 1952 and 1953, the second and third years after the war broke out.

The impact of this delay upon end-item production is shown in Figure 3 which shows deliveries of selected end items. Those chosen are volume items of clothing and equipment and some of the figures used represent averages of deliveries on several items in order to reflect as well as possible a general picture of end-item deliveries. Here is shown dramatically the inability to support troop mobilization during the first year of the war. In fact, on February 16, 1951, Mr. John D. Small, Chairman of the Munitions Board, wrote to Mr. C. E. Wilson, Director of Defense Mobilization, warning that because of shortages of clothing and uniforms the equipping of inductees was seriously threatened. "Planned increases of Army inductees have already been stopped."

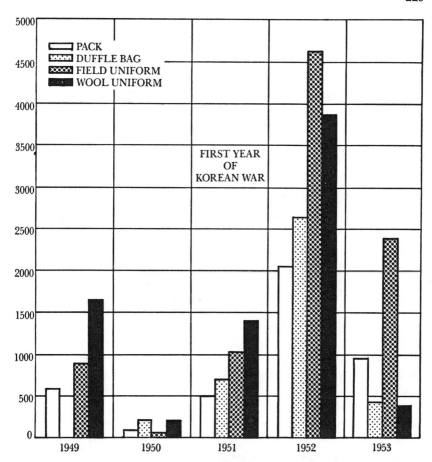

FIGURE 3 DELIVERY OF SELECTED QUARTERMASTER
ITEMS (KOREAN WAR)

Without attempting to place blame, the simple fact is that practically no textile products procured after the war broke out reached troops in the field until after the main fighting had stopped in July 1951. Again, it should be noted there was no shortage of raw wool or cotton when the invasion of Korea occurred; also industry capacity was still adequate in all areas of military-type textiles.

It may be worth answering the inevitable question, "How were our troops in Korea supplied?" The answer, obviously, is "from the large carryover stocks from World War II which constituted, in effect, a very large reserve of almost all items."

Our creeping military involvement in Vietnam created only limited supply problems for support of mobilization. However, this can scarcely be regarded as an archtype of any future mobilization. A more realistic assumption would be that mobilization would come suddenly after a period of prolonged peace, and that mobilization of military manpower would necessitate an increase in the military forces of at least 100 percent in the first year as was necessary in World War II and the Korean War.

Questions that should be addressed would include just how far any reserve would meet the need; whether new weaponry deployed by the enemy might obsolete the protective capability of whatever material was in the reserve; whether there would be a broad industry base to supply the needed military textiles, including capacity obtaining by large-scale conversion from ordinary civilian type production; would there be an adequate supply of raw materials immediately available for producing military textiles; and, also important, if the conflict were prolonged, would the industry base be adequate to meet the needs of both the military and the civilian population?

Changes in the Textile Industry. During the past 10 to 15 years profound changes have been taking place in the United States textile industry and in the textile market which have had an enormous effect upon the capability of the textile industry to provide support in any future mobilization. These changes have so altered the production capabilities of the American textile industry in relation to military requirements that it can be said that the textile industry as it has existed over the past 30 years in which we have fought in three wars simply no longer exists.

Military textiles may be considered as falling into two major groups insofar as their technical requirements are concerned: those for which specific functional performance characteristics are critical or essential and those which conform fairly closely to their commercial counterparts. The technical requirements for the first group are quite inflexible. In large part they relate to the protection, safety and efficiency of combat troops and can be met only by specific types of textiles for which an adequate industry production base, capable of rapid expansion in time of mobilization, is essential to the effectiveness of our military posture.

Almost all military textiles fall into the broadwoven segment of the industry, largely because of the technical requirements for tightness of weave, low air porosity, stability or durability.

While total production in this area is large, military textiles are largely concentrated in a relatively few classes of products: duck, fine cotton goods (combed), worsteds, all of which have a small industry base today, with production in all these areas a downward trend.

The impact of imports over the past dozen years has been serious, not just because they have taken over 15 percent of the U.S. broadwoven goods market but also because our national policy has been pointed toward turning over the growth in our home market to the less developed countries of the world as a first step toward their industrialization. Also the concentration of imports in certain sectors of the market has been highly damaging; e.g. the U.S. woolen and worsted industry has been largely liquidated as a result of competition from knits and other competitive polyester fabrics. As a result, there is no longer a viable woolen and worsted industry upon which the military could count for the quantities of textiles that would be required in a mobilization.

The most serious aspect of this situation, however, lies in the resulting unattractiveness of the broadwoven goods industry as a potential area for capital investment in new production capacity. With the profit margins held down by low-price imports and competition from other types of textiles, there is little likelihood of growth in capacity other than that arising from replacement of equipment by more productive machinery in existing mills. Accordingly, looking into the 1980-85 time frame, this industry will be providing a smaller and smaller part of the U.S. market and in proportion to total consumer demand will have less capacity to meet combined military and civilian consumer demands in a future emergency.

A more potentially serious problem, however, is the shrinking base for production of cotton-type fabrics having the capability of meeting the technical requirements for military textiles of high performance in water resistance and comfort. Current trends in fiber consumption show the rapid rise in utilization of the non-cellulosic, man-made fibers by the U.S. textile industry. This would indicate the desirability for the military services to be able in an emergency to obtain large quantities of textiles made from cotton and wool. From this standpoint, the maintenance of textile manufacturing facilities capable of producing textiles from cotton, and the continued use of textiles predominantly made from cotton by the military, would appear to be in the interests of national security and should be continued as policies of the Department of the Army and the Department of Defense.

Positive actions to reduce the fluctuations in the price of cotton which adversely affect its desirability to textile manufacturers and to assure a carry-over of adequate size to meet possible military needs as to quantity, grade and staple at any time in the crop year would accordingly be in the national interest.

Chapter Fourteen

Public Image of The Textile Industry

OVERVIEW

By The Editorial Staff, Textile Marketing Letter

The public perception of the textile industry plays an essential role in the marketing of textile products.

Without public confidence in quality and reliability, no product or company can long survive in what is one of America's most competitive industries. But the need for public confidence goes far beyond consumer confidence in products. The attitude toward the industry is general, how innovative it is, how essential it is to the nation's economy and how competitive America's textile industry is with others around the world, all play an important role in the overall marketing climate for American textiles.

The textile industry, as one of the nation's largest employers and the provider of some of the most basic needs of mankind, must have the confidence of the general public. An industry or a company needs broad public understanding if it is going to prosper, in this day of increasing public scrutiny and government regulations. It must have the support of the many "publics" who come in contact with it every day.

Public relations, public affairs, communications, by whatever name it is known, is an essential ingredient in the marketing of textiles. It is just as important at times as is design, quality or a good marketing strategy.

In recent years, we have seen what can happen to an industry when it loses public confidence. The so-called "Consumer Movement" has resulted in the removal of entire product lines from the marketplace. Foreign competition has captured large segments of basic markets as a result of

232

declining consumer confidence in the quality and reliability of some American products. Even though American industry has in many cases, become more responsive to consumer demands, there still is a lack of general consumer confidence in some products. If American industry is to regain its traditional role as the best source for quality consumer products, it must first of all, get its house in order from a quality control standpoint and then communicate this to the public.

While some industries must focus on the need to correct a negative image, the American textile industry has a much different problem. Its major public relations problem is a lack of any strong image at all. While everyone is surrounded by textile products, literally, from the cradle to the grave, few people have any perception of the industry which makes all these products possible. It is, in effect, an invisible industry.

For many years, this really did not make much difference. Historically, the textile industry manufactured its products and sold them in an atmosphere insulated from outside influences. Apart from paying taxes and complying with a few basic laws related to working conditions and transporting and selling goods, industry had little involvement with state and federal governments. But with the growth of the consumer movement and the regulatory explosion, all business has become more involved with government. As a result, a company or an industry must have public support and understanding if it is to improve the business climate and enhance its ability to work without undue government regulation.

In 1914 the Federal Trade Commission Act was passed. It was the first of what was to become a series of laws governing the manufacturing and marketing of products. The growth of this type of regulation was slow, at first. Over the next 52 years, Congress passed just six laws which had a direct impact on the textile industry. They were the Clayton Anti-trust Act, the Export Trade Act, the Wool Products Labelling Act, the Lanham Trade Mark Act, the Fur Products Labelling Act and the Textile Products Labelling Act.

Beginning in 1967, however, the situation changed rapidly. In 11 years, 15 more agencies were created to regulate business, including textiles. In all, the Federal government now has 58 regulatory agencies that issue some 7,000 rules and policy statements, 2,000 of which are legally binding. The Federal Trade Commission, alone, now has some 1,700 bureaucrats looking at business practices. The huge Occupational Safety and Health Administration has published literally thousands of regulations covering conditions and practices in the workplace. The Environmental Protection Agency became one of the biggest, and most costly, of the growing federal agencies as the public demanded a massive cleanup of the nation's air and streams. The Consumer Product Safety Commission has cradle-to-grave regulations covering everything from children's sleepwear to coffins.

In this atmosphere, it has become increasingly important for major manufacturing and marketing industries like textiles, to build public understanding of both its products and its manufacturing practices.

In 1975, the American Textile Manufacturers Institute, which is the central trade association for the textile mill products industry, commissioned a public attitude survey by Yankelovich, Skelly & White, Inc., to develop definitive information about the industry's public image. The survey revealed that:

- Overall knowledge of and familiarity with the textile industry by itself and in relation to other industries was low.
- The textile industry was best known by its end-products, primarily apparel and home furnishings.
- The favorable attitude toward these products resulted in a favorable overall impression 'of the industry, despite the fact that the respondents didn't know that much about the textile industry beyond the level of product familiarity.
- The more people knew about the industry, the more favorable was their opinion of it.

One in three of those surveyed said they were at least somewhat familiar with the textile industry. As the researchers pointed out, however, it is probably more important to note that two out of three were unfamiliar with the industry, a high percentage when compared with other industries.

When asked for an opinion of what the industry does, most people could not distinguish between the textile and apparel industries. One in four could not immediately describe the industry. When asked about textile products, half said the industry produced apparel and the other half said "bolts of cloth/fabric." This led the researchers to conclude that many perceive textile and apparel manufacturing as a single industry.

There was a general favorable opinion of the industry among those who had an opinion. Products were viewed favorably, and therefore, there was a positive opinion of the industry. Sixty-one percent said they had a favorable opinion of the textile industry.

This was reinforced by the general opinion that the industry has produced increasingly attractive and durable products over the prior 10 years with the industry getting high marks for alertness to trends, new product development and research. Easy-care fabrics and garments contributed much to this perception.

Although nine out of 10 believed the textile industry to be important to the U.S. economy, most respondents could not distinguish the textile industry from any other on its performance in specific areas. Some positive and negative impressions did emerge, however. People felt it was a good idea to invest in a textile company; that the industry employs more women and minorities than other industries; and that it had improved working conditions over the 10 prior years.

On the negative side, a significant minority—29 percent—felt the industry paid its workers less than other industries, although the majority found textile wage scales on par with other industries. A rather large number of college students, among whose ranks are future textile executives, thought work in the textile industry was monotonous.

In general, however, the study showed the industry to have a non-image. Indicative of this was its mediocre standing when rated against five other major industries in 13 different categories. With only one exception, the textile industry was never rated the highest or lowest in any category, but always came out somewhere in the middle. Textiles were stacked up against steel, food, drugs, plastics and paper in categories such as progressiveness, concern for public and consumers, most satisfied workers and importance to national defense and the economy.

Further, the researchers found that the public was unclear on some important industry characteristics: how many people it employs; the structure of the industry; and the names of specific companies which comprise the industry. "The association of particular companies with the textile industry is weak," the study states, "far below DuPont's association with the chemical industry or IBM's association with the computer industry." When asked to name a specific textile company, only seven were mentioned by respondents.

But the study also revealed that, although the public's general perception is cloudy, the more familiar a person is with the textile industry, the more favorable is his impression. Of those familiar with the industry, 80 percent said they had a favorable opinion of it, 20 percent unfavorable. Of those unfamiliar with the industry, the ratings were almost even with 51 percent rating it favorably and 49 percent unfavorably.

About two-thirds of the general public said they had seen or heard about the textile industry, with television and magazines being the major sources of information. Half indicated that they had learned about textile manufacturing in school. It is interesting to note that of those who had visited a textile mill, the overwhelming majority came away with a very or somewhat favorable impression of textile plants.

Armed with this information, which essentially said: "The more they know us, the more they like us," the textile industry has been focusing its public relations efforts on what the industry is, what it does and how that contributes to the social and economic well-being of the nation. Planned communications programs are conducted by individual companies and their state and national trade associations.

In smaller companies, the communications function is generally centered in the public relations and personnel divisions. A good deal of emphasis is placed on employee communications, since employees are the public most directly affected by the success or failures of a company. Basic communications tools—company newspapers and magazines, bulletin boards, direct mailings and audio-visual presentations—are employed by most companies.

Another important dimension of these communications programs is community relations. Company representatives are active participants and leaders in civic and charitable organizations, church groups and organizations. Companies sponsor Little League teams, company and community softball and bowling teams, provide the leadership for fund-raising drives and some companies own and operate recreational facilities for their employees and communities.

Increasingly, liaison with local news media has become important. Company officials are being interviewed by newspapers and appearing on television and radio "talk shows" in an effort to build a better understanding of the key role their company and its employees play in the economic life of their communities. Plant tours and open houses are helping to acquaint more and more people with the progress the textile industry has been making.

Mid-size to larger companies have full-time public relations staffs who perform a wide range of communications activities designed to improve public acceptance of a company, its policies and its products. Product promotion generally is handled at the divisional level with the assistance of advertising and public relations agencies. Publicly owned companies conduct programs aimed at enhancing the company's standing in the financial community and in the financial press. This has become an increasingly important function, with market implications, in view of the industry's growing need to generate the capital necessary to modernize and at the same time meet government regulations.

The extent of textile company's communications activities varies with the commitment of top management to communications, but, in general, more companies are devoting more of their resources, both time and money, to communications. In some companies there is a multi-faceted program designed to reach the media, shareholders, politicians, community leaders, employees, consumer groups and other special interest organizations. In other companies single groups, such as employees, are considered the most important public, and, as a result, receive most of the attention.

Since the early 1950's the American Textile Manufacturers Institute has conducted a broad public relations program designed to attack the industry's identity problem and build public appreciation for the industry's essential role in the economic and social fabric of the nation. In recent years, these communications, increasingly, have focused on the industry's relations with the federal government.

Over the years, the ATMI program has emphasized the theme that the textile industry, along with apparel, is the largest single employer of manufacturing workers; that it provides more jobs for minorities than the national average; job opportunities are available at a variety of skill levels and that it generates the largest payroll in many small towns as well as some of the larger cities. It also emphasizes the fact that the industry is modern, one of the nation's leaders in productivity and, as such, is making a significant contribution to providing the United States with the highest standard of living in the world.

At various times, all forms of communications, including motion pictures, educational filmstrips and literature, publicity, speeches and special events have been used to convey this story to both special and general publics.

The industry's involvement in international trade serves to illustrate how communications programs have been used to help improve the domestic textile market. Historically, American textile manufacturers have been plagued by competition from products made in low-wage countries under working conditions which would be illegal here. The industry has recognized the need for reciprocal international trade and has been willing to share the growth of the domestic market with foreign countries. However, when imports become excessive and disrupt the domestic market, the industry has called for reasonable regulation through quotas and tariffs.

In view of the "free trade" sentiment in this country, communicating the position of the U.S. textile industry has been a major public relations challenge.

Communications has played a significant role in the industry's expanded export activities. In the late 1970's industry leaders recognized that, if the textile industry in the United States is to grow, much of that growth will have to take place in overseas markets. With domestic consumption of about 60 pounds per capita, the American market is growing at the rate of only about one percent annually. On the other hand, world consumption averages only about 15 pounds per capita, and in some countries it is as low as five pounds.

In 1979, the industry embarked on a major export promotion effort designed to motivate manufacturers to look beyond our shores for new and expanding markets. The effort was well-received by the news media, which gave the effort widespread coverage. Industry leaders wrote magazine articles, appeared on network television and gave numerous newspaper interviews citing the opportunities for market expansion overseas. Exports increased significantly, and U.S. manufacturers are increasingly being recognized as permanent factors in the overseas markets.

Similar activities have been carried out with respect to consumer products. The industry has actively promoted its concern for product safety and its support for programs which provide the consumer with more information, such as care-labeling of wearing apparel and carpets and rugs. Textile manufacturers believe it is sound marketing to provide consumers with information they can use in selecting and caring for textile products. Because it is good business, they strongly support voluntary programs rather than those which might be imposed by government.

Industry communications programs have emphasized the need to educate the public about the problem of fabric flammability, by underscoring the fact that fabric will burn if exposed to fire. At the same time, it must be recognized that the vast majority of fabric-related injuries are due to carelessness by individuals. Highly flammable textile products have been removed from the market, but the problem will be removed only if the public understands and practices fire safety.

The marriage of communications and marketing in the textile industry has a solid foundation and can be expected to take on growing importance in years to come.

J. Marshall Doswell, vice president for corporate communications for Springs Mills, Inc., was the first chairman of the ATMI Communications Action Group comprised of industry public relations professionals who advise the ATMI on its communications programs.

In assessing the relationship between communications and marketing, Doswell pointed out that if a company wants to sell its products in today's marketplace something more than good products is required. A company also needs a good reputation.

"This is an era of consumerism, of government regulation, of rising public expectations of performance. In this environment, the marketing success of every company and every industry is affected by public attitudes.

"It is dawning on more and more companies and industries that they must do more than sell their products; they must also sell themselves. This is forging a vital link between marketing and communications.

"The marketing people sell the products. The public relations and public affairs people sell the integrity, responsibility and validity of the companies behind the products."

The two efforts are inseparable. Their combined value will grow because this is also an era of communication.

65. "CORPORATE PUBLIC RELATIONS"—HOW TO MAKE IT PAY OFF*

By Frank McNeirney, Kurt Salmon Associates, Inc.

Every textile firm has a corporate image, whether it particularly wants one or not. It's an inescapable part of corporate life from the very outset.

Perhaps things would be simpler for advertising and public relations people if a company could somehow postpone having a corporate image— as one might defer building a new dye-house, or getting into doubleknits. But it just can't be done. Nor, for that matter, can a company hide, or limit the extent of, its corporate image.

With this in mind, the least a textile firm can do is to draw up some definite ideas about how it wants to look in the eyes of its present and potential customers. It must then transform these ideas into corporate goals. And recognize that success in achieving these goals depends on

---

*This article first appeared in the March 1971 issue of the *Textile Marketing Letter*.

factors like product quality, style, price, and customer service. And realize that something called a Corporate Public Relations Department, no matter how well staffed or professionally run, cannot in itself insure that these goals are reached.

Before even thinking in terms of a public relations program, every textile firm should try to measure how well the image it *now* projects squares with the image it feels it *should* project; i.e., the one that would best enable it to achieve its short-range and long-range goals.

Admittedly, this is not a simple task. I submit it can be done properly only through scientifically structured and interpreted attitude surveys among a firm's customers and potential customers.

These surveys cost money, they must be conducted by skilled interviewers, and the results must be evaluated by people experienced in the field of behavioral science.

A complicating factor in the case of textile firms is that term "customers" may include not only first-hand purchasers of a firm's products (like apparel manufacturers), but retailers and ultimate consumers as well.

And look at the payoff! Such surveys do several things:

- They uncover and pinpoint significant attitudes held by customers toward your company.
- They enable you to define areas that need improvement.
- They permit you to focus a laser-beam of remedial efforts on those areas that need specific attention.

Isn't this infinitely better than conducting a profusion of public relations activities, some of which may be of no benefit at all, and others of which may actually be of disservice?

As we said, attitude surveys are not a simple matter. They use scientific interviewing techniques, measurement approaches, rating scales, and statistical testing procedures. Needless to say, designing them and carrying them out involve complicated skills in many areas—statistics, data collection techniques, data processing, testing and interpretation.

Non-directive interviewing techniques, for example, are used to increase the likelihood that respondents' opinions will be furnished candidly. Processing the data by computer permits the building up of sizable reservoirs of knowledge about attitudes among similar groups of customers throughout the industry—against which a given marketing situation can be compared.

The attitude survey approach need not be employed only once and then discontinued—nor should it be. Like birth control pills, attitude surveys are most effective not when seized upon in an emergency, but when used on a regular basis. When conducted periodically, they do more than just measure what attitudes exist among consumers at a given time; they also measure how effective management has been in responding to, and acting upon, the findings of previous surveys. Additionally, members of the public relations staff are able to see clearly the results of their work.

The danger of any approach other than a results-oriented one towards corporate public relations is emphasized by recent events. A disastrous business recession has been the signal for textile management to improve efficiency. Many corporate public relations programs and people simply could not prove their effectiveness, and were the victims of large-scale cutbacks.

The results? Disillusionment among many public relations professionals.

One hopes the lesson has been learned, and that in the future the widespread use of attitude surveys and other modern management tools will enable corporate public relations people to concentrate their energies for maximum benefit to their firms. The handwriting on the wall is pretty clear: the days of using a haphazard, scatter-shot approach to corporate public relations are over.

66. WHERE FAMILIARITY BRINGS RESPECT

**Textile Plant Visits Build
Favorable Public Attitudes***

By Jean L. Woodruff, Clemson University

In these times of declining public respect for business in general, it is encouraging to note that a recent study conducted for the American Textile Manufacturers Institute by the research firm of Yankelovich, Skelly & White, Inc., reveals an unexpected promotional opportunity for the textile industry. Simply put, the study concludes that the more people know about the textile industry, the more favorable is their opinion of it and that an important means of building familiarity is through plant visits.

More specifically, important findings of the study were that:

- Attitudes among the public studies were much more favorable toward the textile industry than toward business in general.
- Only one in three Americans show some familiarity with the textile industry, and many confuse it with related industries such as fiber or apparel.
- In general, those respondents more familiar with the

*This article first appeared in the September 1976 issue of the *Textile Marketing Letter.*

textile industry had more favorable attitudes about
it.
- Of those respondents who had visited a textile plant,
about seven in ten received a "very" or "somewhat"
favorable impression of the plant they visited.

The promotional implications of these findings are basically clear, but
there can be several variations on the obvious theme. If favorable attitudes
increase with familiarity and familiarity, in turn, can be built through
plant visits, then the industry should encourage more visitors. This
approach is easily implemented where plants exist so that large numbers of
visitors may visit them—bring the visitor to the plant. However, there are
many urban areas where no textile plants exist, but where great concentrations of people live and work. A novel approach in such areas is to
bring the plant to the visitors (or a reasonable facsimile). Such was the
rationale for the THE MILL at Burlington House opened in 1970 on the
Avenue of the Americas in New York City. Since that time, over three
million visitors have been through the entrance.

THE MILL is a permanent exhibit at Burlington House and one
which is a far cry from the standard, fabric-oriented, static display. Rather,
it is a multi-sensory attraction that takes the visitor on an eight and a half
minute adventure into the fascinating world of textiles.

Two hundred feet long, the exhibit has two levels of working space,
mirrored to give the illusion of a full-scale mill. A visitor entering THE
MILL will spend his first minutes viewing various fibers and learning of
their origins. He then will see full scale textile machinery illustrating how
textiles are made—the spinning of yarn, dyeing, knitting, and weaving.
Several specialized textile processes are represented: the weaving of intri-
cately patterned jacquards, the knitting and boarding of hosiery, the
tufting of carpet, etc. (The realism of the situation is enhanced through the
use of sound tapes with the noise of a textile plant.) The final minutes of
the journey are spent viewing flashing images of the multitude of ways in
which textiles are intimately woven into the life of every human being—in
apparel, the home, and industry. And through the entire experience, the
spectator does not walk a step. A moving walkway carries him effortlessly
through THE MILL.

THE MILL is far more than just another exhibit; it has proven to be a
valuable educational tool as well. For many people who would never have
the opportunity to visit a textile mill, it has helped to develop an
understanding of the complexities of the modern textile industry. For all, it
could be described as Burlington's Ely R. Callaway once referred to it, "the
best short course in textile appreciation ever devised."

It is as though Burlington anticipated the results of the Yankelovich
study. Certainly, THE MILL is an important and innovative step toward
building favorable public attitude for the textile industry by offering a
means through which many can become familiar with the industry.

67. THE VALUE OF GOOD PUBLICITY IN TEXTILES*

James C. Cumming, Consultant

In an article in the Novermber 1970 *Textile Marketing Letter,* we defined Publicity as "an unsponsored, non-paid message—verbal or written—in a public information medium, about a company, its products, policies, personnel, activities or services." We also pointed out that if you try to withhold information the press will probably get it anyway, and will very likely get it in distorted form.

Soon after this was written, and almost by way of confirmation, one of the major textile companies was attacked in a grossly unfair and distorted manner by a self-styled protector of the consumer. Although it is unusual for the press or, as in this case, electronic media to deliberately twist the facts in order to put a company in a bad light, there are times when a reporter will get only a partial story, and that part will come from somebody with an anti-company axe to grind. That's why it's important that the company's side of every story should always be available to the press.

Even this will not always eliminate the deliberate distortion. For that reason it is essential that a continuing program of publicity and public relations be maintained that will offset any damage that may be done by those whose interests lie in other directions from yours. For you don't live in a vacuum. Somebody will always be talking about you, and he may not be friendly.

Among the textile companies that recognize this fact of the market-place and maintain good publicity programs are Burlington Industries, particularly its Galey & Lord Division, DuPont, Eastman Chemical Fibers, and the various divisions of Indian Head.

And, to be even more specific, have you ever noticed the consistently good press enjoyed by Celanese? Publicists working with other fiber companies often wish they could develop for their clients the good image that Celanese has.

There are a number of reasons for this. One of the chief reasons is that Celanese executives are not afraid to talk to the press. When an editor wants information about a fiber situation he knows that he can call, among others, Louis Laun,** president of Celanese Fibers Marketing Co. Mr. Laun somehow is astonishingly available to the press and can be trusted to make a frank and accurate comment.

Good Publicity Starts At the Top. This leads to the obvious observation that the development of good publicity for a company must start with top

---

*This article first appeared in the April 1971 issue of the *Textile Marketing Letter.*

**The current (1981) president of Celanese Fibers Marketing Co. is John A. Fennie.

management. It comes from a deliberate executive decision that the organization should work closely with the press in its broadest sense, and that includes radio and television. Then should come the decision to *seek out* publicity opportunities for the company and to see that your products and your policies get their full share of press attention.

Publicity Should Be Planned. Not *all* publicity has to be handled at such lightning speed. In fact, once the decision is made not to wait for publicity opportunities to come to you, but to seek them out, your publicity should be carefully planned and programmed.

Such planning involves two overlapping activities.

The first requires alertness on the part of your publicity person or people to take advantage of publicity opportunities that develop within the company. This means keeping an eye out for new personnel joining the organization, and issuing the proper information to the press about their backgrounds and their functions with you.

The second activity involves careful planning for as much as a year ahead. This is where imaginative photo backgrounds and news stories have their place.

Your plan, for example, will include publicizing the introduction of your new line. But it's not enough simply to photograph the fabrics or the garments in the line and send them to editors with descriptions. Both the editors and their readers find this sort of thing very dull.

So your plan calls for something more imaginative. If your new line of summer dresses is ready for the market in February, when there's still snow on the ground, fly your models to a south sea island and photograph them against exotic backgrounds. If your new winter coats are introduced to retail buyers in June, check the mountain areas where snow may be available and photograph them there.

The added pick-up by publications and interest on the part of readers will more than pay for the added cost of this kind of imaginative planning. You can even make a TV tape while you're at it, for free showing on television stations. Or you can prepare a "platter" about your line for circulation to radio stations.

In this way publicity for your company can be *created*.

The Editor's Assistant. There's no need to go into such areas of placement as the press conference and the press kit. Your publicity executive will be expert in when and how to prepare and use them.

The important thing is to give him the authority he needs to work as the editor's assistant within your organization. Editorial space, since it is not paid for like advertising space, must be *earned*.

Consider, for a moment, what a hot topic textile and fashion news is today. In consumer interest it is second only to health and beauty.

Think of the tremendous press that is available for textile publicity. There's hardly an industry that has more trade papers, all the way from the technically oriented magazines like *Dyestuff Reporter, Textile World,*

Modern Textiles, Textile Industries and *American's Textile Reporter* to marketing publications like *Women's Wear Daily, Daily News Record, Home Furnishings Daily* and *Men's Wear.*

And there's hardly an industry to which more consumer space is given. Look at the fashion news in *Good Housekeeping, McCall's* and *Ladies' Home Journal.*

That's why an investment in product publicity can be just as important to the textile marketer as his investment in advertising. Publicity should be regarded as a very important part of the textile marketing function.

Chapter Fifteen

Building the Industry's Future: the Management of Resources and Change

OVERVIEW

By Arthur Martin Spiro

The primary resources of any industry are people, fixed assets (machinery, land, buildings, energy, etc.) and finances. These contribute to varying degrees in each of the marketing, manufacturing and support activities of the textile and related industries.

Affected by seasonal cycles, changing fashions, and rapid technological developments in a highly competitive environment, the textile industry provides outstanding opportunities for creativity and the rewards that go with the successful implementation of the creative force in this fast moving business.

The role of modern management requires sound planning in an effort to best anticipate and manage the problems of change while reconciling the market needs with manufacturing capability to produce and deliver the right products at the right time, place and price. This type of planning requires both operational and strategic, qualitative and quantitative direction as to where the organization is going and how it plans to get there, coupled with a system to continually monitor these objectives, shifting gears where indicated and avoiding disasters. Accomplishing these objectives at a satisfactory profit, while maintaining personal and financially sound relationships with customers, suppliers and employees is the primary objective of management and it is towards this end that the delicate balance of optimizing human, fixed and financial resources is dedicated in building for the future.

Human Resources

Our most important consideration is the availability and motivation of the people needed to run businesses at one extreme and the motivation and satisfaction of the consumer at the other extreme. In between, as well as at these extremes, we can anticipate the continued effects of safety and environmental social legislation which will increasingly influence the processes and products of industry.

Improved data processing capability and the design and application of systems to rapidly provide meaningful information will greatly improve market research capabilities. If properly utilized, this will provide management with factual information for making business decisions relative to consumer preferences, introduction and evaluation of new products and the sensible control of inventories to avoid the pitfalls of excesses through the pipeline from manufacturer to consumer.

Labor availability in textile and related industry plants has been on the decline in this country for the past thirty years, largely due to relatively low wage scales compared to other industries plus the economic need for 24 hours of work in plants with high capital intensity and continuous processes. Much has been done by sophisticated management to improve this situation but much more is still needed in the areas of wages and benefits, working conditions and opportunities for advancement. The selection and motivation of personnel will be an important center of sophisticated management attention in building the industry's future.

In the management area, more emphasis will be placed on giving individuals responsibility for running a business and holding them to agreed results through exercises in planning and resource allocation. Men and women of ability do not necessarily all look alike, dress alike, think alike or come from the same schools and in fact, the solid growth of a company may very well depend on having managers who think differently from each other, who do not confuse questions with criticism, or dissent with disloyalty and who, once a decision is made, based on a sound analysis of all the available facts, will all get into the same boat and row hard in the same direction.

Fixed Asset Resources

At the outset, a manufacturing business must decide whether it wants any given facility to be commodity or specialty process and product oriented. For the most part, textile equipment will be made to satisfy either these two directions and those who try to mix the two types of processes and products in the same facility will likely find that costs seek the higher level, while quality and flexibility seeks its lowest level.

Commodity type processes and products demand continuous operations to justify high productivity and payout of highly capital intensive equipment in relatively large, streamlined facilities where there are the advantages of economy of scale and flow to be cost competitive.

Specialty processes and products on the other hand, while often also capital intensive are at the same time usually more labor intensive than commodity products and can usually, if properly merchandised, be marketed with wider gross profit margins than commodity products, thus justifying a much higher degree of flexibility with higher unit costs.

Again, the planning of capital resource allocations will become more important in terms of justifying proposed expenditures before they are made, relative to return on investment and need. Technological innovations are coming forth so rapidly and at such high investment costs that anything less than the most sophisticated analysis of need and return is an invitation to disaster.

The study of materials' handling and flow through sophisticated industrial engineering will continue to be important in terms of reducing the need for non-productive labor costs and speeding up deliveries of product.

Sophisticated technological approaches will continue to be developed to provide on line quality control as well as improved inspection of finished products.

Electronic data processing techniques with improved software systems offer additional opportunities for better controlling and improving delivery schedules to provide better customer service.

Buildings will be constructed with new technology to avoid the need for costly heating. These structures will be air conditioned to remove balanced machinery and body heat through principles of co-generation which will in turn provide energy that can be used to run other types of motors and equipment. All of this, coupled with sophisticated boilers and systems, will create significant reductions in the high cost and use of energy in many textile plants which are energy intensive.

Fixed asset resources are things which are becoming increasingly temporary while by comparison, human resources are much more permanent. As our relationship with things becomes less permanent, for whatever the reasons, the economics of permanence is replaced by the economics of transience, creating both problems and opportunities. In the economics of transience, advancing technology tends to cover the cost of manufacture much more rapidly than the cost of repair work. We may find that in many future instances it will become more sensible to plan building for the short term instead of the long term, and this often makes it difficult to control quality. We are moving gradually towards a "throw away society" with all of its uncertainties. Recognizing the inevitability of these changes but uncertain as to the demands they will impose on us, we must hesitate to commit large resources for relatively inflexible facilities without the most careful analysis and projections.

The choices for spending on fixed assets are many and often confusing. The greatest of care and attention to detail in terms of market, product and process analysis is needed to arrive at the right decisions in this fast moving industry, after which eternal vigilance must be applied to anticipate and recognize change, while protecting the investment. Good management will not settle for anything else.

Financial Resources

As decision making risks become more complex for the reasons already noted herein, the effective management of financial resources becomes paramount. The industry is moving so rapidly that failure to effectively protect the financial structure of an organization can often result in the precipitous collapse of some of our most sacred institutions. It is for these reasons that all of the needed product, market, personnel and fixed asset planning must increasingly flow into and through the financial and administrative areas of the company to then be structured into operating and strategic business plans that are continually monitored to avoid damaging surprises by having failed to anticipate problems and respond to change. Crisis oriented management, as a result of no planning or poor planning will have no long-term place in the future of this industry. Even the most volatile of markets, products and processes must be circumscribed with a best efforts plan to minimize the risk of financial disaster.

The need for capital to provide expansion and operating funds is great and growing. The textile industry has developed and unfortunately retained a cyclical and relatively unglamourous image in the eyes of the investment community during the past two decades and it has become increasingly difficult for many firms to obtain the financing needed to move ahead on all fronts. Thus, we are likely to see continuing shakeouts in the future with the strong, well managed companies getting stronger due to availability of outside financing while the weak will get weaker and fall by the wayside. At the same time, the opportunities will continue to remain good for new innovative entries to obtain the needed financing to exploit specialty concepts when supported by sound business plans, earnings projections, forecasted balance sheets and respectable cash flows.

Inventory management, control and turn has and will continue to be improved through the use of sophisticated data processing systems.

With all of these efforts however, in the end there is no substitute for the financial success arising out of wider profit margins reflecting the difference between cost and selling price. This result comes from the creative opportunities in effectively merchandising products and processes in this fast moving textile and related industry. Success then feeds on itself and with proper controls, the needed financial support should be available from a variety of sources including banks, factors, insurance companies, venture capitalists as well as from the public market sector.

New Horizons

No discussion of future trends would be complete without recognizing the opportunities that exist for the world emergence of our lifestyle, reflected in specialty products at one extreme and commodity products at the other, through the development of a meaningful export business which as time goes on, will then combine with imports under the umbrella of many international trading companies which will be formed in this country. Such operations are new to our relatively young nation, which until recently, has not had to pursue this area since essentially all of our products could be absorbed in home markets. It is clear however, that with the needed Federal Government support to encourage such efforts in the national interest, to create and maintain jobs, improve our balance of payments and protect the international value of our currency, that the U.S. textile industry has much to offer the world to share in this great economic opportunity which has long been enjoyed by older trading nations including the United Kingdom, Japan, Germany, and the Netherlands.

Conclusion

Effective management of change and resources must avoid the heavy cost of violent swings and disasters. The maximum long run profitability of any enterprise is the net result arising from the difference between the profits of successful decisions and the losses of unsuccessful ones. We must use all our resources effectively to increase margins while turning problems into opportunities so that we do not all become firemen in the end. We must increasingly understand and react to the crucial importance of timing, taking the initiative to shape the course of events—rather than be controlled by them. Opportunities cannot be hoarded; once past, they are usually irretrievable.

68. A LOOK AT THE TEXTILE INDUSTRY THROUGH 1990*

By Robert F. Eisen,
Greenwood Mills Marketing Company

I have been asked to use my crystal ball and tell you what I see for the American textile mill industry through 1990. First, let's take a look at what we have now. We employ 910,000 in an industry with annual sales of $38 billion and an after-tax profit of $1.025 billion. Our sales were 2½ percent

*These are the comments made at the Textile Distributors Association, Inc. annual convention at Buck Hill Falls, Pa., June 6, 1979. This article subsequently appeared in the September 1979 issue of the *Textile Marketing Letter*.

of all U.S. manufacturing, but we only accounted for 1.2 percent of the profits. To state it another way, our profits were 3.1 percent of sales and 11.6 percent of stockholders' equity, compared to 5.4 percent and 15.1 percent respectively for all U.S. manufacturing. We will spend $1.17 billion in 1979 for capital expenditures which is 0.7 percent of all U.S. manufacturing.

New textile machinery is sophisticated and expensive. The last integrated spun yarn/weaving plant built in this country was in 1973. Since then, no company has been able to justify the expenditure required for a plant of this type. New weaving plants utilizing filament yarns eliminate the need for expensive spinning equipment. Even so, in these plants the cost of fixed assets per employee is in excess of $100,000, if operated on a three-shift basis. On a four-shift or 168 hour-per-week schedule, this would decline to $80,000 per employee and production units would increase by about 21 percent.

By 1990, our industry will have fewer companies and they will be operating fewer plants. However, the plants will operate a greater number of hours per year. Four-shift operators will be commonplace. During the next decade, the number of mergers and/or acquisitions will increase. Some older plants requiring substantial expenditures, either to comply with Government regulations or to remain competitive, will close. Some companies will be acquired at prices attractive to the seller, but the buyer will also think he has gotten a bargain. This is so because some textile stocks that are publicly traded are selling at below 40 percent of the book value. In an inflationary economy, book value is a very conservative figure.

To replace some of the textile plants built within the past 20 years, the current cost would possibly be three or four times the original cost, and some of these plants are well depreciated. Jay Meltzer recently made an interesting comment, namely, that although the textile mill industry's return on equity is poor, if you buy a stock at 50 percent of its book value, your return on equity is doubled. Textile stocks can be attractive as possible acquisition candidates and/or as investments.

If you can't build a plant because of the current high costs, the alternatives are to modernize older plants, acquire other plants, or acquire other companies. However, not all older plants are good candidates for acquisition. Some are too far gone and would require expenditures substantially out of line with potential estimated profits over a reasonable period of time. Companies, regardless of size, who have good management, are generating adequate profits, and continue to modernize, will be able to compete in the marketplace and generally prosper.

Textile labor averaged $4.52 per hour, plus fringe benefits, in early 1979. By 1990, using an average annual increase of eight percent (and this may be too high), wages would be $11.37 per hour. Obviously, labor-saving machinery is desirable. High-speed water and air jet looms producing two and one-half to three times as much cloth as a fly shuttle loom are a reality. High-speed carding with improved quality is available, as is high-speed twisting. We expect further improvements in open-end spinning, particularly in rotor speeds and in the building of more durable machinery to lower the cost of spare part replacement. Robots are being built for use in America and the automotive industry is studying their use for assembly lines. Although it is not easy to visualize how a robot could replace a textile mill worker, it is not outside the realm of possibility that some of the more tedious and fatiguing tasks could be so automated.

Cloth inspection and color matching have been two of the troublesome areas in the industry. Several years ago Ford Aerospace and Communications Corp., a subsidiary of the Ford Motor Co., introduced their computer-controlled laser inspection system called Textilscan. It was a modification of a system which they developed to inspect sheets of glass used in automobiles. Springs, Burlington, Greenwood, and other companies purchased this system for the inspection of gray cloth. Hopefully, in the future a laser inspection will be available for finished cloth in white and solid colors.

Recently, this subsidiary of Ford introduced an on-line color analyzer called Qualscan which will be built under license from Greenwood Mills. In phase one, Greenwood Mills, in conjunction with Clemson University, developed a digital color scanner designed to produce a quick reading when a swatch of cloth was inserted in the machine. The color scanners that were available on the market generally had three prisms and were relatively slow. Qualscan has 16 prisms, works instantaneously, and gives reliable readings over a range of colors.

In phase two, the color scanner was mounted on the exit end of the thermosol-pad-steam dye range. It moves across the cloth every six seconds when range is operating at 100 yards per minute, and makes three readings—left, center, right—and transmits the data to a CRT terminal located at the head dyer's station. In addition, on every eighth scan a print-out is made and this is a permanent record. The computer is programmed with the acceptable tolerance both for the run and for side to center to side shading. If the scanner indicates the cloth is outside of the tolerance, an out-of-control flashes on the CRT alerting the dyer that he must make adjustments to bring the shade back into tolerance. Every 30 minutes the scanner head automatically moves to the side and calibrates itself.

The Qualscan device is being offered to the industry by Ford and a number of companies have visited our plant to see it in use.

The third phase, still to be developed, will be of interest to apparel manufacturers. It is to fully instrument the variable points on the thermosol-pad-steam dye range and with readings from the scanner, put a computer to work to program the dye range to stay on shade. If this can be accomplished, it will help the quality minded apparel manufacturer who ply marks the component parts before assembly in his sewing room. This tedious job could be eliminated.

If a computer controlled inspection system for finished cloth can be developed, it will be possible for the finishing plant to put up cloth on large rolls and ship it to the garment manufacturer along with a magnetic tape indicating where all of the defects are located in the roll. A computer controlled cutting head in the garment plant could be programmed by the magnetic tape from the cloth mill and would cut around the defects in the cloth. This system, however, would only be feasible if high-speed, single ply cutting can be made economical.

Our industry is consuming 12½ billion pounds of fiber per year, with cotton accounting for 24.3 percent, the lowest percentage in the history of our industry. By 1990, I expect that cotton will continue to decline to less than 15 percent. Cotton dust standard is one reason. Another possible factor is toxic chemicals which are under intensive study. At this stage, no one knows whether formaldehyde, the necessary chemical for imparting crease resistant finishes to cellulosic fiber fabrics, is or is not carcinogenic. If later studies show that this chemical cannot be used, it will drastically change fabrication, because a number of cloths that contain cotton or rayon require crease resistant finishes to make them salable.

There is a long-range battle of the yarn forming systems going on, namely, filament yarn versus spun yarn. Fiber companies produce staple by extruding filaments and cutting it. They ship the cut staple to the mills and we spin it into yarn. The economies have been in favor of taking continuous filament yarn and bulking it with air, steam, and/or false twist texturing to simulate a spun yarn. Efforts being made in this area are slowly but surely succeeding. Therefore, I visualize that the use of filament yarns, particularly textured polyester filament yarn, will increase. One reason would be if we have to move away from spun yarns made with cellulosic fibers because of toxic chemical related finishes. Another reason is the economy of manufacture that has been achieved in textured polyester yarns in the past ten years. Partially oriented feed yarns permitted higher extrusion speeds, the use of the more economical continuous spin/draw process, and increased texturing speeds. In sight are texturing speeds of 900 meters per minute, and machines are being built with winding speed capabilities of 1,000 meters per minute. The use of air entanglement jets on textured polyester yarn has permitted this yarn to be substituted for more expensive ply twisted yarn and/or substituted for singles yarn as a twist-free yarn. All of these efficiencies mean that textured polyester yarn is being produced more economically and the quality is better. On the other hand, the breakthroughs in spun yarn have been limited. I mentioned open-end spinning and high-speed carding, but these developments are less significant than the breakthroughs on filament yarn. I predict that capital expenditures for spinning equipment in the next decade will primarily be limited to those mills who have to replace older equipment. It is estimated that 66 percent of the yarn (on a poundage basis) used in apparel fabrics, is spun yarn. I believe that eventually the use of filament yarn will exceed spun yarn in these cloths.

There is also a long-range battle of the fabric forming systems going on, namely, wovens, knits, nonwovens. Each has its place and each is trying to enlarge its share of the market.

Nonwovens have not succeeded in gaining a foothold in apparel shell fabrics and the limited attempts to date have met with failure. However, nonwovens are replacing wovens and knits in a number of end uses including diapers, sanitary napkins, substrates for coating, wallpaper backing, etc.

Knit fabrics, particularly double knits, several years ago took a bite out of the woven apparel fabrics market, but high-speed looms have beaten back this challenge. Single knits in polyester/cotton spun yarns in solids, yarn dyes, and prints have been profitable and should continue to grow. High style double knits made from exotic blended yarns are a small but profitable part of the market. Nylon tricots have done well in the automobile industry as a headliner and until something better or less expensive comes along, they should be able to retain this business. The profitability of nylon tricot apparel fabrics seems to be in direct relationship to the supply of nylon yarn. If the yarn market is in tight supply, tricot fabrics will continue to do well. Velours made on both circular and warp knit machines have been one of the "hot" style fabrics for the past several years. Over the next ten years, their profitability will depend on whether the fabric is "in" or "out" as a style item.

Textured polyester double and single knits will remain competitively priced until the supply of polyester filament yarn tightens up. Feed yarn accounts for a high percentage of the cost of textured polyester woven and knit fabrics, and for this reason yarn procurement is of vital importance. Knit fabric plants are needed by diversified textile mills who can run substantial, texturing operations, inasmuch as knits help consume poundage, and when combined with wovens, permit large-scale purchases of feed yarn from fiber companies, thus insuring strong relationships.

Thirty-six and 40 cut textured polyester double knit fabrics have been introduced into the market and if quality problems can be overcome, these cloths will be interesting competitors against the fine denier textured polyester woven crepes.

What does our industry need to achieve our goals for the future?

We need a consistent and sustained effort on the part of the President of the United States and his Administration to control imports of textile mill and apparel products to reasonable levels.

We need a much greater effort on the part of the American textile machinery manufacturers to produce equipment that will be competitive in design, performance, and price, with machinery produced elsewhere. Much of the machinery being purchased today is made in Europe in plants utilizing labor that is paid rates equal to or higher than the U.S. Why can't American machinery companies develop equipment we need?

We need help from the man-made fiber companies. We are not looking for a new fiber. We are looking for an improved fiber, namely, a polyester fiber in both staple and filament yarn, at a reasonable price, with adequate strength, pill resistance, crease resistance, that can be aqueous dyed on a range in full spectrum of colors at economical speeds without the use of a carrier and without the use of pressure. The so-called easier polyesters that are on the market are not adequate. If we had a fiber with the specifications that I outlined, we could eliminate the thermosol units on our continuous dye ranges and by so doing make it easier to schedule dye runs in our plants. Also, as the industry moves toward greater use of textured polyester yarns, we do not want to give up the economies of range dyeing associated with spun yarn fabrics. Thermosoling of textured polyester wovens has been tried but the heat tended to destroy the bulk of the yarn. When the changeover was made from pin spindle to friction textured yarn, the new yarn had less bulk which made it still more difficult to thermosol dye this type of cloth. With easier dyeing polyester we could build aqueous dye ranges to process textured polyester woven cloths. It is also possible that a range of this type could handle polyester taffetas. If the latter were successful, the economics would permit the replacement of nylon taffetas as the big outerwear shell fabric. Give us this easier dyeing polyester fiber and the door will be opened to many new processing techniques.

Printed fabrics are an important part of the U.S. apparel fabric market, accounting for an estimated 15 percent. Although steady progress has been made by rotary screen machines in increasing speeds and the fineness of the patterns, what the industry needs is a revolutionary development: a printing machine of reasonable cost that can print cloth in a full range of printing techniques at speeds in excess of 300 yards per minute, require only one operator, be easy to operate, and produce quality fabrics. Is this impossible? With the sophisticated solid state programming that is available, nothing is impossible. If such a machine were available, it would have interesting repercussions in the marketplace, particularly if it could print at lower cost than cloth can be dyed. We would then see prints gaining a larger share of the market, particularly in children's wear and other areas where price is a factor.

Finally, let me discuss distribution. There are three channels of distribution of cloth to the apparel industry: direct sales, through converters, and through jobbers and/or importers. This distribution will continue into the forseeable future. As long as the converter supplies skilled styling, selling, and service, he will continue to perform an important function in the industry. Apparel manufacturers want to buy the "hot" print patterns, the "desirable" colors, and the "needed" fabric types, all of which, when put together, become that magic word "style." The U.S. is not a state-controlled economy. Therefore, style and the converting industry will be just as important in 1990, if not more so, than they are today!

69. CLEARING THE ROAD TO EFFECTIVE MARKETING PLANNING*

*By Carl T. Hoffman, Director, McKinsey &
Company, Inc., Management Consultants*

The Textile Industry of America is not alone in feeling the impact of the new technology. Established firms in all parts of the civilized world are having the same experience. As a result, they are taking a long, hard look at their competitive positions in today's markets and are taking steps to maintain or to improve upon those positions in the future.

Because of this situation, McKinsey and Company recently undertook a research project to determine the answers to the following three basic management questions:

1. What is the importance of forward market planning in the process of managing a business at a profit?

2. What approaches are being followed by most managements? Which approaches are working and which are not?

3. Why are some companies getting a real payoff from their marketing planning and why are others spinning their wheels, wasting a lot of time and money, and getting nowhere?

This McKinsey Study was conducted with the full cooperation of over 40 industrially-based corporations all listed in Fortune Magazine's top 500 American corporations. It was sparked by the observation that while many enthusiastically endorsed marketing planning, only a limited number of these firms could point to substantial benefits. This study confirmed the belief already held by McKinsey directors and many others that marketing

---

*This article summarizes the talk given by Mr. Hoffman at the AATT Symposium in Greenville, South Carolina on October 23, 1969. It highlights the necessity for corporate planning to keep pace with the new problems and oportunities brought about by the new textile technology. While McKinsey and Company is perhaps best known to the textile industry for its contributions to the du Pont Company and other large textile firms, it should be pointed out that Mr. Hoffman speaks from a worldwide perspective. His firm is now acting as marketing and management counsel to many of the world's leading corporations from the vantage point of McKinsey offices located in New York, Washington, Chicago, Cleveland, San Francisco, Los Angeles, Lisbon, Paris, Amsterdam, Dusseldorf, Zurich, Milan, Melbourne and Toronto.

This article subsequently appeared in the December 1969 issue of the *Textile Marketing Letter.*

planning for the future is indeed a problem area for most corporations. The most common symptoms and complaints of such planning are:

1. The excessive time which many corporation executives put into the job plus the enormous paper flow which results from it.

2. The disruption of the normal processes of running the business while the study is underway.

3. The lack of any substantial improvement in profits or in competitive market positions as a result of the study.

The Findings. We wanted to know why. Our study showed that the four most common causes of unsatisfactory results from marketing planning boiled down to the following:

1. Overemphasis on the "system" or the mechanics of planning rather than the "substance" or ideas going into the plans.

2. Planning for the future on the basis of facts that were linked solely to the past. Many corporations took the position that since they had always been "No. One" in their field and had always had a competitive edge in foreign and domestic markets that it was fair to assume that it always will be that way. They failed to take into account the whole new set of conditions which were reshuffling the competitive standings in their respective industries.

3. There was the question of inconsistent organizational assignments. Too many people were asked to do things which they were not qualified to do or unable to do because of inadequate delegations of authority.

4. In many cases there was a failure to integrate marketing planning with the overall management process. There appears to be no question that the two things must operate side by side and move in the same direction, guided by the same basic philosophy.

Form Over Content. What do we mean by overemphasis on the system? Our study showed that most people were at least generally familiar with the basic mechanics for forward planning. Despite a general understanding of what needed to be done, we encountered entirely too much preoccupation with format rather than content. With the frequent failure on the part of top management to weigh probable actions and reactions one against the other, and to challenge estimates which were usually too optimistic, many reasonably simple planning projects bogged down because too much time and paperwork were being devoted to fairly unimportant details. Finally, we discovered a great deal of corporate planning was being based on wishful thinking rather than on current competitive performance in the marketplace.

The result of this frequent overemphasis on the system was in many cases a series of highly structured plans with no substance, and no commitment to do anything that would not have been done in any event.

Then there was a third thing and this, of course, was quite understandable on the part of corporations that have reached maturity. It has to do with planning that was tied wholly to the past history of the corporation; probably the most common problem that we encountered.

Underlying Economics Misjudged. It was revealing to note how many otherwise competent executives could look at a chart showing a steadily declining share of the market or profit picture and assume that this matter could correct itself with no substantial changes in strategy or programs. When planning for the future is tied to the past there is nearly always an attempt to project the brilliant performance of the past into the future by means of forecasting. In doing so, planners frequently overlook or misjudge the underlying economics of changes in the marketplace, or in the technology of their industry, which are vitally affecting their position as well as the position of present and future competition.

Corporate executives who tie future performance planning to past performance are almost always blinded to the possibilities inherent in other alternatives and other opportunities. This entire approach emphasizes form rather than idea. In many cases, it was difficult to avoid the conclusion that management was deliberately steering clear of new ideas, either because it felt more comfortable with the ideas of the past or wasn't sufficiently conversant with the new technology and the new economics to project ideas on the basis of them.

Planning which starts with a thoughtful and comprehensive statement of "where do we want to get in the next few years," and is then followed by an imaginative consideration of all the ways of getting there, cannot help but be dynamic and vital. Such planning is not linked to the past. It considers only the future. It is quite content to consider major new marketing strategies in no way limited to existing products or markets.

In all fairness to those doing the planning, it should be stated that the information structure in many companies is such that it fails to produce the marketing and economic facts necessary for effective planning. It is also true, however, that even with the necessary facts available, many planners never really understand the business system that they are dealing with or the opportunities for the future which that system makes possible.

Three Basic Mistakes. Earlier in this study, we mentioned inconsistent organizational assignments as one of the problems most frequently encountered in doing a good job of advance marketing planning. Some of the situations we encountered could be compared to a baseball team with four catchers and no pitchers. It must be obvious to any serious student of corporation activities that organizational assignments always play a crucial role in successful marketing planning.

The three mistakes which we encountered most frequently in this area were:

1. The separation of the responsibility of planning from the responsibility of executing the plan.

2. The fact that many marketing groups are given absolutely no authority to encourage what we choose to call "marketing myopia," that is, structured to think in terms of products rather than markets.

3. The fact that many planners are given absolutely no authority to insure the very necessary inter-functional coordination which must be brought about in any corporation, if practical results are to be achieved.

It has been our observation that in this process of planning, for the company's leadership position, the choice of alternatives and other basic decisions must always remain with the responsible line executive. If this is not done, planning becomes a parallel activity to the job of running the business, and not the basis for it. Fact gathering and paper work can be delegated, but management responsibilities cannot be.

Further, there is a frequent failure to integrate market planning with the overall top management process. Overall goals and the size and growth rate, volume and profits must be agreed upon and established. Management decisions must be made regarding the products and markets to be emphasized for the immediate and more distant future. As a next step, guide lines must be established as to the assets of the corporation to be committed to the project; the availability of those assets; the return expected, and the payout requirements.

Finally, top management must always be actively involved in the challenge and evaluation of the plans and in the ultimate selection of alternatives.

Conclusions. The conclusions we have drawn from this study of 40 of the top 500 corporations are as follows:

1. Many companies are trying to solve, or at least think they are solving, their marketing problems through systematic planning, but regrettably few are succeeding.

2. Successful marketing planning requires these
   ingredients:

   a. Top management involvement and leadership.

   b. A thorough evaluation of opportunities.

   c. A planning program that embraces all critical
   functions and particularly research and
   development and manufacturing.

   d. Every successful planning project must be
   spearheaded by line executives. The plan
   must be the basis for running the business.

   e. All emphasis on the study must be on
   substance and not form.

70. WHAT LEADS TO SUCCESSFUL PLANNING?*

*By Robert E. Coleman, President,
Riegel Textile Corporation*

In *The Way of All Flesh,* Samuel Butler says that "A life will be successful or not, according as the power of accommodation is equal to or unequal to the strain of fusing and adjusting to internal and external changes." In other words, and most executives would probably agree, people and organizations will prosper to the degree that they are successful in "managing change." Whether we should or should not manage change does not appear to be the crucial question. Rather, the real question is how to manage change. Consider just a few aspects of this complex question

From a practical viewpoint, companies usually deal with change in one of two ways. Either they jump from crisis to crisis as urgency dictates, or they try to head off crises (or at least minimize their frequency) through good planning. In all fairness, though, those companies which seem to go from crisis to crisis probably do not design it that way. As many executives would be quick to point out, well-thought-out planning is certainly a justifiable objective but it nonetheless is difficult to achieve. Too many obstacles stand in the way.

In the first place, the pressures of day-to-day business simply do not leave much time in which to wonder and day-dream about what is going to happen 20 years from now. And secondly, even if there were enough time

---

*This article first appeared in the April 1974 issue of the *Textile Marketing Letter.*

to plan adequately, the problem would hardly be solved. For planning involves dealing with the uncertainties of an ill-defined future and the methodology of forecasting is far from being a precise science. A final obstacle to good planning stems from the very nature of the effort.

It is much more difficult to work with an uncertain, ill-defined future than it is to work with a current crisis. A crisis, e.g., a building falling down, is a problem with more finite and certain dimensions and thus the temptation is to procrastinate planning and work with the better-defined crisis. In the case of a building falling down, it would certainly be reasonable to devote your energies to that problem. But in many situations the problem takes on crisis proportions only as an escape from the rigors of planning.

Thus, to become successful in the management of change, management must answer with a resounding "Yes!" to the question: "Are we willing to do the work necessary for effective planning?" For PLANNING is the key to managing change. Consider just a few of the following questions which one deals with in the planning process and it becomes even more apparent why it is such a vital element:

- What are the goals of the organization?

- What threats and opportunities exist which will help or hinder the progress toward the organizational goals?

- Which alternatives for the allocation of resources (people, material, machinery, money) exist and should be chosen?

- Are the decisions currently being made consistent with overall organizational goals and objectives?

Unfortunately, perhaps the answers to the above and other similar questions are unique to every organization. Therefore, a "road map" which will automatically lead to successful planning is not available. All is not hopeless, however, for there are certain aspects which are common to almost every planning effort. The following discussion focuses on three such aspects: (1) the planning environment of the organization, (2) the availability of computer based assistance in planning administration, and (3) monitoring the plan.

The Planning Environment

No organization can successfully plan unless every level of management is willing to support the effort and create the kind of environment in which the planning process can grow and prosper. Once this has been done, the development and preparation of specific "plans" (road maps) will naturally follow and their format will tend to fit the special needs of the individual organization. Some of the characteristics of such a climate are:

FULL-TIME ASSIGNMENT. A significant portion of top management time is devoted exclusively to the questions posed at the beginning of this article (as well as to other questions which relate to the future in which the organization wants to live). One effective way to start could be to assign a trusted and effective member of the chief executive's staff to this effort on a full-time basis.

GOOD COMMUNICATIONS. Frequent conversations take place between line management and corporate management dealing with, among other things: (1) options available to the various parts of the organization, (2) the development of priorities, and (3) the resolution of conflicting objectives.

In order to have this process develop effectively, it is essential that conflicting points of view have their "day in court." Most areas that deal with the future do not lend themselves to clear-cut answers and opportunities to discuss different possibilities in a positive environment must be provided.

The environment must be healthy enough to permit the evaluation of "sacred cows"—those products or policies which were very successful in the past but which have outlasted their usefulness. This can be effective if the decision makers (the real planners) can discuss these areas without fear of recrimination. The chief executive has to decide when there has been enough "talk" and he must, if necessary, choose among the alternatives available.

A way in which this process can be encouraged is to tie-in management bonus compensation to the effectiveness with which planning is done as well as to performance against the plan.

CONTINUOUS EVALUATION. Deliberately increase the amount of time spent analyzing results in terms of the implications on future results. Rather than asking how current results compare with last year's results, keep asking the question: Are current results in line with planned results?

As the cultivation of this all-important climate continues, certain changes tend to take place. First, more and more members of the management team, both staff and line, develop a clearer understanding of the organization's goals and objectives. Second, more and more management time becomes available to refine and expand organizational goals and objectives. Third, management tends to be faced with fewer surprises. In addition, management becomes better prepared to develop alternative courses of action as required.

Computer Based Assistance

The planning process involves, among other things, a great deal of number manipulation, particularly in those situations where a number of options need to be considered. During the last several years, effective computer assistance in this area has been developed. This assistance makes it possible to:

1. Specify different relationships among data with a minimum of effort.

2. Develop the effect on goals and objectives as changes in these relationships occur.

3. Develop detailed reports (plans) which can be effectively used to monitor deviations from the plan.

Again, successful development of computer assisted planning depends more on the organizational climate than on the particular software packages that might be acquired. (Developing this capability is an invaluable stimulus to increasing the awareness of more and more people on the specifics of what needs to be done in order to achieve the established goals and objectives.)

The odds are more in favor of success when the particular individuals who are committed fully to the planning effort take the responsibility for making these kinds of software packages work. This will work better than a "joint venture" between the planning staff and the software specialist regardless of whether the software specialist is a member of the organization or whether he is an outside consultant.

Conflicting goals can also be highlighted. For example, the goals might include: (A) inventory turnover rate of 15, and (B) on-time shipments to customers 98 percent of the time. When the various concerned individuals learn how much inventory will be permitted, they may realize that the customer service goal is not achievable because of the seasonality of demand. The ideal result of such a conflict would be the development of a list of various options available for top management to review.

Monitoring the Plan

Once an agreement has been reached as to what the goals and objectives are to be and how they are to be achieved, actual results need to be monitored so that deviations from the plan can be noted, capitalized on, or corrected, as necessary. Deviations need to be noted in several areas: (1) Are planned events taking place as scheduled? and (2) Are the financial results being achieved?

The process of investigation which has to take place in order to uncover the reasons for deviation again provide invaluable learning experiences for the individuals involved. In addition to improving current results, this activity will insure that the next planning cycle will result in improved plans which, in turn, will increase the chances for the organization's long-term prosperity.

Conclusions

1. In planning, the substance of the effort exists primarily in the development of the process and secondarily in the development of specific annual or long-range plans.

2. Commitment to planning can be made effective by the dedication of an increasing amount of top management time exclusively to the effort.

3. Involvement in planning is a responsibility of all levels of management.

4. Planning is not a once-a-year exercise but is a continual year-round effort.

71. DYNAMIC NEW APPROACHES TO TEXTILE MANAGEMENT*

By Peter G. Scotese, Springs Mills, Inc.

The title of my talk, as printed on the program, could be a little misleading. It sounds as if I am supposed to descend from the rafters amid fire and lightning, clutching a list of 10 new do's and don'ts of management carved in stone. That's really not the case, and maybe I ought to explain. You could probably call it "Dynamic New Approaches to Speech Titles."

A couple of months ago, when the matter first came up, it was suggested that my topic would be, "The New Role of a Major Worldwide Textile Supplier for the Balance of the 1970's." Now there's a nice umbrella. You can take a title like that and say almost anything you want to. However, Dick Frankfort wanted something snappier. He came up with "An Inside Look at a Turnaround," which was very flattering to us at Springs Mills, Inc., but probably a little premature. Dick said he wanted something from me on the general subject of management, so we continued with this title: "Textile Management for the Seventies." Not enough sex appeal, said Dick. We thought the word "dynamic" had sex appeal. And certainly anything "new" would sound intriguing. Dick agreed. So your program today lists my talk as "Dynamic New Approaches to Textile Management."

---

*This article is the unabridged text of Mr. Scotese's address before the American Apparel Manufacturers Association meeting in New York City on November 16, 1972. It subsequently appeared in the January 1973 issue of the *Textile Marketing Letter.*

Professional Management. You deserve to know this background, because, now that you've been lured by a title with sex-appeal, I'm going to level with you. I'm going to talk about what I want to talk about. And my views on management could probably best be described as "Getting Back to Basics." That's not very sexy, but it's mine. Coach Vince Lombardi used to say that any team which executed the fundamentals of football—the basics—consistently and well would be a winner. The basics are the key to what I know as professional corporate management. They're only dynamic. in the sense that when executed consistently and well, they usually produce good results, and only their refinements are really new.

Perhaps it's the application of professional management fundamentals to textiles and apparel that's new. We represent very traditional industries. We represent industries that are largely products of individual entrepreneurs and family ownership. We represent industries that are often asset-rich and return poor. I think professional management can help the textile and apparel industries change that picture.

We have seen the beginnings of professional mangement in our industries. We need to see much more. Return on equity in the textile and apparel industries is woefully low compared to the all-manufacturing average. And that, to me, is the name of the game we are in as managers— maximizing the return on our stockholders' investment whether we're the sole stockholder or not.

Key to Success? Some people say the name of the game is selling goods, and I agree that this is all-important. But to borrow a catch-phrase from my retailing experience, "You can't sell goods from an empty wagon." You must have the goods, and you must market them profitably. Anybody can give away goods.

Others in our industry insist that the name of the game is fashion— and fashion is an important element in our business. But only if it produces an acceptable return. The high cost of producing fashion isn't worth a minimal profit; tax-free municipals would be a better investment. Still others say the key to success in textiles and apparel is modern, efficient manufacturing—and improved productivity is surely needed in our business. But plant and equipment must produce an acceptable return. To do that, it must be flexible, geared to the opportunities unearthed by successful marketing strategies.

No one element in the operation of our businesses holds the exclusive answer to this question of how to maximize return on investment. Gerald Zornow of Eastman Kodak described the situation quite aptly in a talk before the New York Sales Executives Club. He said: "The manufacturing people would like to make one product millions of times. The marketing people would like to make millions of products once. The distribution people would like just enough of whatever does get made...but they have to have it yesterday."

To keep our companies operating and producing effectively requires a dynamic balance and interaction between all these functions. Maintaining that balance and promoting that interaction is the job of professional management. How does professional management go about this? What's so different about a professional manager?

Earlier, I talked about getting back to basics. The professional manager makes certain basic assumptions, and makes use of certain basic principles, in his efforts to produce the best return for his company and stockholders. We've done this at Springs Mills, Inc. We did it when I was with Federated and Indian Head. Other managers do it at many other companies. To a large degree the assumptions and principles used are the same regardless of the type of business you're managing.

Over the years, I have developed a point of view toward management that I'd like to share with you—per Dick Frankfort's suggestion. I might point out that I also share this point of view with the key managers of our company—not to impose a management style on anyone, but to insure a unified commitment to the philosophy and principles we think are essential in building the kind of corporation we want to operate.

Planning. First, I believe in the science of professional management, and the art of making it work. This means producing planned results by establishing and accomplishing specific objectives, goals, priorities and strategies for both the near-term and the long-term. This is not limited to the small group at the top; it should permeate all layers of the corporation. Division results should contribute to corporate objectives. Department results should contribute to division objectives. Continous, in-depth, long-range planning is the process which provides a blueprint for achieving objectives. And this is what it's all about.

The starting point in any planning process is the corporate objective— what is the corporation trying to achieve?

You'd be surprised—or maybe you wouldn't—to discover how difficult it is for people within a company, people who've worked side by side for years, to agree on the purpose of the company. Often, they've never really thought about it before. In other cases, Joe wants to go in one direction and Sam wants to go in another. Whatever the case, it is perhaps the most difficult part of the planning process to hammer out agreement among corporate management on the primary objective. But a specific objective— whether it's to increase the value of the common stock, or to add a certain increment each year to earnings per share, or to increase share of market by a certain amount—is absolutely necessary. It charts a definite course for the corporate ship.

The primary objective of the corporation is to focus on the plans, budgets, goals and strategies of the corporation's individual components. And the long-range planning process shouldn't be limited to the top corporate management and the planning director. All the key executives on the corporate staff and in the divisions should be involved. It is something they must do as an extension of their day-by-day operating duties necessary to run their businesses. We call these people our "key mistake-makers"—they are the executives in any company who can influence profit and loss in a significant way.

In addition to providing targets to aim for, the planning process is very valuable in other ways. It enables managers to participate in goal-setting, and this is important in motivating the individual manager and allowing him to relate his function to the rest of the operation. It also forces upon him the discipline of weighing alternatives, and supporting his recommendations with strong, factual arguments.

While I'm on the subject of planning let me give a plug for the American Management Association's Center for Planning and Implementation at Hamilton, New York. Springs has conducted all its long-range planning sessions there, and I'm convinced there's no other place quite like it in the world—in terms of providing the structure for the proper kind of planning.

Management by objectives, of course, requires extensive and frequent measurement and evaluation of results. Managers should take whatever action seems indicated by measurement to stay on plan, or get back on plan.

Often, this involves computerized information systems. My own view is that the test of such a system is not cost, nor personnel reduction, nor glamorous sophistication—it is whether it provides managers data that is both timely and actionable. If it doesn't meet this test, you're wasting your money.

I also believe in management by exception. This requires that operational decision-making be delegated as far down the line as possible. A manager's style can be his own. And as long as he is adhering to generally accepted basic principles and achieves planned results, he should be left alone. Attention should be focused on the exceptions—the areas that are not performing as planned or expected.

Personnel. A second principle of professional management involves people. Producing superior results requires superior people. Highly capable people are motivated by the opportunity to demonstrate their ability. I think it is desirable to establish a system of goals and rewards which recognizes this, and compensates, beyond base salary, those individuals whose performance produces superior results. This would include such items as bonuses, incentive compensation, stock plans, profit sharing and the like.

I also expect my managers to help recruit, develop and identify strong people, in order to place them on a faster "career track." Any manager's "Number Two" man or woman should be interchangeable with his boss. This is how you develop executives capable of guiding future growth. One way of insuring this is to establish systematic personnel evaluation procedures, outside training and planned advancement programs.

To many people, this probably sounds like you have to add layers of people and mountains of paperwork. That's the easy way. The trick is to keep the business simple, with as few layers of people as possible. What you really want are people who can concentrate on things that actually contribute to the profitability of the business. "Playing office" and engaging in "paper warfare" are unproductive.

Professional management calls for a lean, qualitative group of people who avoid "busy work," paper shuffling, and a perfectionist approach which results in investing time and effort beyond the real value of a given job. These are creative, innovative people, people who seek challenge, and who work well in group situations At Springs, we are building an organization which encourages that kind of person. We have found that bringing together people with different areas of expertise—as characterized by our Corporate Management Committee—produces valuable synergism, and a clearer understanding of broad objectives and strategies.

Your own personnel needs, organizational structure, planning processes and compensation systems should be predicated on one idea—that managers at all levels identify with the interests of the stockholder.

Profit Center. A third principle is the profit center concept. Profit centers should be established wherever practicable as a means of bringing a product to market.

This concept clearly establishes profit and loss responsibility. It also facilitates marketing the product, and evaluating its acceptance. And it provides a vehicle for delegating opportunity to a group of managers. There is a great deal of latitude for innovation in the profit center concept, within the context of the corporate long-range plan.

Marketing Orientation. This concept complements a fourth principle, which is a marketing orientation. Management should begin with an assessment of consumer needs, and work back from there in developing and delivering products to fill those needs at an acceptable profit.

This requires strong market research, not only to provide actionable data in terms of consumer needs and long-term trends, but to develop information about our competition. You don't necessarily want to follow a competitior's lead, but you certainly don't want to act out of ignorance of what he is doing. It also requires strong product management, with profit-and-loss responsibility centered in the individual product manager. This involves proposal and development of new products, as well as bringing them to market in profitable, innovative ways. And a strong marketing orientation involves determining whether it is more profitable to buy and resell, or to produce goods in a given situation.

ROI. Fifth, and last, and most importantly, we come to the principle which I think should be the operating motto of the organization— "What's the return on investment?"

The successful professional manager thinks like a stockholder, whether he is one or not. This means placing emphasis on capital turnover, inventory turnover, improving gross margins on products, investment in low-cost, high-yield markets, increasing the productivity of existing assets, and divesting those assets which are not providing an acceptable rate of return.

One way to accomplish this is to institute strict capital budgeting systems. Relate the anticipated return on any proposed project to the cost of corporate money on the outside market. Limit the allowable payout times on capital projects. Establish ceilings on total new annual investments in fixed assets. Make a case for a project's profitability through the components of your company before you as a corporation finance it. At Springs, we expect every manager at all levels to think "return on investment" constantly. It is the single most important fundamental that managers and their associates must consider. We simply must make more money on an investment than it costs us to finance it.

So there you have one professional manager's views on professional management.

It can be stated much more simply. Experience has shown me that three basic rules can be applied to all operations:

1. In the near-term, avoid catastrophe.

2. In the intermediate term, maintain the operation.

3. For the long-term, improve the operation.

A professionally-managed company, in my judgment, is market-oriented, with specific objectives. It has superior, innovative people, a commitment to long-range planning, a lean, loose organization and a thorough knowledge of its operating environment. And it has a management team strongly unified by its understanding of corporate objectives and principles—and who think "return on investment" all the time, just like the stockholders.

72. THE MANAGEMENT OF CHANGE*

By Arthur M. Spiro, Executive Vice President,
Waumbec Mills, Inc.

Perhaps the first step in the *Management of Change* is to appreciate that all technological change is not for the good of man or society. Massive technological failures too often go unrecognized until we find that many of the right questions were not asked soon enough, as illustrated by the

*We are grateful to Mr. Spiro for permission to reprint these highlights from the great speech which he gave before the Textile Distributors Association at Pocono Manor, Pa., June 16, 1971. To the best of our knowledge, this is the first time that any responsible textile marketing executive has undertaken to analyze the respective impacts of fashion and technology on textile marketing, and to put each in its proper place. Few men are as well qualified as Mr. Spiro to undertake an assignment of these dimensions. He has been a leader in the world of fabric fashions for many years. He knows production and he knows

U.S. Supersonic Transport Airplane, Low-Calorie Diet Beverages and Corfam Poromeric Products.

Gardner writes that societies and organizations, like people and plants, have a life cycle, with a green and supple youth, a time of flourishing strength and a gnarled old age—but the life cycle of organizations is not predictable.

The increased rate of technological change and the resultant necessary decision making processes, tend to shorten the life span of societies that are not equipped for the *Management of Change.*

Gardner further emphasizes that an organization, capable of continuous renewal through the *Management of Change,* must be interested in what it is going to become, not what it has been!!

Our worst examples of frustration and failure are in those societies of big government, big school systems, big businesses, big labor unions and big religious organizations which have become prisoners of procedures with the rule books growing fatter and the valuable ideas growing fewer.

The Daily News Record carried an article on May 5th, 1971, headlined "Technology Stars at Knitted Outerwear Exposition in Atlantic City—With Fashion Sidelined!!"

In addressing the Annual Meeting of the Knitted Outerwear Association, Ben Heller said that we are making too much of the same—"we are making frankfurters not fashion and that road leads to indigestion!"

In speaking on the subjects of Knits—Promises and Problems at the American Society of Knitting Technologists Meeting in May 1971, Ely Callaway said that the day will soon come when the number of knitting machines a company owns and operates will not be nearly so important as it seems to be now.

Herb Koshetz writing in the *New York Times* on Sundays, May 2nd and May 16th, 1971 expressed industry concern over deficiencies in quality and performance characteristics of knits and we see similar articles appearing almost every day in trade publications.

Recently, a very important customer of ours asked to see what we had in the way of raschels and we in turn asked *Raschel What?*

Reconciling these items suggests that technology is managing us to the extent that we have forgotten our business is fashion and the creation of stimulants to the purchase of soft goods in the battle for textiles' share of the consumer dollar. Technology should stimulate and serve fashion, not replace it!!

---

marketing. He has received degrees from both Clemson University and the Massachusetts Institute of Technology.

Following a series of quotations which emphasize recent changes confronting the textile and apparel businesses and which deal with the influences that bring about fundamental changes in any business organization or society are Mr. Spiro's twenty basic questions and answers dealing with today's marketing problems.

This article appeared in the March 1972 issue of the *Textile Marketing Letter.*

Fashion, like art and fine cuisine, is an expression of man's reaction to his environment, however the source of strength and reasonable longevity must come from an aesthetic center of authority. When that center of authority becomes so over powerfully techonological that we become more concerned with the machine than the product, the tail wags the dog.

Occasionally we achieve an unusual, major technological break-through and for a time, as in the recent double knit machinery develop-ment, the resultant products generally coincide with current fashion needs. There are times, however, when a significant new development can get somewhat out of hand, as for instance: we have steamrollered European technology into a trend that has made most other medium to heavyweight apparel fabrication seem like..........some form of social disease.

There is no long-term license to print money in the textile business! The payoff still goes with creativity, hard work and a contribution to fashion, value and quality, the understanding of which does not come in packages with instructions accompanying the machinery!

In the race to expand our domestic markets, we have provided an umbrella under which European and Far Eastern countries have been able to find a very profitable home for the best of their otherwise distressed and surplus fiber, fabric and garment production in the U.S.A. on the basis of price, style and quality—in wovens and knits of textured filament polyester yarns. Make no mistake about it, these imports, often supported by export subsidies in their country of origin, will be difficult if not impossible to dislodge.

Extremism in any form is no virtue and to suggest that the fancy warp business now has the same and very unusual type of growth potential that double knits had a number of years ago, is another form of wishful thinking that does not reveal an understanding of facts.

Warp knit machines are relatively inflexible in styling capability and almost two thirds of domestic capacity is concentrated in the hands of a very few firms which are equipped to think and deal in volume, whether plain or fancy. This is not to suggest that opportunities are not bright for new and relatively small, fancy, warp knit fabric suppliers but it seems clear that such possibilities are relatively limited because of the basic conflicts that exist in terms of quality and cost, each of which seeks its most undesirable level when the mix gets so big as to be difficult to manage.

Questions and Answers

1. Why are some elements of the garment and fabric business such as men's and ladies' footwear, accessories, men's shirts, neckwear and slacks now doing so well?
   Suggested Answer: Fashion, which did not come about as the result of any given technological machinery development but as an expres-sion of life stimulated by central authorities in such places as New York, California and Europe.

2. Why have some elements of the garment and fabric business such as men's tailored clothing and ladies' dresses been so poor of late?

   Suggested Answer: Lack of a new central fashion trend to provide direction and stimulate retail and consumer purchasing in spite of the availability of all kinds of new and sophisticated technical equipment.

3. Will the men's tailored clothing business and the women's dress business improve and if so, when?

   Suggested Answer: You betcha! The women's dress business is already staging a comeback, sponsored by fashion authority, and as soon as the construction of men's tailored clothing reveals a new and long overdue, more comfortable look and performance, commensurate with our environment, it too will come back strong in woven goods as well as knits.

4. Are fashion trends predictable?

   Suggested Answer: Only when there is a central trend of authority to provide direction from which we can draw inspiration! It makes little difference whether it is Paris, London, Florence, or Seventh Avenue so long as it is a recognized direction that fits the times!

5. Generally speaking, have we been in a period of fashion stagnation in women's wear?

   Suggested Answer: Yes! We occasionally do go through such characteristically recognizable periods of confusion which rob innovators of their main weapon for earning profits. In rebelling against all sources of authority, we have tried to torpedo the small conspiracy of creators who in turn provide us with the nucleus of needed direction.

6. What happens when we torpedo the fashion innovator?

   Suggested Answer: Technology takes over as the sole remaining weapon in the fight to gain competitive supremacy, with emphasis on utility. We are in that stage today—which is yesterday for the forward looking!

7. What are the signs that signal the revival of fashion at the expense of technology?

   Suggested Answer: The print business. Here the talents are fewer, the risks are greater. The print business is hot! Once this is overdone, as it cyclically always is, we will see the emergence of new looks—perhaps "Linens with a new look."

8. Do people still want to look smart and pretty?

   Suggested Answer: Most definitely! Those kids with denim dungarees and long hair think they look smart and pretty and I believe they do. Their dress is an expression of a return to nature at the expense of technology and keenly observant manufacturers have made fortunes by "getting with it." Don't knock it—join it—and when they all start looking the same, that fashion look, too, will pass. That's the name of the game.

9. Where do we look next for fashion inspiration?

Suggested Answer: Look at the times and surroundings for inspiration; nature and ecology. Cleanliness will go with it. A rebellion against technology is as much a part of fashion as it is against beer cans and disposable bottles!

10. In rapidly changing times, what is the most important basic virtue of expensive textile machinery?

    Suggested Answer: (Flexibility)—To produce what the market needs! Machines only pay off when they run—and not for making unwanted inventory.

11. Is the double knit machine a flexible piece of equipment?

    Suggested Answer: "YES," very much so in terms of potential styling capability within certain limits, providing one has the capacity to put the material to good use and the market wants it. Suggested Answer Two: "No," it is one of the most inflexible pieces of textile manufacturing equipment ever devised for its price, relative to the ability to economically compete on a wide variety of basic fabric concepts.

12. Are warp knit machines more flexible than double knit machines?

    Suggested Answer: Technically, "YES" because it is theoretically easier to change needles and gauge, practically speaking, "NO" unless one wants to have a bigger warping department than knitting department. Circular machines are ideal for short runs; warp knit machines for long runs.

13. Are single knit circular machines flexible?

    Suggested Answer: More so than double knit or warp knit machines providing the product has competitive value!

14. Is weaving more flexible than knitting?

    Suggested Answer: Yes! With respect to the ability to pay off in a vastly wider variety of basic constructions using a wider range of yarns on any given loom, but for only relatively long runs as in the case of warp knitting. A knitting needle has severe limitations compared to the drop wires and needles of a loom and it is infinitely easier to change harnesses and loom reeds than to change needles, dials, cylinders and gauge on any knitting machine.

15. What is the most flexible way to achieve fashion style trends in fabric?

    Suggested Answer: Printing! For those with talent and strong stomachs!

16. Is the weaving business dead?

    Suggested Answer: Read and understand if you will, Ely Callaway's remarks delivered to the American Society of Knitting Technologists, on May 7, 1971.

17. Aside from new generation replacement machines, do we have an oversupply of double knit machines installed and on order in this country?

    Suggested Answer: Same as the previous answer.

18. Relative to the number of very expensive jacquard double knit machines in place and on order for this country, can we estimate our

supply of design and mechanical talent needed to take optimum advantage of this capability to produce fancy goods?

Suggested Answer: A good "guesstimate" is less than twenty percent. Parenthetically, there is probably not sufficient demand to continually take advantage of much more than this unless we want to compete with prints. Think about that one for a while before spending $50,000 to $60,000 for a relatively inflexible piece of highly sophisticated equipment that produces about 1,000 to 1,500 yards per week!

19. Is there too much fabric making equipment of all types, installed and on order in this country now, relative to our needs?

Suggested Answer: Yes! Surgery will be needed to eliminate much of the same in all sectors of weaving and knitting and to replace some of what is left with more efficient and more flexible equipment. This will be further complicated as new and important fabric forming techniques continue to be developed. The danger is that many patients will die by throwing the cost book away before calling the doctor; thus creating depressed market prices that will carry the disease to others. THE SHAKE OUT IS HERE IN SOME AREAS AND COMING FAST IN OTHERS.

20. What is the most important consideration in the future of the textile business in the U.S.A.?

Suggested Answer: People and the motivation of them in our businesses at one extreme, as well as consumerism at the other extreme. In a recent address, Gabriel Hauge, Chairman of the Manufacturers Hanover Trust Company refers to it as "REWRITING THE SOCIAL CONTRACT." Products and processes will be increasingly influenced by these needs.

Successful fashion evolution can provide reasonable longevity. Evolution can be compressed with care, but when the squeeze explodes into fashion revolution, we have chaos in our business as in other societies. Instant fashion brings instant successes and instant failures, which equals nothing for those who are dedicated to style, quality, service and value. We do not want a continuing fashion dictatorship from any source, but given the choice of extremes, as Machiavelli wrote in politics, society will prefer tyranny to anarchy! The search for leadership in fashion is as important as it is in government.

Fashion instability derives from social instability, the roots of which are many and complex in our societies. Having provided relative abundance so quickly, towards the improvement of basic living conditions for most of our society, and with goals and plans set to bring full achievement soon, our forward social momentum creates a restless search for new priorities and values. There is an awakening for a new emphasis on the quality of life, which in turn will provide needed direction for those in our industry who are keen enough to be inspired and take action.

Information and communication advances in our better informed society places a greater responsibility on the media to provide us with needed, proper information. I wish we could join together, as their readers and customers, to advise our friends of the fourth estate that their continued creation of controversial confusion is damaging to our business. We need protection from this kind of friendship and we know that they can and should be more constructive in responding to our needs.

It is recognized that the world's current and future crises are created by the inability of institutions to control technological change and economic development, while all of mankind struggles to strike a balance between its goals and the ability to achieve them. The textile industry is cyclical enough, with its successes tied to a host of imponderables, including weather conditions and the fickleness of women, so that we cannot also afford to over accelerate technological development as we have done of late, unless we are bent on self destruction!

As one who has been identified with advancing the cause of bench technological development in this industry for more than 25 years, and who has benefited immeasurably from the same, I am now suggesting that the time has come for us all to stop abusing technological developments, by imposing some needed self-restraints, relative to our human ability to cope with the job *Through the Management of Change.* I am afraid that we cannot constructively sort out all the technology at the rate it is being delivered by the machinery people and the media—and when we try to do so, it is inevitably at the expense of giving needed attention to fashion, which is much more important to the continuing needs of all concerned!

The demise of a textile firm or the closing of a mill no longer seems to be the news it used to be, but rather just another disposable object on an already littered field.

As the title of Patricia Griffith's novel put it, "THE FUTURE IS NOT WHAT IT USED TO BE!"

Biographical
Sketches

NANCY C. BOITER

Nancy Boiter is currently stylist in charge of design and styling for the Cavel Division of Collins and Aikman Corporation. She has been extensively involved in all phases of creative development, design, and marketing of fabrics for the furniture, home furnishings, and automotive industries. Previous to her present position she was creative merchandiser with the LaFrance Division of Riegel Textile Corporation. She also was head stylist with LaFrance.

Nancy has traveled extensively in the U.S.A. and abroad in developing new design ideas and in seeking new markets. She has lectured in North Carolina State University, Clemson University, and the University of Georgia in the areas of textile and fabric design.

She is a graduate of the University of Georgia with a degree in Interior Design, a past scholar in the artists-in-residence program in Cortona, Italy, a member/student in the Ossabaw Island Project, and she holds a Master's Degree in Fabric Design from the University of Georgia. She has consulted and taught weaving and fabric design for numerous groups and is currently a member of several professional and trade groups in the textile industry.

275

JOHN A. CAIRNS

John Cairns got his first exposure to textile marketing in the fall of 1925 when he became an advertising copywriter in the Service Department of Fairchild Publications. He finished his active career in textile marketing some 50 years later when temporary illness forced him to resign from his job as executive director of the American Association for Textile Technology. In his earlier years in the industry, Mr. Cairns handled the advertising of Snia Viscosa Rayon at a time when its sales in this country exceeded those of any domestic producer. He also handled the advertising of Cisa, which was generally considered to be the first to introduce spun rayon to this market. In 1927 Mr. Cairns became vice-president and copy chief of an advertising agency whose clients were all in the textile or related industries, many of them in the woolen and worsted business, foreign and domestic. Mr. Cairns started his own advertising agency, John A. Cairns and Co., Inc. in the summer of 1930 and started John A. Cairns of Canada Ltd. a few years later. The war years saw him commuting at regular intervals between his headquarters in New York and his newly established offices in Montreal and Toronto. In later years he had correspondent agencies in a number of European countries to serve the needs of clients in those countries as well as American companies with interests abroad.

In January of 1966 Mr. Cairns started the *Textile Marketing Letter* as a public relations medium for the firm of which he was then Chairman. Shortly after that he joined forces with Dr. Wallace D. Trevillian, Dean of the College of Industrial Management and Textile Science at Clemson University in establishing Clemson's annual "Textile Marketing Forums" which lasted for several years. He retired as Chairman of Chirurg and Cairns, Inc. at the end of 1967 and arranged to have them present the *Textile Marketing Letter* to Clemson University in January of 1970. Mr. Cairns went along with the new set-up as one of the *Letter's* contributing editors, and still spends a major portion of his time on matters relating to the *Textile Marketing Letter* and to its new companion piece, *Handbook of Textile Marketing.*

JIM H. CONNER

Jim H. Conner was born in Atlanta, Georgia on November 10, 1937, and attended public schools there. He graduated from Georgia State University with a B.B.A. degree in 1962 and received an M.B.A. degree from the same school in 1968.

Following graduation from college in 1962, he joined Armstrong Cork Company as a marketing representative with assignments in Lancaster, Pennsylvania, and Atlanta, Georgia. In 1966, he joined the Georgia Textile Manufacturers Association, where he served as secretary of the organization until July, 1972 when he was named executive vice-president of the American Yarn Spinners Association, the national trade association of the sales yarn industry. In addition to his duties with AYSA, he serves as executive director of the Association of Synthetic Yarn Manufacturers, the Carpet Yarn Association, and the Durene Association of America.

His interest in international affairs goes back to his college days when he was a delegate to the Auburn Conference on International Affairs. He currently serves on a number of U.S. Government advisory committees including the Exporter's Textile Advisory Committee, the Management-Labor Textile Advisory Committee, and the Industry Sector Advisory Committee for Multi-lateral Trade Negotiations. In addition he served as an advisor during negotiations of the Multi-Fiber Arrangement, the Tokyo Round trade negotiations, and some 50 bilateral trade negotiations over the last several years. He organized two highly successful trade missions to Europe and the first textile trade missions to Hong Kong and the Peoples Republic of China. These missions were aimed at introducing U.S. yarn products in overseas markets.

He is a former director of the Gastonia Rotary Club, a life member of Delta Sigma Pi professional business fraternity, and a member of the Legion of Honor of the Order of Demolay. During college, he was named to Who's Who in American Colleges and Universities and served as student body president.

KAY CORINTH

Kay Corinth has had a varied career in the fashion world, including a close association with apparel and home furnishings textiles. She is presently a free-lance writer and contributing editor of *Fabricnews*, an international textile trade publication, and has written many articles for other trade media.

Her textile background includes serving as fashion director of William Skinner & Sons, one of the country's oldest mills, where she styled fabrics, colors and prints, traveling to Europe each year for ideas.

As merchandising director of *Seventeen* magazine, she planned and executed fabric and home furnishings promotions for teenage girls in the country's leading retail stores.

She is author of *Fashion Showmanship*, a book on how to plan and produce fashion shows, published by John Wiley & Sons. With Mary Sargent, she is co-author of *All About Entertaining* and *Male Manners: The Young Man's Guide*, both published by David McKay Company.

Ms. Corinth holds an M.S. Degree from New York University, an A.B. Degree from Oklahoma City University in her native city, and a certificate with honors from Tobe-Coburn, a fashion merchandising school. She has received the "Distinguished Alumni Award" from OCU, the Lane Bryant and Alumnae Club Awards from NYU, and the "Mehitabel" award from Tobe-Coburn Alumnae.

She is currently serving on the Merchandising Committee connected with the New York State Board of Education "Futuring Project," a two-year study of the curricula in marketing and distributive education.

She is active in a number of professional organizations for women executives, including The Fashion Group, National Home Fashions League, New York Women in Communications and Trends. She resides in Manhattan with her husband Thomas Corinth, son of the noted painter Lovis Corinth.

MICHAEL JAMES DREWS

Mike Drews' expertise in textile chemicals comes from several years of work and research in textile chemicals, dyes, fibers, and flame retardants. He is presently an Associate Professor of Textile and Polymer Science at Clemson University where he has taught and carried on an active research program since 1972. He received his doctorate from North Texas State University and his B.S. from the University of Wisconsin. He has published widely in journals, given many presentations to groups throughout the world, and held numerous research grants and contracts to conduct basic and applied research in textile chemistry. He is currently a member of the American Association of Textile Chemists and Colorists, and the American Chemical Society.

ROBERT F. EISEN

Robert Eisen is president of Greenwood Mills Marketing Company, a division of Greenwood Mills, Inc. of Greenwood, South Carolina.

Mr. Eisen began his career in textiles in 1937, and with the exception of the years 1942-1946, when he served on active duty with the U.S. Navy as a Lieutenant Senior Grade, he has spent his entire business career in this field. He graduated from St. John's University in 1942 with a degree of B.B.A.

Mr. Eisen is a member of the Management-Labor Textile Advisory Committee of the U.S. Department of Commerce. He serves on the Textile Market Committee, International Trade Committee and the Economic Affairs Committee of the American Textile Manufacturers Institute. He is a member of the board of directors of the Textile Distributors Association, Inc.; a member of the Mid-Manhattan Advisory Board of the Manufacturers Hanover Trust Company; a Trustee of the Union Dime Savings Bank; serves as an arbitrator for the American Arbitration Association.

He resides in Garden City, Long Island with his wife, Louise.

THOMAS H. GUNTER, D.B.A.

Dr. Tom Gunter is a native of Atlanta, Georgia and was educated at Georgia Tech (B.S.I.M.) and Georgia State (M.B.A., D.B.A.). He has both industrial and academic experience in his field of marketing and management.

Presently Dr. Gunter is Professor of Marketing and Dean of the School of Business and Economics at USCS. He has taught at Clemson University and Old Dominion University. He has consulted with over thirty organizations in the areas of consumer behavior, long-range planning and corporate strategy. His research interests of lifestyle and psychographic analysis and personnel selection have appeared in several dozen publications. Dr. Gunter is on the editorial board of the *Textile Marketing Letter*.

J. MICHAEL MC DONALD

Mike McDonald has varied experience related to textile marketing. For the past several years, while teaching in Clemson University's College of Industrial Management and Textile Sciences, he has consulted and conducted research mainly in the areas of personnel, labor relations, and public perception of the textile industry. He has published articles in several textile-related publications, including the *Textile Marketing Letter*. He is presently an Associate Professor of Industrial Management. He received his B.S. degree from Georgia Tech, and his Ph.D. from the University of Georgia.

EDWARD MORSE

Edward Morse's career has been centered on communication. From a newspaper reporter, first on *The New York Press* and then on the *New York Evening Sun* he went to Lord & Taylor as assistant advertising manager in charge of advertising for The Man's Shop; later he was named the store's advertising manager. From Lord & Taylor he went to the newly opened Saks-Fifth Avenue as advertising manager. His direct association with fibers and fabrics started with the reorganization of merchandising of Pacific Mills where his title was "Assistant Sales Manager in Charge of Advertising." From cotton and woolens he went to Celanese Corporation of America as advertising manager, then about to launch a full-scale campaign for its synthetic textile fibers and fabrics. At Celanese he directed participation in cooperative advertising at all levels of distribution—mill customers of its yarns, converters marketing fabrics containing Celanese yarns, with cutters using such fabrics and with retail stores for both piecegoods and ready-to-wear departments.

JULIA MORSE

Julia Morse has had extensive experience in the marketing of textiles. She started as a copywriter for Marshall Field of Chicago, and later joined Peck & Peck as its publicity director. At Chirurg & Cairns, an advertising agency with offices in New York, Hartford and Boston, she was a vice-president, chairman of the Women's Point of View Committee and a member of the board of directors. She supervised such textile-oriented accounts as Dan River Mills, the Lurex Division of the Dobeckman Company and the International Silk Association.

Her authority on fashion as a marketing factor in textiles is under-scored by her service in the International Fashion Group, New York, as a vice-president and in Boston as a director of the regional Fashion Group. Most recently she has been an Instructor in Advertising at the Chamberlain School of Retailing, a junior college in Boston.

JOHN B. RUSSELL, JR.

John Russell's expertise in the marketing of textiles has come from a long career in textiles. He recently retired from Dan River, Inc. where he served as assistant to the chairman and chief executive officer.

Russell joined Dan River in 1969 as executive vice-president of marketing and a director of the company. In this capacity, he served as Dan River's senior executive in the New York area until 1979. During this period, he was also responsible for the Dan River International Corporation, an export subsidiary which directs sales activities in some 25 foreign countries.

During 1979 Russell undertook a special assignment to expand Dan River's activities in the export sales area. He spent a number of months in Hong Kong and was responsible for establishing the company's first distribution structure in the Far East.

During his career with Dan River, Russell has been very active in industry affairs, and has served as chairman of the American Textile Manufacturers Institute, the industry's central trade association. He has also served as chairman of the Export Subcommittee of the International Trade Committee of ATMI. For a number of years he has represented the textile industry on the General Arbitration Council, and currently is chairman of this organization. He is also a member of the Management Labor Advisory Committee of the U.S. Department of Commerce.

Russell began his textile career in 1946 as a salesman for Folkard & Lawrence. From 1951 to 1955 he served as a merchandise manager for Dan River before joining Burlington Industries as general merchandise manager for the company's Mooresville Division. He subsequently was named vice-president of the division in 1958 and its president in 1959.

He assumed increasing responsibilities during his career at Burlington and, before joining Dan River, was serving as president of the International Division of Burlington and a member of Burlington's Management Committee.

LEON E. SEIDEL

About half of Leon Seidel's 36 years of textile business life has been spent studying and applying softgoods marketing principles. Before engaging in this activity, he was educated as a textile engineer at the Philadelphia College of Textiles and Science, with his last year spent doubling as student and faculty member. During his academic period, he was given the opportunity to work in two mills, a worsted weaver and a vertical cotton mill.

Seven years of synthetic yarn weaving mill experience in the New York and Allentown, Pa. areas came next, culminating in plant's management.

Modern metallic yarns always held a special fascination for Seidel and it was in this business that he spent the next 14 years with the Dobeckmun Co. In this work he formalized and communicated a technology for the infant industry, did technical service and formulated quality standards for metallic yarn manufacture.

When Dobeckmun was purchased by Dow Chemical Co., Seidel was transferred to the Williamsburg, Va. headquarters for two years of marketing management training. After this, he returned to New York, first as merchandising manager, then as field sales manager for filament yarns.

For the following six years, Seidel was vice-president—marketing for Metlon Corp., a producer of metallic and plastic yarns. He joined Textile Industries as marketing editor in 1969, wrote the hardback book, *Applied Textile Marketing*, later, and to the present, added fibers and fabric forming editorial duties to his senior editor status.

JANE TOWLER SMILEY

Jane Smiley is the Director of Special Events, Fashion Activities, and Publicity for all 19 Burdine's Department Stores in Florida. (Burdine's is owned by Federated Department Stores.) Her responsibilities encompass all aspects of her store's public relations, community activities and all store promotions which can run the gamut from fashion shows to home store events to selection of the Burdine's float for the Orange Bowl Parade which is seen on national television.

Mrs. Smiley's career started with the executive training program at Macy's New York, continued at Lord & Taylor and, in turn, led to becoming the Marketing Consultant for *The New Yorker* magazine where she made repeated research trips to more than forty major U.S. markets, as well as European centers. In addition her work included covering men's and women's apparel markets, furniture and home furnishing markets and also preparing selective marketing and advertising programs for manufacturing concerns. Upon leaving the magazine Mrs. Smiley became the first woman national brand Sales Manager in the domestics industry as Martex Sales Manager at West Point-Pepperell, Inc.

Her professional activities have been varied: They include serving on the board of directors of "The Fashion Group, Inc.," and in other capacities in the "National Home Fashions League," and "Advertising Women in New York," and as past president of "TRENDS" the prestigious and exclusive fashion executive group in Manhattan.

ARTHUR MARTIN SPIRO

Art Spiro has had extensive experience in many areas of the textile industry. He is currently vice-chairman of the board, Carleton Woolen Mills, Inc., and president, A.M.S.-TEX Enterprises, Inc. and Spiro Fane Corp. He also operates his own consulting business serving textile and related industries in management, marketing, technology, and finance through A.M.S.-TEX. He was previously corporate vice-president with United Merchants and Manufacturers, Inc.; director and executive vice-president for marketing with Waumbec Mills, Inc.; director of merchandising for the Industrial Rayon Corporation; and vice-president of merchandising for Colonial Mills, Inc.

He attended Clemson University, Cornell University, and M.I.T. and taught at M.I.T. as well. His authority in so many wide-ranging textile areas has led him to service as marketing editor, *Encyclopedia of Man-Made Textiles*. His publications have appeared in numerous trade publications and magazines. He has lectured at various textile schools and industrial seminars and has appeared periodically before the New York Society of Security Analysts to discuss textile trends. Mr. Spiro also developed two successful patents for man-made fiber manufacturing.

He is the winner of the industry award, the Textile Veterans Association Achievement Award of 1972 (naming a scholarship after him at Clemson and M.I.T.). As testimony to his wide-ranging expertise he has served as the chairman of the board, president, and board member of the Textile Distributor's Association; as chairman of the Operating Committee of TEXPO; as president of the American Association for Textile Technology, Inc.; as an active arbitrator with the American Arbitration Association; as a member of the American Textile Manufacturer's Association; as a member of the board of governors of The Weaver's Club; and as a member of the advisory board for Textile Curriculum and Seminars for the Fashion Institute of Technology.

JEAN L. WOODRUFF

Jean Woodruff, editor of the *Textile Marketing Letter,* is also on the faculty of the Department of Industrial Management at Clemson University where her primary teaching area is marketing. She has published several textile-related articles and received a grant in 1977 to study public perceptions of the textile industry. Ms. Woodruff received her B.A. from the University of North Carolina at Greensboro, her M.B.A. from Emory University, and has worked on a Ph.D. at the University of Georgia. She has also studied at the University of Oslo, Oslo, Norway. Ms. Woodruff is listed in several biographical publications, including *Who's Who in the South and Southwest, The World's Who's Who of Women,* and *The International Who's Who of Intellectuals.*

Recently Ms. Woodruff has accepted a position at Western New England College in Springfield, Massachusetts as an Assistant Professor, Department of Marketing.

Index